AN EXPERIENTIAL
LEARNING APPROACH TO
EMPLOYEE TRAINING SYSTEMS

AN EXPERIENTIAL LEARNING APPROACH TO EMPLOYEE TRAINING SYSTEMS

Ronald R. Sims

Q

QUORUM BOOKS
New York • Westport, Connecticut • London

Library of Congress Cataloging-in-Publication Data

Sims, Ronald R.
   An experiential learning approach to employee training systems /
Ronald R. Sims.
      p.   cm.
   Includes bibliographical references.
   ISBN 0–89930–526–1 (lib. bdg. : alk. paper)
   1. Employees—Training of.   2. Experiential learning.   I. Title
HF5549.5.T7S557   1990
658.3′124—dc20   90–32648

British Library Cataloguing in Publication Data is available.

Library of Congress Catalog Card Number: 90–32648
ISBN: 0–89930–526–1

First published in 1990

Quorum Books, 88 Post Road West, Westport, CT 06881
An imprint of Greenwood Publishing Group, Inc.

Printed in the United States of America

The paper used in this book complies with the
Permanent Paper Standard issued by the National
Information Standards Organization (Z39.48-1984).

10 9 8 7 6 5 4 3 2 1

Contents

Illustrations   vii

Preface   ix

1. Training Systems   1

2. Why Training?   17

3. Determining Training Needs   35

4. Collecting and Analyzing Data on Jobs: The Role of
    Job Analysis in Training   55

5. Designing Training Programs to Develop Pivotal
    Skills and Competency Levels   73

6. Establishing Training Objectives and Determining
    Program Content   93

7. Training Program Design and Selection of Training
    Methods   109

8. Selecting Trainees: Understanding Individual Differences,
    Learning, and Learning Styles   125

9. Selecting Trainers   145

10. Enhancing the Effectiveness of Training Programs   161

11. Planning Evaluations of Training Programs: A Systems
     Analysis Approach   187

12. A Selected Recapitulation   219

Bibliography   233

Index   249

Illustrations

FIGURES

1.1	Heating System in the Home	3
1.2	An Instructional System	7
1.3	A Training Systems Model	9
3.1	Training Needs Assessment Model	39
3.2	An Example of a Questionnaire for Identifying Training Needs	43
3.3	Comparison of Job Demands and Skills for Engineering Manager	47
3.4	The Five-Step Needs-Assessment Model	52
5.1	The Experiential Learning Model	80
6.1	Training Objectives Worksheet	101
8.1	Factors that Affect Motivation in Training Programs	129
10.1	The Importance of the Match between Training Contributions and Inducements in the Psychological Contract	176
11.1	Designing a Training Program Evaluation	191
11.2	Evaluation Matrix	195
11.3	Research Designs	199
11.4	Training Plan and Evaluation	202

11.5   Example Cost-Benefit Analysis
        for a Training Program   215

TABLES

2.1   Who Gets the Training   28
2.2   General Types of Training   29
2.3   General Types of Training by Industry   30
2.4   General Types of Training by Size
        of Organization   31
2.5   Specific Types of Training   32
6.1   Examples of Instructional Objectives   98
6.2   Criterion Scoring Guide   102
6.3   Standards for Checking Adequacy
        of Training Objectives   104

EXHIBITS

8.1   Using Learning-Style Data in the
        First Training Session   143
10.1   Decision to Attend a Training Program   179

Preface

What distinguishes successful employee training programs from unsuccessful ones? In many cases, the distinction can be found by critiquing the extent to which those responsible for designing training programs successfully use the key phases of any training endeavor: preassessment, training needs analysis, development, implementation, and evaluation. However, with the changing of times and the increased appreciation of the importance of human resources to an organization's ability to remain economically viable and respond to the demands of an ever-changing and global marketplace, no organization can afford not to manage its training programs appropriately.

This book has been designed to help human resource management specialists responsible for their organization's training programs to manage training programs more effectively. With this in mind this book emphasizes the importance of viewing training programs from a systems perspective and the value an experiential learning approach can provide in more effective training in organizations. Toward this end, the book provides a step-by-step guide through the use of important experiential learning concepts to the preassessment, needs analysis, design, implementation, and evaluation of training systems. The book is not intended to be completely prescriptive; however, it does present a systematic and practical experiential learning approach to the design of a training system.

The experiential learning training principles and procedures presented in this book have been thoroughly and extensively tested in a variety of training environments with a wide range of trainees and objectives. They have without a doubt proved to be workable, effective, and generalizable.

To be more specific, the application of the experiential learning systems approach to training in public and private organizations over the past eight years has resulted in enthusiastic responses by trainees, other trainers, and organizations. Many of the suggestions I have received over the years have been incorporated into the book you have before you.

While the professional literature on training is staggering in volume, it is hoped that this book will fill a void in the literature on training, for it attempts to present a complete view of the more significant aspects of the training endeavor within a framework of experiential learning. This book is addressed to those individuals, either present or future, in business, government, military, and other organizations, who must ensure that the ever-increasing budget committed to training is, indeed, maximized. The content should also be of interest to those who must evaluate the contributions of a training activity to the purposes and objectives of the organization. In reality, members at all levels of an organization should, therefore, find this book helpful. This book should offer insights that will help human resource management specialists do their jobs better.

While a single name is given as author of this publication, it was not a solitary effort. The School of Business Administration at the College of William and Mary deserves considerable recognition for its cooperative and wholehearted support of this undertaking. My appreciation and thanks are extended particularly to Herrington Bryce, the Life Insurance of Virginia Professor at the School of Business Administration, College of William and Mary, who provided encouragement and moral and intellectual support. In addition, I am grateful to David Kolb, Chairman of the Department of Organizational Behavior, Case Western Reserve University, whose fine mind, encouragement, and infinite patience were largely responsible for freeing me to appreciate the value of experiential learning.

Thanks must also go to the support staff of the School of Business Administration who worked with me in the production process. Melissa Reagan bore with my endless cutting, pasting, and copying requests, and Nancy Smith helped with the production of camera-ready tables and figures.

My wife pitched in, too. Serbrenia helped do library research, challenged my faulty thinking, smoothed the rough edges of my phraseology, and flawlessly performed the thankless task of reading each chapter of each draft.

Training Systems

INTRODUCTION

The success of the scientific teams in the military in World War II was outstanding both in Great Britain and in the United States. As a consequence, after the war there was a rush to apply the same kind of thinking, which then was called "operations research," to various nonmilitary problems, and in particular to industry. At first the problems considered were rather small. The scientists studied production as well as some minor problems of marketing and finance. A few sporadic attempts were made to solve some problems in transportation, for example, the design of roadways. But luckily along came a computer that was an enormous aid to the scientist. At first the computer itself was used in a relatively insignificant role, for example, in tasks like bookkeeping. Then people began to see that computer capability as it was opening up in the 1950s suggested the possibility of using the computer as a way of processing enormous amounts of information. Thus came the idea for the SAGE system, a system that would supply to the defense agencies of the United States information about the locations of our own aircraft and of all enemy aircraft, and about suspicious objects in the air. The computer had started to grow up.

As the scientists' perspective widened, they began to think of this approach as the "systems approach." The scientists saw that what they were chiefly interested in was characterizing the nature of the system in such a way that decision making could take place in a logical and coherent fashion and that none of the fallacies of narrow-minded thinking would occur.

Furthermore, using their scientific knowledge, the scientists expected to be able to develop measures that would give as adequate information as possible about the performance of the system. More recently, however, the systems approach has been applied as a managerial innovation in a variety of situations and problems (political, economic, social, military, and industrial). These systematic procedures can be, and have been, employed in designing training systems.

The purpose of this chapter is to present an overview of several training systems models, a generalized, integrated, and conceptual picture of the major steps to plan, design, develop, conduct, and evaluate a training system. Toward this end, the chapter will highlight the importance of viewing the development of training from a systems perspective.

The development of an organizational training system requires an examination of many systemic issues. A training system is linked to other organizational units and must be taken into consideration in each step of the training process. In turning to the task of this chapter it is important first to develop a definition of a system.

SYSTEM DEFINED

What is a system? Gane (1972) has provided one definition of a system: *a set of elements which, with some objectives, uses processes to transform inputs into outputs*. To define such a system one needs to define four things—the inputs, the outputs, the processes, and, most importantly, the objectives. Thus an engineering system, say a generating plant, has coal as its principal input, and transforms it into electric power as output. The objective is to do so with the greatest possible efficiency, and the processes may be burning the coal to raise steam and using the steam to turn the turbine, which rotates the generator armature.

A data-processing system may have inputs of rates of pay, hours worked, and tax rates and produce outputs of pay slips and checks, using electronic computer processes. The objective may be to produce accurate and timely payrolls and reports.

A navigating system has inputs of position desired and present position and produces outputs of desired courses, leading to later positions.

When defining a system in this manner, it is often very useful to simplify thinking about it by asking: What are the objectives? What are the outputs? What are the inputs? What processes are used to transform the inputs into outputs?

Another definition of a system, provided by Cohen, Fink, Gadon, and Willits (1988) is: *any set of mutually interdependent elements*. Mutual interdependence means that a change in any one element causes some corresponding change in the others. In turn, those changes will have an impact back on the original changed element. An example of a simple physical

Figure 1.1
Heating System in the Home

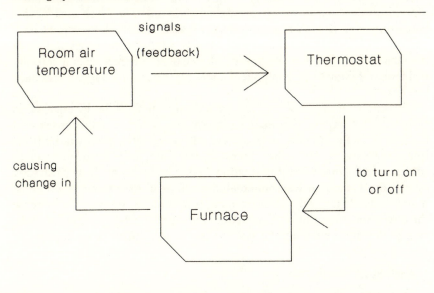

system is the heating system in a house. It consists of a source of heat, a thermostat, and a means of delivering heat to various parts of the house. Drops in temperature below a preset level cause the thermostat to send a signal to start the furnace, which delivers heat until the temperature rises in the house; this registers on the thermostat, which then turns off the furnace until the temperature drops again, and so on in a repetitive (and, these days, increasingly expensive!) cycle. The constant interplay among these elements, mutually adjusting to maintain a roughly constant temperature in the house, demonstrates a system achieving equilibrium, in which the system parts are constantly tending toward a particular steady state.

In order to achieve equilibrium, the system depends upon various feedback mechanisms. The thermostat cannot make the "decision" to turn the furnace on or off without "information" from the surrounding air (Figure 1.1). Imagine, for example, if a member of the household hung a warm coat over the thermostat in a cold and drafty room. The feedback cycle would be disrupted; the thermostat would receive inaccurate information ("the room is very warm") and would signal the furnace to shut off irrespective of the actual temperature of the air (now blocked off by the coat) in the room. The control mechanisms that maintain equilibrium in any system are dependent upon accurate feedback from various parts of the system and its surrounding environment.

Tracey (1971, 1984) presents another definition of systems as: *a combination of human and material resources, including the organization and procedures required to coordinate their functioning, employed to achieve a mission or objective*. A true closed-loop system has the following characteristics: (1) it is an organized and orderly whole with clearly definable boundaries, (2) it has a mission or objective, (3) it has several interdependent and interacting components, and (4) it has some type of feedback mechanism.

Ultimately all organizations are open loop systems—that is, engaged in constant transactions with their environments, which usually consist of a number of other systems. Any system will make adjustments in policies, rules, regulations, and other operating behavior in order to attempt to survive and maintain itself in relation to its environment. In general, any system must make at least minimal alterations in its internal operations, based on feedback from its environment, in order to survive. To increase the effectiveness of the system, frequent and delicate adjustments are necessary: the more complex the system, the more difficult the adjustments.

Analysis of Training Systems

The systems approach to training has been a fashionable catch-phrase for some time now. It has not always been clear what its advocates meant by it, nor was there any clear idea of what a training system looked like. There was, and still is, some value in the idea of trying to describe training activities as though they were systems.

Training systems analysis is the process of breaking the whole training process into its component parts and relating these parts to each other and to the organization as a whole. The objective of training systems analysis is to enable trainers (in the remainder of this book, the term *human resource management* (HRM) *specialists* will be interchanged with the word *trainer*) to acquire better understanding of the behavior of the whole training system by studying the behavior and interactions of its parts. Training systems analysis should be viewed as a strategy for improving decision making (for example, prioritizing training needs and allocating resources to meet those training needs).

Effective use of training systems analysis will allow HRM specialists to make choices that will achieve maximum internal operating efficiency of the training components that make up the training system. More specifically, the goal of training systems analysis is to plan, design, develop, conduct, and evaluate the utilization of available training resources in such a way as to achieve organizational goals by the most efficient and effective means possible.

Training systems analysis requires an examination not only of current and planned projects and training needs but also of many systemic issues.

Essentially training systems analysis involves a series of carefully sequenced activities as follows:

1. Assess organizational objectives
2. Assess nature of current or anticipated training needs
3. Select trainees
4. Establish training goals
5. Determine how to conduct the training
6. Select appropriate training techniques and personnel
7. Select evaluation design for training program
8. Conduct training program
9. Monitor training program
10. Formally evaluate training program

Training is a highly complex system; and where there is system complexity, there is a need for models to permit proper understanding, control, and management of the system.

TRAINING SYSTEMS MODELS

A model is a representation of a system. The model is not the system; the model represents, in simplified form, selected features of the system under study. The system is always more complicated and richer in detail than the model.

Training systems models traditionally concentrated on four factors:

1. Assessment, and identification, of organizational training needs (macrolevel)
2. Assessment of job training requirements (microlevel)
3. Program design
4. Evaluation or feedback

The great virtue of the early models was that they supplied newcomers to the training function, of whom there were many in the 1960s, with an understandable and commonsense overview of an emerging professionalism.

The increasing complexity of training activities and the findings flowing from admittedly limited research pointed to the need for extension of these models. Attempts have been made to extend the relevance of the earlier models by modifying the format. Cole (1986) uses a spiral configuration in his Systematic Training Basic Cycle, which starts with "Training Policy" and goes on to argue the need to "Establish a Training Organization," "Identify Training Needs," "Plan Training," "Carry Out Training" and

"Evaluate Training." The evaluation activity in this model then leads back to the "Identify Training Needs" part of the cycle.

Extension of the early training models has also led to an increased emphasis on the interaction among several phases (assessment, training and development, and evaluation) of training programs. In most of the training systems models developed since the early 1970s one can find the three phases mentioned in some form, as evidenced in Goldstein's (1986) model presented in Figure 1.2.

In the assessment phase, the need for training is determined and the objectives of the training effort are specified. Looking at the performance of clerks in a billing department, a manager might find that their typing abilities are weak and that they would profit by having typing instruction. An objective of increasing the clerks' typing speed to sixty words per minute without errors is set as the criterion against which training success is to be measured and represents the way the objective is made specific.

In the next phase, training and development, the clerks would be given a typing test, and the billing supervisor and a HRM specialist would work together to determine how to train the clerks to increase their typing speed. A programmed instruction manual might be used in conjunction with a special typing class set up at the company. Then the training is actually conducted.

Finally, if both the assessment phase and the training phase have been done competently, then the evaluation phase should present few problems. Evaluation is crucial and focuses on measuring how well the training accomplished what it set out to do. Evaluation must provide a continuous stream of feedback that can be used to reassess training needs, thereby creating input for the next stage of employee development.

Viewing training from the system's perspective requires the existence of individuals to work together and raises a series of fundamental questions or dilemmas, which must be resolved in order to accomplish the training program's mission. Imagine what takes place to get the complex job of training done:

1. Training goals must be determined, agreed upon and disseminated
2. Some way of making decisions about training goals and all subsequent tasks must be found
3. The various tasks necessary to achieve the training goals must be divided and allocated
4. Capable people must be found, employed, trained, and assigned to the tasks that make up the training effort
5. Timely information must somehow be conveyed to those who need it to do their tasks
6. A way must be found to get all parties (for example, trainees and trainers) to the training program to do the necessary work

Figure 1.2
An Instructional System

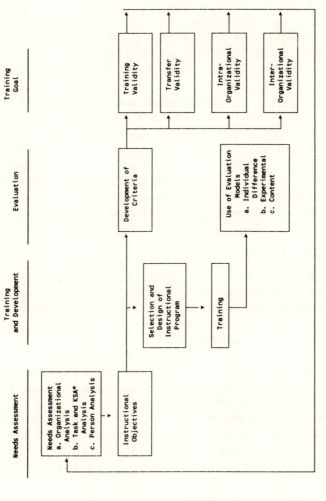

* KSA = Knowledge, Skills, Abilities.

Source: From I. L. Goldstein, TRAINING IN ORGANIZATIONS: NEEDS ASSESSMENT, DEVELOPMENT, AND EVALUATION, 2nd ed. (Monterey, California: Brooks/Cole, 1986) p. 16. Reprinted by permission of the publisher.

7. A way must be found to ensure adequate performance of the tasks

8. A way must be found to ensure coordination of the many tasks of the training effort

9. A way must be found to measure and modify all of the above when the conditions leading to the original training goals are not being met or changed

The problems of trying to decide what should be done, who should do it, and how they should divide the work, coordinate efforts, and so forth, provide many challenges for those in training. The training systems models depicted so far in this chapter and the system diagram presented in the next section can help those in training respond efficiently and effectively to the fundamental questions and dilemmas that confront every training effort.

Figure 1.3 presents the training system model on which this book will focus. Although the degree of emphasis changes for different training programs, most of the components of this model are considered important to any training system. The remaining chapters in this book will discuss in more detail the material related to each component of this model and its importance in understanding and enhancing training efforts. The remainder of this chapter provides an overview of the complete training system depicted in Figure 1.3 and the relationship among the components.

Preassessment Phase

Some training systems assume that it is feasible to go straight into the organization-wide assessment of training without having previously considered such essential factors as: the availability of financial resources, management and other key players' attitudes, professionalism of HRM specialists, and, most important of all, the potential capacity of the organization to undertake change within the cultural constraints of the current value system. These are the factors that will largely determine the extent, content, and viability of subsequent assessments and the acceptability and potential for success of future training activities.

The training system presented in this chapter does not imply that training is assessed on the basis of an open-ended budget when it is a known fact that budgets generally precede training and that HRM specialists, to be credible, must work within prescribed financial constraints. Resource availability will also determine the capacity of the organization and its training personnel to undertake evaluation, as well as the type and level of sophistication of evaluation that can be realistically expected within the organization environment.

The attitudes of management and other key players, particularly toward training, can, as Kenney and Reid (1986) argue, be either a major resource or a potentially crippling disability, in that the wrong attitudes may deter-

Figure 1.3
A Training Systems Model

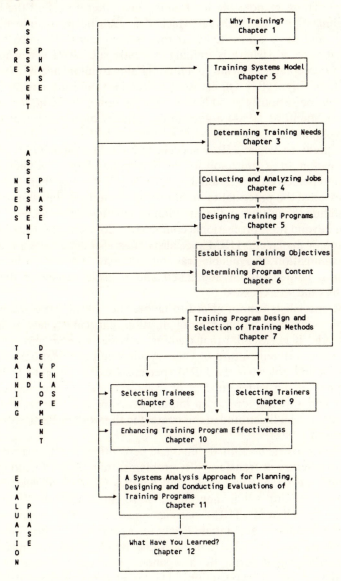

mine both the extent to which HRM specialists will attain human and
financial resources and the organizational levels at which training will be
acceptable; whether it will be used to determine and meet actual training
requirements, or will be merely a formalized activity based on the repetition
of historically determined, low-risk, low-value training (e.g., operations
training). Those responsible for training must therefore find the level in
the organizational hierarchy at which it is realistic to assume they can
operate, and have a sensitivity to the "sacred cows" that exist in any
organization (e.g., where is training currently successful and where is it
totally unacceptable?) prior to initiating the training needs assessment
phase (Donnelly, 1987). Otherwise the assessment and subsequent training
efforts can be seriously at odds with organizational expectations and attitudes, as Mumford (1984) argues in the context of management training
and development.

The extent to which HRM specialists have the capacity to generate
change within an organization will be determined largely by their acceptability and perceived professional competence. They must therefore ensure
that they have the potential to undertake projected areas of assessment or
they will find themselves in the situation of isolating future areas of activity
that are beyond their professional competence, for example, internal training of senior managers. HRM specialists must also undertake a preassessment examination of available training resources: there is little point in
going into battle without a detailed and realistic survey of their own
strengths (and weaknesses).

HRM specialists cannot afford to ignore the values, expectations, and
perceptions of those within the organization, particularly at top management levels. It is essential that training activities contain and reflect the
actual organizational culture or value systems and expectations of the organization and not what the HRM specialists feel it "ought" to be. The
importance of the wider concept of organizational culture has relatively
recently come to the fore as an important factor at all levels of training
efforts and is well illustrated in this context in the work of Pettigrew, Jones,
and Reason (1982).

Sensitivity to organizational values and perceptions has been a continuing
source of re-entry or transferability problems: trainees are forced to reject
or modify the knowledge, skills, and abilities (KSAs) inculcated during
off-the-job training when they enter, or re-enter, the back-home work
environment. Therefore HRM specialists must ensure that, where possible,
training assessments are initiated only in organizational situations where
the assessors have knowledge of the value system of the organization, so
that material gained during the assessment phase can be based on actual,
rather than assumed, expectations. The intent is not to argue that assessment efforts and outcome reports should comprise a purely reactive con-

tent; they must help to challenge the accepted order but within the bounds of cultural acceptability and the capacity of the organization to change.

The rest of this book will focus on a more detailed discussion of the training system model presented in this chapter. Chapter 2 will present a brief history of training, a definition of training, purposes of training, poor and good reasons for training, the importance of training for accomplishment of organizational goals, and the variety of ways employees and organizations benefit from training. The remaining chapters will be presented with a focus on the training phases of needs assessment, development and implementation, and evaluation.

Needs Assessment Phase

As Figure 1.3 demonstrates, the needs assessment phase includes the determination of training needs, collecting and analyzing jobs, designing training programs, establishing training programs, and determining program content. A more detailed description of each step of the needs assessment phase will be presented in the following paragraphs.

Determining Training Needs. This phase of the training process is to determine precisely what training needs exist currently and to project future training requirements. There are three levels of analysis for determining the needs that training can fulfill: organization, job, and employee performance analysis (McGehee and Thayer, 1961; Schuler and Youngblood, 1986). Training needs might surface in any one of these three broad areas. Chapter 3 will describe the three levels of training needs analysis in more detail, several specific methods for determining training needs (i.e., performance discrepancy analysis, nominal group process, team problem-solving analysis, etc.), and procedures for selecting a method.

Collecting and Analyzing Data on Jobs. Job analysis represents a fundamental starting point for training as well as other human resource management activities. Organizations can use a job analysis to specify both the training an employee requires for effective performance and the type of training current employees may need to become promotable. In addition, a complete job analysis will reveal whether a new employee needs additional training in certain areas to perform the job successfully. This can usually be discerned by comparing the employee's past work history and training to the tasks specified in the job analysis. By providing, through job analysis, a definition of what constitutes a job, the supervisor can easily explain to a new employee the boundaries of the employee's unit of work. In any work situation it is difficult for an employee to perform well if there is confusion about what the job is and what is supposed to be done. Only by examining the skills required for a job can the organization train and promote employees in conjunction with its human resource needs.

Training programs must be constructed with a keen eye to what should be taught and its purpose in meeting organizational needs. Efficient use of the millions of training dollars spent each year is directly tied to the collection of data from jobs. For organizations to reap the benefits of training programs they must be based on sound data collection. The source of valid and reliable job data is job analysis. The extent to which jobs are appropriately analyzed and training needs determined will result in effective, yet efficient, employee training programs.

If training systems are not based on a solid foundation of objectively collected job data, the inevitable consequences are the inclusion of irrelevant content, the omission of important content, misplaced emphasis, and, ultimately, an inadequate or overtrained product. The form in which this data can be collected will be described in Chapter 4.

Designing Training Programs (Development of Pivotal Skills and Competency Levels). The criteria used by the HRM specialist as a basis for selection of training objectives must ensure that the resulting training program is designed to develop important pivotal skills and the competency levels necessary for successful back-home performance by the trainee. A training program is a planned system of goals and objectives based on a needs assessment (e.g., completing a thorough job analysis), program content, learning principles, division of labor (trainer-trainee), a definable set of training activities or experiences to include specific training methods and aids, and procedures for evaluation of the training program. The extent to which these systemic elements can be structured in an orderly and rational manner will have much to do with the training program's eventual success or failure.

Job analyses detail the full dimensions of a particular job with all its variations, caused by the organization in its efforts to achieve overall strategies and goals. It would be unrealistic and extravagant, in terms of time, personnel, money and other resources, to provide the amount and kind of training required to equip every graduate of a training program to perform every job task (pivotal or peripheral) associated with a particular occupation or skill in any position anywhere. For the same reason, it is often impractical to train employees to the level of proficiency required in some positions. Some training is more realistically and more practically conducted on the job. Consequently, it is essential for the HRM specialist to select from the total list of job performances those that are most appropriate and feasible for formal training—and to decide what standards or levels of proficiency or competency will be required for successful completion of the training program. Training priorities for specific job duties and tasks (pivotal skills) must also be assigned to ensure that the most critical skills are taught even if reductions in the length and cost of the training program are necessary.

Chapter 5 will discuss the importance of good training design, along with principles that should be considered when designing a training program (structure, relevance, specificity, generality, reinforcement, in-process evaluation and feedback, openness and flexibility, linkage, involvement, cost effectiveness, redundancy, synergy, and training for psychological wholeness of learning and for transferability and compatibility). It will introduce the concepts of pivotal skill and competency development, discuss Kolb's (1984a) Experiential Learning Model (ELM), and review corresponding learning styles as key variables in the design of training programs.

Establishing Training Objectives and Determining Program Content. The next step in the development of a training system is to select training objectives from the needs analysis (i.e., from data collected in the job analysis). Chapter 6 discusses the importance of selecting, writing, and organizing training objectives, determining program content, and establishing criteria for the selection of the optimum method, technique, or medium to achieve training objectives. While training course outlines, programs of instruction, or training guides may be available to the HRM specialist, most of these documents are of limited help in planning tailored training activities.

The effectiveness of the training system depends on the efficiency of the HRM specialist in selecting and writing meaningful training objectives. Training objectives must be stated in performance terms. In this form, training objectives describe clearly what the trainee must be able to do, the important pivotal skills, and the standard or competency level of acceptable performance. Chapter 6 describes the importance of selecting, writing, and organizing training objectives and selecting training methods to conduct the actual training program.

Training and Development Phase

Training Program Design and Selection of Training Methods. Training methods can be classified in three ways: information presentation, simulation methods, or on-the-job training. Lecture, conference, demonstration, and performance methods have been used in training from the beginning. New training methods appear every year. While some are well-founded in learning theory or models of behavior change (e.g., behavior modeling), others result more from technological than from theoretical developments (e.g., video-tape, computer-based business games). The decision to use one strategy or another must be made on the basis of careful analysis of the training situation from several standpoints: training objectives, training program content, trainee population, training staff, space, facilities, equipment, training materials, time, and costs.

Chapter 7 will discuss the importance of someone's assuming responsibility for the training effort, as well as the legal aspects that can impact training design. In addition, the chapter will highlight several training methods and discuss the importance of the selection of training methods.

Identifying Trainees: Individual Differences, Learning, and Learning Styles. Anyone who has participated in training realizes that there are no two individuals exactly alike, and no two training programs exactly alike. Individual differences are glaringly obvious in the training environment. Trainees differ from one another in looks, interests, likes and dislikes, understanding, and rate of learning. In addition, there are variations in learning patterns that are the result of differences in ability and motivation among trainees. Therefore, in planning learning activities that provide the optimum motivation, the HRM specialist needs to recognize that individual differences stand out as a critical factor.

The greatest single factor in the determination of training program content is that individual differences must be recognized. It is also important that trainers understand the learning process and principles of learning. Chapter 8 discusses the importance of learning, learning principles, and individual differences (learning styles) of trainees as keys to the potential success of the training effort. Chapter 8 also provides a detailed discussion of several learning-style models that can be used to assess individuals' learning preferences. Chapter 8 also describes the usefulness of information about learning styles in understanding trainees.

Selecting HRM Specialists (Trainers). Those responsible for the design and implementation of training programs should take care in choosing trainers. A key variable in the eventual success of the training effort is the effectiveness of the trainer. Personal characteristics (learning and training style, the ability to speak well, to write convincingly, to organize the work of others, to be inventive, to inspire others to greater achievement) are important factors in the selection of trainers.

Chapter 9 describes the importance of understanding the role of the trainer, important factors in trainer selection, what makes a good trainer, some common trainer pitfalls, and trainer styles. In addition it discusses the purpose, issues, and benefits of using a team (internal-external) approach in training programs.

Enhancing Training Program Effectiveness. Management of those aspects of the training program that influence the learning process is important in fostering employee development. Learning is an interactive process that involves both trainers and employees. Enhancing this interactive process should be beneficial to the overall success of a training effort. The goal of Chapter 10 is to present the importance of adapting training methods to particular employee learning styles and of developing the learning climate in training programs. The chapter will stress the importance of creating training activities and training environments that should enhance and improve the effectiveness of training programs in organizations.

Kolb's ELM will be presented as a viable system for managing the learning process in Fry's concept of the learning environment (Fry, 1978). Chapter 10 will emphasize that any training program, training course, or training session can be viewed as having degrees of orientation toward each of the four learning modes in Kolb's ELM—labeled as affective, perceptual, symbolic, and behavioral, to connote the overall climate they create and the particular learning skill or mode they require (Kolb and Fry, 1975). Thus an affective training environment emphasizes the experiencing of concrete events; a symbolic training environment emphasizes abstract conceptualization; a perceptual training environment stresses observation and appreciation; a behavioral training environment stresses action-taking in situations with real consequences. Any particular training experience can have some or all of these orientations, to differing degrees, at the same time.

Chapter 10 will also describe a series of psychological contracting activities intended to facilitate the "start-up" phase of a training program for adult learners and will present a vehicle for HRM specialists to contract with members of training programs to build their own versions of a training (learning) environment. In a sense the intent is to help HRM specialists see the value of using the approach presented in this chapter as a catalyst for conversations among training staff and trainees directed toward building and maintaining a highly effective learning community.

Evaluation Phase

A Systems Analysis Approach for Planning, Designing, and Conducting Evaluations of Training Programs. In the eyes of the trainee, training ends when trainer and trainee go their separate ways. Upon returning to the job duties, the employee hopes to perform more effectively or, perhaps, be better prepared for promotional opportunities. When direct involvement in the program has ended, as far as the employee is concerned, training is over. But though the instruction has ended, the training process has not yet run its full cycle.

One very important question remains: Was the training effective? This often overlooked question involves the third and final phase of training—evaluation (it must always be understood that training evaluation occurs throughout the training process). The ultimate evaluation questions regarding training programs evolve around utility. More specifically, is the gain to the organization in increased performance greater than the cost of the training to justify the investment? Answering this question requires that dollar values be placed on various levels of performance and that various training costs be computed.

The purpose of evaluation in the training process is to determine whether trainees actually gained new knowledge, skills, and abilities as a result of the training program. Chapter 11 is limited to identifying precisely *what* is to be evaluated, *who* should do the evaluating, and *when*, *why*, and *how* the evaluation is to be done.

There are a variety of training program evaluation techniques available to the HRM specialist; Chapter 11, however, describes in detail the training audit and cost-benefit analysis techniques, obstacles/pitfalls and opportunities of evaluating training programs, and a systematic approach for planning, designing, and conducting training program evaluations.

Training Systems: What Have You Learned?

Chapter 12 will provide a review and recapitulation of the important points emphasized throughout the book. In addition, Chapter 12 will pay particular attention to viewing training as a systems effort, as discussed throughout this book. Finally, the chapter will highlight some important concerns that HRM specialists must address.

SUMMARY

Effective training in organizations requires viewing training as a system. The extent to which HRM specialists understand and treat training efforts as a system will, in the end, increase the potential success of training programs. In addition, the development of an organization's training system requires examination and analysis of the other organizational units linked to the training system and of the training system itself.

A more effective training system should result from the development of a model that represents the training system. The model should include the following phases: preassessment, assessment, training and development, and evaluation. The problems of trying to decide what should be done, who should do it, and how they should divide the work, coordinate efforts, and so forth, can be addressed by viewing training as a system.

2

Why Training?

INTRODUCTION

As the demands of foreign competition, increased efficiency, and the second industrial revolution spread, organizations are coming to regard training expenses as no less a part of their capital costs than plants and equipment. Total training outlay by U.S. firms in 1986 was $30 billion—and rising (American Society for Training and Development, 1986, July). In 1987 private-sector employers spent an estimated $32 billion providing approximately 38.8 million employees (31 percent of the total civilian labor force) with 1.2 billion hours of formal training and development (Lee, 1987). A more recent study, by *Training* magazine (1989), estimated that organizations with one hundred or more employees would spend $44.4 billion for formal training that year, up from $39.6 billion spent in 1988. In addition to the above figures, most organizations pay employees for 100 percent of the time they spend in training, and 82 percent of total training hours take place on company time (Gordon, 1986). This represents a significant investment in the human resources of this country. Training is big business and getting bigger.

At the level of the individual organization, Motorola typifies the rising commitment to and investment in training. Motorola has committed itself to a training budget of 2 percent of each employee's salary. It spent $44 million in 1986 alone. Eight hundred Motorola employees have full-time training duties, while 200 training vendors (outside suppliers) and 360 in-house subject-matter experts assist. Motorola budgets about 1 percent of annual sales (2.6 percent of payroll) for training. It even trains workers for its key suppliers, many of them small- to medium-size organizations without the resources to train their own people in such advanced specialties as computer-aided design and deficit control. Taking into account training expenses, wages, and benefits, Motorola's total annual training cost amounts to about $90 million. The results have been dramatic, according to a company spokesperson: "We've documented the savings from the statistical process control methods and problem-solving methods we've trained our people in. We're running a rate of return of about 30 times the dollars invested—which is why we've gotten pretty good support from senior management" (Brody, 1987, p. 87).

A study by the Work in America Institute confirms that organizations have also realized the benefits of retraining their employees. The study found that retraining current workers for new jobs is more cost-effective than firing them and hiring new ones—not to mention the difference that retraining makes to employee morale (Brody, 1987). And in "downsizing" industries where there are no alternatives to furloughs, unions are working with management to help retrain displaced workers (Cascio, 1989). This chapter presents a brief history of training, a definition of training, and the purposes of training; it also discusses poor and good reasons for training, the importance of training to the accomplishment of organizational goals, and the variety of ways employees and organizations benefit from training.

History of Training

Worker training can be traced back to biblical times, with ancient Egyptians overseeing hordes of slaves being "trained" as well as driven by foremen, often of the slaves' own nationality. Training was direct, task-oriented, and on-the-job. The evaluation of that training was simple and based entirely on the outcomes of the employees' efforts. Orientation, a major form of twentieth-century worker training, was also provided in biblical times although less systematically than it is now. Similarly, on-the-job, task-oriented training was made available through apprenticeship programs primarily for manual and artistic work (Hawthorne, 1987a).

The beginning of the Industrial Revolution was characterized by a substantial growth of human knowledge and rapidity of change, as evidenced by the number of patents in the first half of the nineteenth century (Steinmetz, 1976). Despite the creativity and originality that fostered the Industrial Revolution, references to training during that period failed to address such approaches to production or to business, attending more to specific task learning. The formation of "factory schools"—Hoe and Company in New York in 1872 is one example—coincided with the building of factories requiring skilled workers, such as trained machinists for manufacturing printing presses, during a period when business was good. Similar schools were subsequently started by Westinghouse, General Electric, and Baldwin Locomotive Works in 1888, 1901, and 1907 respectively (Steinmetz, 1976).

Prior to World War I, training was largely a local matter. Employment patterns were characterized by seasonal fluctuations and high turnover prior to the Depression. While the data are fragmented, less than 50 percent annual turnover was unusual, and the median in normal times was 80 percent. Turnover could be as high as 125 percent of unskilled and semiskilled workers. Orientation and training of workers was essential to industrial firms in order to maintain some corporate stability. Frederick Taylor's industrial engineering concepts influenced the technical, skill-specific training methods (Hawthorne, 1987a).

Furthermore, retraining was important, since many employees moved from industry to industry, a pattern that adumbrated the retraining concerns for skilled and semiskilled workers as the Depression came to an end. What makes retraining somewhat different in the 1980s is the widespread retraining needs of white-collar, college-educated employees, in contrast to blue-collar workers.

Partly because of the wartime emphasis on the supervisor's role, as well as the advancement of the behavioral sciences (e.g., Vroom, 1964; Likert, 1961; McGregor, 1960) and the growth in the size of corporations, interest in management development increased during the 1950s. The focus was on liberal education experiences for top-level executives. It was thought that technically trained managers needed exposure to the liberal arts to develop into sophisticated corporate leaders. Colleges and universities were the major source of that kind of corporate education; well-known programs were offered by Dartmouth College and Princeton University (Hawthorne, Libby, and Nash, 1983). Harvard University offered its first Advanced Management Program in 1945 (Mahler, 1976). In 1955 General Electric offered the first long-term internal executive education program, which lasted nine weeks (Mahler, 1976).

In 1958 orientation was the most common corporate education program; it was developed to stem attrition as well as to foster loyalty to the firm (Clark and Sloan, 1958). Sharp and Oughton, Inc., conducted a survey in 1968 and found that orientation, safety programs, supervisory training, and management training were the most frequent offerings (Quackenboss, 1969). The 1960s were characterized by growth and diversification in business, and the entry of women and minorities into business not open to them until then (Hawthorne, 1987a).

A dominant theme of the 1970s in training and education was the growing formalization of coursework. A few corporations formalized their courses into traditionally styled "corporate colleges" (Hawthorne, Libby, and Nash, 1983) while others developed company-sponsored courses that earned collegiate credit from the American Council of Education and from the New York Board of Regents, both of which operate programs that accredit courses sponsored by noncollegiate organizations (Pitre, 1980). During the early and middle 1980s, training became more of a systems approach in which the training unit served less as a deliverer of education than as a broker and consultant on education and training to managers and officers (Lusterman, 1985). Changes during the past few years have required training at all levels in organizations to make a powerful impact on the nature of organizations and training itself. Because training administrators and executives in general view training as playing a significant role in the success of the organization, training should continue as an integral and important part of organizations.

WHAT IS TRAINING?

The primary impetus for training in organizations is change. Managers of privately owned companies must enhance their organizations' profits and their stockholders' returns by increasing sales or reducing operating costs or both. Government administrators and private-sector executives at all levels have come under increasing pressure to change and provide more effective and efficient services. In addition, leaders of voluntary organizations, such as the United Way and the American Cancer Society, likewise seek ways to grow and prosper as critical financial resources become more and more difficult to obtain. Today's organizations must respond to demands for change while at the same time realizing that advances in technology and knowledge are rendering many traditional employee skills obsolete, while simultaneously developing needs for new ones. There have even been comic remarks that a college degree should be written in disappearing ink, since technical material has an ever-decreasing half-life (the time it takes for one-half of the material to become obsolete) (Leap and Crino, 1989). A recent analysis of corporate training programs sponsored by The Conference Board (Lusterman, 1985) cited one training director who remarked that since the half-life of an engineer is about five years, "a twenty-five-year-old graduate will have to be reeducated eight times in the course of a forty-year career" (Lusterman, 1985, p. 2).

Engineering is not the only profession experiencing a continuing need for re-education and retraining. New or present employees who draw their expertise from a knowledge base (accountants, computer technicians, nurses) will have to keep pace with advances in this knowledge base during their careers. Change and the impact of technology have affected training needs for other levels of workers as well. Clerk-typists of old must now become word processor operators, using micro, mini, and mainframe computers in their daily work. In addition, they must master a constantly changing software base that may include electronic mail, word processing, spreadsheet, desk-top publishing, graphics, and data-base management programs (Leap and Crino, 1989). Cashiers are leaving simple mechanical cash registers behind, as computerized cash registers make it possible to check on the customers' credit histories, keep track of inventory, and maintain sales records for departments and stores (Lusterman, 1985). As change continues and foreign competition intensifies, training will have to broaden an employee's range of skills to accommodate the new job demands (Olsen, 1986).

To many people, for many years, training had connotations of rote or mechanical learning, but it is used here to mean a systematically planned approach to learning knowledge, skills, abilities (KSAs), and attitudes, with certain important features. Training is a systematic process of changing the KSAs, attitudes, behavior, and/or motivation of employees to improve the match between employee characteristics and employment requirements (e.g., the demands of the job). The systematic process of training consists of planned programs designed to improve competence and performance at the individual, group, and/or organizational levels. Improved competence and performance, in turn, implies that there have been measurable changes in KSAs, attitudes, behavior, and/or motivation. The need to improve individual and group competence and performance, and to achieve goals as effectively as possible, is common to all organizations, private and public, small and large.

Reasons for Training

The most obvious reason for training is that it should meet a need; however, many Human Resource Management (HRM) specialists must still answer the question: "How do you tell the difference between good and bad training?" In many training situations it may be apparent that some training programs provide better results than other training, but it is not always obvious what makes the difference. Organizations expect employees who are responsible for the completion of certain work to complete that work properly; as a result, organizations want to have only the good kind of training, rather than the bad. Thus, they must find out what makes the difference.

It is much easier to define the results of good training than to define the action of good training. If, after training, the employee can do what he or she couldn't do before the training, and if the training did not take too long and didn't cost too much, we conclude that the training was "good" (Broadwell, 1975). On the other hand, if, when the training is over, the employee still cannot do the job for which he or she was trained, then the training may have been all "bad." "May" can be used because the training may have been all right, but other conditions—such as location, attitude and motivation of the employee, time of the day, or the employee's lack

performance. Second, managers knowingly hire and promote employees who need training to perform at standard levels. When the number of applicants is small, management has little choice but to hire or promote an applicant with few or no job skills and to remedy that lack through training. Third, many times management hires employees who possess the aptitude to learn and then trains them to perform specific tasks. For example, in hiring new employees for its manufacturing operations in Louisville, Kentucky, the General Electric Company uses an aptitude test that measures general manual dexterity and motor coordination skills. To learn a specific assembly job, new employees undergo company-provided training that may last for periods ranging from a few hours to several days.

4. *To solve problems.* Managers report they must achieve their goals through both scarcity and abundance: a scarcity of financial, human, and technological resources and an abundance of financial, human, and technological problems. Managers are expected to attain high goals in spite of personal conflicts, vague policies and standards, scheduling delays, inventory shortages, high levels of absenteeism and turnover, union-management disputes, and a restrictive legal environment.

Organizational problems are addressed in many ways. Training is one important way to solve many of those problems. Training courses may concern personnel, marketing, accounting, finance, manufacturing, purchasing, information systems, general management, etc. Training personnel, universities, and training consultants assist employees in solving problems and performing their jobs effectively.

5. *To prepare for promotion.* One important way to attract, retain, and motivate employees is through a systematic program of career development. Developing an employee's capabilities is consistent with an organization's human resources policy of promotion from within, and training is important in a career-development system. Training enables an employee to acquire the KSAs needed for a promotion and eases the transition from an employee's present job to one involving greater responsibilities. Organizations that fail to provide such training often lose their most promising employees. Frustrated by the lack of opportunity, achievement-oriented employees often seek employment with organizations that provide training for career advancement. Training can increase both the employees' level of commitment to the organization and also their perceptions that the organization is a good place to work. By developing and promoting its human resources through training, management can supervise a competent, motivated, and satisfied work force.

6. *To orient new employees.* During the first few days on the job, new employees form their initial impressions of the organization and its managers. These impressions may range from very favorable to very unfavorable and may influence their job satisfaction and productivity. Therefore,

many administrators make an effort to train new employees during orientation to the organization and the job.

Training for the right reasons can lead to greater employee commitment, less turnover, and less absenteeism, thus increasing top management support for training and ultimately the organization's productivity. In the end, training must provide a benefit to employees and, at a broader level, contribute to the well-being of the organization. The implication is that training should be evaluated in terms of its contribution to organizational effectiveness.

Benefits of Training

Training benefits the organization, the group, and the individual. Perhaps the easiest way to summarize these benefits is to consider training as an investment the organization makes in employees. That investment pays dividends to the trainee, to the organization, and to other workers. Some of the more common benefits of employee training for the organization, the individual employee, human relations, intra- and intergroup relations and policy implementation are listed below. (From M. J. Tessin, "Once Again, Why Training?" *Training* 15, 2 [February 1978], p. 7. Reprinted with permission from the February 1978 issue of *Training*, the Magazine of Human Resources Development. Copyright 1978, Lakewood Publications, Inc., Minneapolis, MN [612] 333–0471. All rights reserved).

How Training Benefits the Organization

—Leads to improved profitability and/or more positive attitudes toward profit orientation

—Improves the job knowledge and skills at all levels of the organization

—Improves the morale of the work force

—Helps people identify with organizational goals

—Helps create a better corporate image

—Fosters authenticity, openness, and trust

—Improves the relationship between boss and subordinate

—Aids in organizational development

—Learns from the trainee

—Helps prepare guidelines for work

—Aids in understanding and carrying out organizational policies

—Provides information for future needs in all areas of the organization

—Organization gets more effective decision making and problem solving

—Aids in development for promotion from within

—Aids in developing leadership skill, motivation, loyalty, better attitudes, and other aspects that successful workers and managers usually display

—Aids in increasing productivity and/or quality work

—Helps keep costs down in many areas, e.g., production, personnel, administration, etc.

—Develops a sense of responsibility to the organization for being competent and knowledgeable

—Improves labor-management relations

—Reduces outside consulting costs by utilizing competent internal consulting

—Stimulates preventive management as opposed to putting out fires

—Eliminates suboptimal behavior (such as hiding tools)

—Creates an appropriate climate for growth, communication

—Aids in improving organizational communication

—Helps employees adjust to change

—Aids in handling conflict, thereby helping to prevent stress and tension

Benefits to the Individual Which in Turn Ultimately Should Benefit the Organization

—Helps the individual in making better decisions and effective problem solving

—Through training and development, motivational variables of recognition, achievement, growth, responsibility, and advancement are internalized and operationalized

—Aids in encouraging and achieving self-development and self-confidence

—Helps a person handle stress, tension, frustration, and conflict

—Provides information for improving leadership knowledge, communication skills, and attitudes

—Increases job satisfaction and recognition

—Moves a person toward personal goals while improving interaction skills

—Satisfies personal needs of the trainer (trainee)

—Provides trainee an avenue for growth and a say in his/her own future

—Develops a sense of growth in learning

—Helps a person develop speaking and listening skills; also writing skills when exercises are required

—Helps eliminate fear in attempting new tasks

Benefits in Personal and Human Relations, Intra- and Intergroup Relations and Policy Implementation

—Improves communication between groups and individuals

—Aids in orientation for new employees and those taking new jobs through transfer or promotion

—Provides information on equal opportunity and affirmative action

—Provides information on other governmental laws and administrative policies

—Improves interpersonal skills

—Makes organization policies, rules, and regulations viable

—Improves morale

—Builds cohesiveness in groups

—Provides a good climate for learning, growth, and coordination

—Makes the organization a better place to work and live

Perhaps the easiest way to summarize these benefits is to consider training as an investment the organization makes in employees. That investment pays dividends to the employee, to the organization, and to other workers (Tessin, 1978; Werther and Davis, 1989). The increasing frequency of training being offered and the variety of job-specific training is evidence that organizations have begun to realize the benefits of training.

Who Benefits from Training? In an exhaustive study of training activities in U.S. organizations, Gordon collected data from CEOs, personnel directors, and training directors from 991 organizations ranging in size from 50 to over 1,000 employees in twelve industries (Gordon, 1986). Gordon's study found that the types of training most frequently provided were: new employee orientation (80.8 percent), performance appraisal (66.2 percent), new equipment operation (57.2 percent), leadership (54.2 percent), and time management (47.1 percent). Table 2.1 lists nine categories of employees and shows the percentage of U.S. organizations with 100 employees or more that provide some kind of training (formal) for each group (*Training*, 1989).

Purposes of Training. The number of organizations that provide training for production workers did not increase from the previous year, and in fact, the percentage dropped to the same level discerned in 1987. A little more than one-fourth of U.S. organizations provided training to production workers. In the 1989 *Training* magazine Industry Report, more production workers per organization (189, which is up from 175 in 1988) received training and each one received more hours of training (33.6 mean number of hours spent training production workers, which is up from 31.7 in 1988 and 39.1 in 1987). Office/clerical employees, another group at the low end of the training totem pole, averaged just 18.9 hours of training annually, a pittance compared with the rest of the groups. On the other hand, a little more than three of five organizations provide some sort of training for their customer-service people (31.2 training hours, which has risen steadily since 1987) (*Training*, 1989).

Table 2.2 lists 15 general types of training and the percentage of U.S. organizations that offer each one (*Training*, 1989). Management training and development lead the pack, and remedial basic education tags along

Table 2.1
Who Gets the Training

Job Category	Organizations Providing Training (%)[1]	Mean Number of Individuals Trained[2]	Projected Number of Individuals Trained[3] (in millions)	Mean Number of Hours Delivered[4]	Projected Total Hours of Training Delivered[5] (in millions)
Professionals	56.1	76.2	6.28	36.4	228.75
First-line Supervisors	69.7	38.4	3.93	36.3	142.83
Salespeople	37.4	72.4	3.98	36.2	144.10
Middle Managers	71.5	25.7	2.70	35.5	95.90
Executives	64.6	7.5	0.71	34.3	24.43
Senior Managers	55.9	13.5	1.11	33.6	37.28
Production Workers	26.9	188.5	7.45	33.6	250.46
Customer Service People	42.9	86.0	5.42	31.2	169.22
Office/Administration Employees	60.1	44.7	3.95	18.9	74.64
Total			35.55		1,167.60

[1] Percent of U.S. organizations with 100 or more employees that provide formal training to people in these categories.
[2] Average number of individuals trained per organization, based only on those organizations that do provide some training.
[3] Total number of people trained in all organizations (in millions).
[4] Average hours of training per individual, based only on organizations that do provide some training.
[5] Total hours of training (in millions) delivered by all organizations to all employees in these categories (one person receiving training for one hour equals one "hour of training").

at the rear. Tables 2.3 and 2.4 dissect the general type of training presented in Table 2.2 by industry and size of organization.

There is no one industry that's likely to provide more of every kind of training. Rather, certain kinds of training are more common in certain kinds of industries. Take public administration, for instance. It's at or near the top of the list when it comes to management skills and development, supervisor skills, technical skills, communication skills, basic computer skills, clerical and secretarial skills, and even personal growth and wellness courses. Where does it trail? Logically enough, it does very little sales skill training, customer relations and services, and customer education (*Training*, 1989).

In the same vein, nearly two-thirds of organizations in the health services field offered wellness courses to their employees, while just two-fifths of business services firms did so. Large organizations are generally more likely than smaller organizations to provide most kinds of training. But in the areas of management skills and development, the difference is slight. And in customer relations and services, only the smallest organizations (100 to

Table 2.2
General Types of Training

Types of Training	% Providing[1]	In House Only (%)[2]	Outside Only (%)[3]	Both (%)[4]
Management Skills/Development	84.2	14.7	15.0	54.5
Supervisory Skills	79.9	18.2	9.0	52.7
Technical Skills/Knowledge	79.8	28.9	6.7	44.2
Communication Skills	75.7	21.0	9.1	45.6
Basic Computer Skills	69.3	18.8	11.8	38.7
New Methods/Procedures	68.8	34.7	4.0	30.1
Customer Relations/Services	66.4	22.9	8.3	35.2
Clerical/Secretarial Skills	65.4	19.9	15.1	30.4
Personal Growth	61.9	14.8	13.0	34.1
Executive Development	61.6	6.5	24.1	31.0
Employee/Labor Relations	52.1	17.8	11.2	23.1
Wellness	47.7	18.1	10.3	19.3
Sales Skills	46.8	15.2	7.3	24.3
Customer Education	42.2	21.3	3.5	17.4
Remedial Basic Education	31.7	9.1	10.7	11.9

Of All Organizations With 100 or More Employees . . .

[1] Percent that provide each type of training.
[2] Percent that say all training of this type is designed and delivered by in-house staff.
[3] Percent that say all training of this type is designed and delivered by outside consultants or suppliers.
[4] Percent that say training of this type is designed and delivered by a combination of in-house staff and outside suppliers.

499 employees) were less likely than the largest ones (more than 10,000 employees) to offer training (*Training*, 1989).

Finally, Table 2.5 offers a look at specific types of training. Training in interpersonal skills, which was provided by 56.6 percent of organizations in 1989, was up from 45.1 percent in 1988. Interpersonal skills training moved to fourth place in 1989, up from 18th place in 1988. Decision making, which was in 20th place in 1988, moved up to 10th place in 1989 (*Training*, 1989). What is perhaps most striking about the data in Tables 2.1 to 2.5 is the breadth and depth of training provided in U.S. industry.

The important thing to keep in mind, however, is that while the programs shown in Tables 2.1 to 2.5 can contribute to improved productivity, quality of work life, and bottom-line performance, they can do so only by adhering

Table 2.3
General Types of Training by Industry*

Types of Training	Manufac-turing	Transportation/ Communications/ Utilities	Wholesale/ Retail Trade	Finance/ Insurance/ Banking	Business Services	Health Services	Educational Services	Public Adminis-tration	All Industries
Management Skills/ Development	82.2	88.3	85.4	85.0	84.1	90.8	79.5	88.3	84.2
Supervisory Skills	72.9	85.8	85.0	82.8	75.2	90.4	72.5	88.5	79.9
Technical Skills/ Knowledge	78.3	80.4	79.7	84.5	74.1	83.5	74.8	85.5	79.8
Communication Skills	63.8	82.5	78.8	77.0	76.0	80.4	76.8	86.2	75.7
Basic Computer Skills	64.0	74.2	66.7	70.3	65.0	62.6	76.2	78.5	69.3
New Methods/Procedures	59.0	68.3	71.1	73.8	63.9	75.8	68.7	77.7	68.8
Customer Relations/ Services	58.7	68.2	87.1	85.7	63.3	68.3	57.3	50.9	66.4
Clerical/Secretarial Skills	57.6	65.9	60.2	61.9	62.2	63.5	76.3	79.5	65.4
Personal Growth	51.1	63.1	60.2	57.8	61.4	70.9	71.2	69.7	61.9
Executive Development	60.8	70.0	71.1	58.0	50.6	58.2	63.2	72.3	61.6
Employee/Labor Relations	51.3	50.4	62.0	45.5	48.8	53.2	45.4	66.5	52.1
Wellness	40.1	55.9	41.3	40.5	39.7	63.2	56.4	60.8	47.7
Sales Skills	59.4	52.8	73.4	69.5	44.3	20.0	29.5	9.6	46.8
Customer Education	48.6	33.1	60.5	44.8	44.1	33.6	42.7	24.2	42.2
Remedial Basic Education	34.2	32.3	32.5	31.4	25.7	26.5	41.1	27.5	31.7

* Percent of all organizations within each industry that offer these types of training.
Reprinted with permission from the Oct. 1989 issue of TRAINING, the Magazine of Human Resources Development. Copyright 1989, Lakewood Publication Inc., Minneapolis, MN (612) 333-0471. All rights reserved.

Table 2.4
General Types of Training by Size of Organization*

Types of Training	Number of Employees				
	100–499	500–999	1,000–2,499	2,500–9,999	10,000 or more
Management Skills/Development	82.8	88.6	89.7	89.8	89.9
Supervisory Skills	78.2	86.7	86.2	87.1	87.8
Technical Skills/Knowledge	78.0	86.9	86.6	88.2	87.5
Communication Skills	73.9	79.8	85.0	85.5	86.4
Basic Computer Skills	67.3	76.4	76.2	78.9	81.5
New Methods/Procedures	68.0	71.7	71.9	72.2	75.2
Customer Relations/Services	65.1	71.0	72.3	70.8	68.1
Clerical/Secretarial Skills	63.9	71.7	69.7	72.4	73.8
Personal Growth	60.3	65.7	69.0	69.6	75.2
Executive Development	59.4	70.0	69.5	70.6	75.8
Employee/Labor Relations	50.1	57.6	59.9	66.4	66.8
Wellness	45.4	53.3	59.4	58.3	60.4
Sales Skills	46.2	47.9	48.2	51.5	54.3
Customer Education	42.0	41.7	41.7	46.2	51.1
Remedial Basic Education	30.9	32.6	36.0	38.6	45.4

* Percent of organizations providing these types of training.

to the basic principles of training design, as discussed later in this book. In terms of costs, as mentioned in the introduction to this chapter, aggregate 1989 budgeted training expenditures in U.S. firms were around $44.4 billion. These costs included hardware budgets (e.g., VCRs, computers), off-shelf budgets (expenditures for prepackaged programs), custom-design budgets, and outside services budgets. These costs do not include salary costs of trainers and trainees. If included, the total cost to business to provide job training is approximately $200 billion per year (*Training*, 1989).

The realization of training benefits is dependent upon the acceptance of training as a systematic process. It is the thesis of this book that the systematic procedures of training can and should be employed by human resource and training personnel in designing training systems. Toward this end, the purpose of this book is to help human resource and training personnel to maximize their training efforts. The book is essentially a step-by-step guide to plan, develop, design, conduct, and evaluate training systems. Although the book is not intended to be completely prescriptive,

Table 2.5
Specific Types of Training

Types of Training	% Providing[1]	In-House Only(%)[2]	Outside Only(%)[3]	Both(%)[4]
New-Employee Orientation	72.1	62.3	1.2	8.6
Performance Appraisals	65.2	38.6	4.1	22.5
Leadership	60.4	14.3	9.6	36.5
Interpersonal Skills	56.6	15.3	7.8	33.5
Hiring/Selection Process	54.6	23.0	7.3	24.3
New-Equipment Operation	54.4	27.5	3.7	23.2
Train-the-Trainer	53.8	15.4	16.5	21.9
Listening Skills	53.6	14.9	8.3	30.4
Time Management	51.5	12.7	10.6	28.2
Decision Making	51.1	15.9	11.4	23.8
Delegation Skills	51.1	15.0	11.3	24.8
Motivation	51.1	13.8	8.5	28.8
Goal Setting	50.1	17.0	7.0	26.1
Personal Computer Applications	49.6	17.0	6.1	26.5
Stress Management	49.6	11.7	13.5	24.4
Word Processing	49.4	17.4	9.5	22.5
Product Knowledge	49.2	33.2	2.6	13.4
Team Building	48.5	13.2	9.2	26.1
Problem Solving	46.8	12.3	5.7	28.8
Computer Programming	46.6	10.9	11.6	24.1
Public Speaking/Presentation	44.5	12.8	11.7	20.0
Writing Skills	41.7	10.2	13.8	17.7
Safety	41.1	16.1	2.3	22.7

	Percent provide[1]	In-house[2]	Outside[3]	Combination[4]
Data Processing	40.6	12.5	8.1	20.0
Managing Change	40.5	10.9	8.7	20.9
Planning	40.3	12.7	4.8	22.8
Conducting Meetings	38.6	17.0	6.9	14.7
Negotiating Skills	37.4	9.1	11.6	16.7
MIS	35.6	8.5	7.8	19.3
Marketing	33.8	9.3	9.0	15.5
Strategic Planning	33.8	7.8	8.4	17.6
Substance Abuse	33.2	7.8	9.5	15.9
Finance	33.0	7.6	11.8	13.6
Smoking Cessation	32.3	8.2	13.9	10.2
Quality Control	29.9	13.1	3.2	13.6
Outplacement/Retirement Planning	27.8	13.0	7.0	7.8
Ethics	26.6	10.7	4.0	11.9
Creativity	25.6	7.5	5.4	12.7
Purchasing	22.3	9.3	5.7	7.3
Reading Skills	17.1	5.0	6.5	5.6
Foreign Language	12.0	2.5	4.5	5.0
Other (Topics Not Listed)	9.6	2.5	5.0	2.1

OF ALL ORGANIZATIONS WITH 100 OR MORE EMPLOYEES . . .
[1]Percent that provide each type of training.
[2]Percent that say all training of this type is designed and delivered by in-house staff.
[3]Percent that say all training of this type is designed and delivered by outside consultants or suppliers.
[4]Percent that say training of this type is designed and delivered by a combination of in-house staff and outside suppliers.

Reprinted with permission from the Oct. 1989 issue of TRAINING, The Magazine of Human Resources Development. Copyright 1989, Lakewood Publications, Inc., Minneapolis, MN (612) 333-0471. All Rights Reserved.

it does present a systematic and practical approach to the design of training systems based on the training systems model presented in Chapter 1 (Figure 1.3).

SUMMARY

Economic and technological trends provide clear signals that training is a growth industry. The pace of innovation, change, and development is faster and faster, year by year. Obsolescence bedevils all of us. Perhaps the Paul Principle expresses this phenomenon most aptly: *Over time, people become uneducated, and therefore incompetent, to perform at a level they once performed at adequately* (Armer, 1970). Training is an important antidote to obsolescence. In addition to the many productivity-enhancing training programs provided (as presented in the tables throughout this chapter), many firms are also offering the kinds of training that will enhance quality of work life as well (e.g., personal growth, career planning, and safety). This trend is likely to continue. What is also likely, however, is continued research that will provide stable and accurate estimates of the percentage improvements in job performance and productivity expected from various kinds of training interventions (Guzzo, Jette, and Katzell, 1985). Such estimates are crucial to the widespread application of utility analysis in training evaluation. This type of research will someday enable us to provide managers with accurate estimates of dollar gains in productivity of alternative training strategies, and it can also guide training HRM specialists in adjusting their programs so as to make them attractive from a cost-benefit viewpoint (Cascio, 1989).

3

Determining Training Needs

INTRODUCTION

Training is needed whenever organizational goals can be furthered by improved employee performance. Training is one of the major ways in which employers develop employees to meet organizational objectives and business plans. The success of organizational training can be enhanced when training is *planned* by the organization. It does not just happen. Planning implies a process of analysis, consideration of alternatives, and decision making.

Planning is particularly crucial in training because, without careful and complete planning, resources are certain to be wasted. Without sound planning, training programs are not likely to support the plans and objectives of the organization as a whole. Too often, training programs have reflected fads, expediency, even caprice. They have been initiated in response to the quick sell or a desire to "keep up with the Joneses." These get-rich-quick schemes increase the likelihood of ineffective training programs, and eventually they must be replaced by more systematic approaches.

The next step in planning an effective training program, after the preassessment phase, as discussed in Chapter 1, is to determine what training is needed throughout the organization. Any discussion of training, therefore, must begin with an analysis of the need for training and a specific plan. In effect, the HRM specialists are preparing a training forecast, which is a major step in a training systems model. The fact that the Human

Resource/Personnel literature is filled with literally hundreds of articles dealing either in whole or in part with training needs assessment is testimony to its importance (Leap and Crino, 1989). The bottom line is that the assessment of training needs is important because other organizational decisions hinge on it (McGehee and Thayer, 1961).

To provide an adequate return on investment, a training course must produce results that exceed its costs. Given finite training budgets, HRM specialists must make difficult trade-offs to determine which type of training will produce the greatest return for the organization. The potential for such a return on investment begins with careful and informed preparation and planning as discussed above. This preparation and planning begins with an analysis of the need for training.

ANALYSIS OF TRAINING NEEDS

Many companies, as mentioned in Chapter 2, allocate large sums of money to training. IBM, for example, spends more than one-half billion dollars per year educating and training workers (Bernstein, Ticer, and Levine, 1986). Some money goes to train 10,000 workers for new jobs. Other expenditures update technical and scientific workers (Werther and Davis, 1989). Still other outlays prepare workers and managers for future challenges. If IBM is to get maximum benefit for this staggering expenditure, then efforts must concentrate on the employees and situations that benefit the most (Beckhard, 1982).

Establishing the need for training takes time. Since training is one way to achieve an optimal person-job-organization fit, a starting point is to analyze the three components of fit. To decide what training is needed, IBM's trainers assess its organizational, job (operations), and employee needs. Organization, job, and employee analysis are the three levels of analysis (the assessment phase of training systems models) for determining the needs that training can fulfill (McGehee and Thayer, 1961; Schuler and Youngblood, 1986).

Organizational analysis focuses on identifying where within the organization training is needed and begins with an examination of the short- and long-term objectives of the organization and the trends likely to affect these objectives. By definition, training is intended to further the goals of the organization. At a general level, an assessment of training needs must begin with an examination of the organization. Training needs must be analyzed against the backdrop of organizational objectives and strategies. Unless this is done, time and money may well be wasted on training programs that do not advance the cause of the company (Moore and Dutton, 1978). Employees may be trained in skills they already possess (as happened to members of a machinists' union of a major airline not long ago); the training budget may be squandered on "rest and recuperation" sessions, where employes are entertained but learn little in the way of required job skills or job knowledge; or the budget may be spent on glittering hardware that meets the training director's needs but not the organization's.

A thorough needs analysis might look at organization maintenance, efficiency, and culture. *Organizational maintenance* aims at ensuring a steady supply of critical skills. If succession plans point out the need to develop managerial talent, training may include transferring high-potential employees through a variety of positions and locations to ensure broad exposure to a variety of responsibilities.

Organizational efficiency might include checking on the degree of goal achievement, the extent to which current employees are performing well enough to achieve organizational goals. There are a number of indicators: productivity, accidents, waste, labor costs, quality of product or service output, employee performance, or various other organizational measures. Examination of the organization's strategies, the results of employment planning, and the major variance between the units' successes and failures can help determine the role training could play. The organization's goals can be analyzed for an entire organization or for an organizational unit such as a department or division. Information on the goals and objectives can be used to identify the scope and content of the training. For example, to meet the goal of increased sales, training in new-product knowledge and new-customer development may be needed.

Organizational culture includes the value system or philosophy of the organization. Like the analysis of efficiency indexes, it can help identify where training programs may be needed and provide criteria by which to evaluate the effectiveness of the programs that are implemented. Training can be designed to impart the organization's philosophy or values to employees (Argyris, 1982).

Assessing training needs at the organizational level presents problems and future challenges to be met through training. For example, changes in the external environment may present an organization with new challenges. To respond effectively, employees may need training to deal with these changes. The comments of one training director illustrate the impact of the external environment:

After the Equal Employment Opportunity Act in 1972 changed the Civil Rights Act of 1964, we had to train every interviewer in the personnel department. This training was needed to ensure that our interviewers would not ask questions that might violate federal laws. When managers in other departments heard of the training, they too wanted to sign up. We decided that since they interviewed recruits, they should also be trained. What was to be a one-time seminar became a monthly session for nearly three years.

Trends in union activity, governmental intervention, productivity, accidents, illnesses, turnover, absenteeism, and on-the-job employee behavior all provide relevant information at the organizational level. The important question becomes: "Will training produce changes in employee behavior that will contribute to our organization's goals?"

Job analysis information is a valuable source of data to establish training needs. Because the organizational needs analysis is too broad to spot detailed training needs for specific jobs, it is also necessary to conduct a job needs analysis. Several approaches to analyzing jobs identify training needs (Bownas, Bosshardt, and Donnelly, 1985). Task analysis, work sampling, critical incident analysis, and task inventories in which employees indicate how frequently they carry out a particular activity and the importance of each activity to the job are all ways to analyze the training needs of a particular job. Job analysis requires a careful examination of the job to be performed after training.

Job analysis involves: (1) a systematic collection of information that describes exactly how jobs are done, so that (2) standards of performance for those jobs can be determined; (3) how tasks are to be performed to meet the standards; and (4) the knowledge, skills, abilities, and other characteristics necessary for effective task performance. Chapter 4 will provide more detail on the importance of job analysis in training needs analysis and the training systems model.

Employee performance analysis determines how well each employee is performing the tasks that make up his or her job; it can be accomplished in two different ways. Employee performance deficiencies may be identified either by comparing actual performance with the minimum acceptable standards of performance or by comparing an evaluation of employee proficiency on each required skill dimension with the proficiency level required for each skill.

Many employers use performance evaluation to identify developmental needs for individual employees. At this level, training needs may be defined in terms of the following general idea: the difference between desired and actual performance is the employee's training need. Performance standards, identified in the job analysis phase, constitute desired performance. Employee performance data, diagnostic ratings of employees by their supervisors, interviews, or tests (job knowledge, work sample, or situational) can provide information on actual performance against which each employee can be compared to desired job performance standards. A gap between actual and desired performance may be filled by training.

A thorough organizational training needs analysis should look at the organization, job, and employee. But to ask productive questions regarding training needs; an "integrative model" such as the one shown in Figure 3.1 is needed (Cascio, 1989).

Assessing the needs for training does not end here. To evaluate the results of training and to assess what training is needed in the future, needs must be analyzed by utilizing the methods of gathering needs analysis data.

Figure 3.1
Training Needs Assessment Model

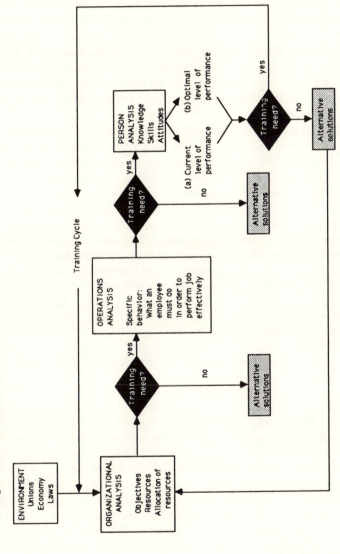

Source: From W.F. Cascio, MANAGING HUMAN RESOURCES: PRODUCTIVITY, QUALITY OF WORK LIFE, PRODUCTS, 2nd ed. 1989. New York: McGraw-Hill, p. 237. Reprinted by permission of the publisher.

Methods of Needs Assessment

In some cases, the determination of training needs is a fairly straight-forward process that may be conducted without an extensive analysis of the organization. For example, all new employees normally undergo orientation training. An impending technological change such as the introduction of new computer hardware will automatically require the need for training those affected. On the other hand, determining training requirements to resolve deficiencies in skills or to address career developmental needs necessitates much greater analysis by training personnel. To identify the training needs that result from performance problems, the HRM specialist must systematically collect and analyze employees' output, product quality, and attitudes.

Training-needs information may be gathered using a variety of methods. Some of these methods work equally well for organizational, job and employee level assessment, and include the following (this list is adapted from Carrell, Kuzmits, and Elbert, 1989; Steadham, 1980; Newstrom and Lilyquist, 1979; Dilauro, 1979; and Moore and Dutton, 1978):

1. *Attitude surveys*. These are useful for gathering general-level information on employee satisfaction, and other attitudes. These surveys seldom provide information in sufficient detail for the design and planning of training programs but can offer information on employee perceptions of the work place, including current training efforts, promotion preparation, retraining programs, and the like.

2. *Advisory committees*. An organization may seek to establish one or more advisory committees to review job skill demands and the quality of current training and selection programs relative to those demands. These committees may be composed of management personnel and employees. The membership of these committees should be determined by who can best provide the appropriate insights.

3. *Performance appraisals*. Depending upon the degree of detail and job relevance of the appraisal, this source of information can be very valuable. Employees who consistently fail to perform certain tasks satisfactorily may require training in order to do so. This will be discussed in more detail later in this chapter as performance discrepancy needs assessment. Time and costs are low since the data are regularly gathered. And because both the employee and supervisor are involved, an emotional commitment to training is often an additional benefit of this method.

4. *Skill tests*. These tests provide an assessment of current employee skill levels. A test of necessary skill, such as typing, computer programming, or driving may also be used to measure training needs. Test results are then directly compared against established skill requirements for the various positions. When using skill tests for needs assessment it is critical that the tests be job-related and measure those skills and abilities required for successful job performance.

5. *Observations of behavior*. HRM specialists or supervisors may directly observe employees' behavior to identify training needs. Observations can be as technical as time-motion studies or as functionally or behaviorally specific as observing

a new employee at work. This method is generally limited to the assessment of technical skills and behaviors. Its primary drawback is that it is time-consuming, costly, and requires a highly skilled observer with both process and content knowledge (unlike an interviewer who needs, for the most part, only process skills).

6. *Actual performance of the job.* In this method of data collection, a trained analyst actually performs the job. From this experience the analyst determines the KSAs required for proficiency. This method can provide useful data on very straightforward jobs. However, the higher the organizational level, or more complex the job, the less useful this method will be. Job analysts are not capable of performing all jobs in the company, especially those that require significant levels of specialized KSAs. Nor is it always possible for the analyst to remain with a job until all possible tasks are performed. There are some jobs where particular tasks, although important, are performed only rarely.

7. *Performance-related documents.* These include productivity reports, absenteeism records, turnover reports, and other performance indicators. These documents are usually collected as a routine part of organizational data collection and provide insight into areas where training may be necessary. A major shortcoming of this approach is that the data simply indicate the existence of a problem and do little to specify its cause. Only a careful analysis will determine whether or not training will solve the problem.

8. *Management requests.* Occasionally, a member of management may request that an employee or employees receive training. With this approach, care must be taken to ensure that the problem is actually a training problem and that the training needs have been accurately diagnosed.

9. *Employee interviews.* This method generally involves a discussion between the HRM specialist and individual employee. Interviews can be formal or casual, structured or unstructured, or somewhere in between. Although employee interviews are good for specifying individual training needs, they are also time-consuming, and the results can be difficult to analyze and quantify. This method is little used compared to other, less costly methods.

10. *Assessment centers.* Used mostly for management development, the assessment center requires participants to undergo a series of exercises and tests to determine their strengths and weaknesses in performing managerial tasks. Although the assessment center is used primarily to predict success in a managerial role, its use in measuring training needs is increasing.

11. *Group discussions.* This method generally involves meeting with employees who represent a specific work area. A primary benefit of group discussions is that the employees are emotionally committed to the training as a result of their active participation in the assessment process. In addition, this method permits on-the-spot synthesis of different viewpoints. A problem with this method is that it can be rather time-consuming (therefore initially expensive) both for the HRM specialist and the organization.

12. *Client or customer feedback.* This source of information is very valuable, as it represents feedback from those upon whom the organization is depending for success. It can also be sufficiently detailed to be of direct use for training planning.

13. *Exit interviews*. A high turnover rate may spell organizational problems and a need for training, particularly in the area of supervision. Many employees who are leaving an organization are willing to provide candid assessments of organizational deficiencies. Included among potential deficiencies may be the current selection process and the preparation provided by training programs. The validity of exit interviews greatly depends on an unbiased and skilled interviewer and on honest answers from the employee who is leaving.

14. *Job descriptions, job specifications, task analyses*. These documents can be reviewed in order to determine which knowledge, skills, and abilities (KSAs) were considered necessary by a formal job analysis.

15. *Questionnaires*. Questionnaires may be given to employees, supervisors, and any other organizational personnel who might be able to provide useful data. The questionnaire generally specifies important skill areas, the importance of the skill, and the employee's perception of training needs for each area, useful training techniques, and program content. The cost of this technique is relatively low because a great deal of data may be collected in a relatively short time. Often, questionnaires are of limited utility in getting at causes of problems or possible solutions. An example of such a questionnaire is shown in Figure 3.2.

As noted above, there are many different methods for collecting training needs information, each with its own advantages and disadvantages. Those responsible for conducting a training needs assessment must be aware of these limitations. In addition, HRM specialists should evaluate the range of alternative methods to assess training needs according to the following criteria: employee involvement, management involvement, time required, relative cost, and the degree to which the data can be quantified (Newstrom and Lilyquist, 1979).

Trainee involvement is desirable to provide the necessary motivation to undertake training and to use the newly acquired behaviors on the job. Management involvement is necessary to provide the support and encouragement for the trainee to implement the new behaviors and provide the rewards for doing so. Although no single method emerges as clearly superior, this research does provide a perspective on the differences among the various methods. HRM specialists may find that such a systematic examination of methods will allow for more directly useful data collection in their organization.

No one can overestimate the importance of trainee involvement and managerial support. According to a recent survey, the most commonly cited reasons for training failures included a lack of managerial support for the new behaviors and a lack of sufficient employee involvement (The Conference Board, 1985). Other reasons were: no on-the-job rewards for behaviors and skills learned in training; insufficient time to execute training programs; inaccurate training needs analyses; and changes in training needs changed after program had been implemented. Thus, training decisions must consider the trainees' supervisors and coworkers, to see that the new

Figure 3.2
An Example of a Questionnaire for Identifying Training Needs

POSITION: Clerical

Employee _____   Department _____

Supervisor _____   Date _____

INSTRUCTIONS:

In column A, rate the skill necessary to perform the job. Use the following ratings: 1 - very important; 2 - moderately important; 3 - not important.

In column B, rate the need for training for each skill area which received a rating of 1 or 2 in column A. In assessing training needs, use the following ratings: 1 - no need for training; 2 - moderate need for training; 3 - immediate, critical need for training.

Skill	A How important is the skill?	B Employee's need for training?
Ability to read and comprehend rough-draft material		
Typing speed		
Typing accuracy		
Proofreading skills		
Ability to use office machinery		
Filing skills		
Ability to compose letters and memos		
Oral communications		
Ability to organize daily routine		
Human relations skills		

behaviors are applied and rewarded on the job (Milkovich and Boudreau, 1988).

Although alternatives for systematic needs assessment abound, in reality it is only rarely used. Digman (1980) found that 81 percent of companies surveyed identified training needs only by reacting to problems that cropped up. Fewer organizations even claim to have regular ongoing processes for defining training needs. However, there are some needs assessment methods which are used by many organizations and newer ones finding their way into the systematic process of training.

Performance Discrepancy Needs Analysis (Performance Analysis). Performance discrepancy needs analysis is one of the more frequently used needs analysis methods at the employee level. Analysis at this level is based upon either a comparison of current employee performance to organizational performance standards (performance discrepancy), or a comparison of anticipated employee skill needs to current skill levels. Performance discrepancy assessment requires that some measure of performance be taken for an employee. That performance appraisal is then compared to the appropriate performance standards. In most situations a discrepancy indicates that further analysis is necessary and suggests training needs. This additional analysis should reveal whether the performance is due to a skill or knowledge deficiency (or other trainable deficiency) or to another problem. The organization may have made a poor selection decision that cannot be salvaged through additional employee training. The employee may have a chemical dependency or personal problems that adversely affect performance. Supervision may be inadequate or the job may have been poorly designed. In any case, it must be determined whether training can improve employee performance. To the extent that training can improve performance, the organization should consider providing it to the employee (assuming that the cost is reasonable). Other options available to the organization include the transfer of the employee to a position for which he or she is better suited (placement/transfer option) or termination due to poor performance. This is the performance discrepancy approach to individual-level needs assessment.

By observation, asking, and listening, a HRM specialist is actually conducting a performance analysis (Michalak and Yager, 1979). There are a number of specific steps that are taken in using a performance analysis to determine training needs. The steps that are used in conducting a performance analysis are:

Step 1: Behavioral discrepancy. The first step is to appraise employees' performance. How are the employees doing now and how should they be doing? If Ms. Doe, a secretary, is using a word processor to prepare budgets and takes an average of 7.5 hours to complete the work, this record of performance can be used to assess her performance. This performance may be 2.0 hours over what is expected. Thus, there is a behavioral discrepancy—a difference between actual and expected.

Step 2: Cost/Value analysis. Next the manager must determine the cost and value of correcting the identified behavioral discrepancy. Is it worth the cost, time, and expense to have the secretary prepare the budgets in less than 7.5 hours?

Step 3: Is it a can't- or won't-do situation? It is important to determine if the employee could do the expected job if he or she wanted to. Three questions need to be answered: (a) Does the person know what to do in terms of performance? (b) Could the person do the job if he or she wanted to? and (c) Does the person want to do the job? Answering these questions requires observation, listening, and asking skills on the part of the person conducting the performance analysis.

Step 4: Set standards. A secretary who doesn't know what the standard is may underperform. Establishing a standard and clearly communicating it can improve performance.

Step 5: Remove obstacles. Not being able to complete budgets on time may be caused by frequent breakdowns of the equipment (the word processing system) or not receiving a job on time. Time, equipment, and people can be obstacles that result in behavior discrepancies.

Step 6: Practice. Practice, practice, practice may be one avenue to performing a job better. Does the manager permit the employee the needed practice time?

Step 7: Training. If the performance analysis indicates that behaviors need to be altered, training became a viable consideration before any training approaches can be weighed and considered as being best-suited to correct the behavior discrepancy.

Step 8: Change the job. Redesigning the job through job enrichment, job simplification, or job enlargement may be the best solution.

Step 9: Create a motivational climate. In some cases a skilled and able employee may not want to perform the job as required, posing a motivational problem. A manager may then have to use a motivational approach that converts this under-motivated person into a motivated high performer. Rewards, punishment, discipline, or some combination may be needed to create a positive climate that results in the employee utilizing his or her skills optimally.

Step 10: Transfer or terminate. If all else has failed, the employee may have to be transferred or terminated.

A performance analysis is a sound procedure that can provide insight into training needs and objectives. The gap between the actual state of an individual's performance and the ideal or desired state of performance forms a basis for training needs diagnosis and the design of training interventions. Such an analysis may also illustrate that training is not the best solution to the behavior discrepancies identified. If this is the case other solutions will surface as the performance analysis is conducted (Haig, 1984).

Adaptive Competency (Person-Job Interaction) Needs Analysis Approach. The adaptive competency needs analysis approach, like the performance discrepancy approach, takes place at the individual employee level. The adaptive competency needs assessment approach focuses on the employee's repertoire of skills as they relate to the specific demands of a job. Tyler (1978) summarizes two major advantages of this approach:

First, competencies cut across boundaries. Instead of assessing intelligence and achievement in school children, skills in job applicants, and symptoms in psychiatric patients, we can examine what each person in any of these categories can and cannot do. One can capitalize on the developed competencies and set up situations in which competencies not now present can be acquired, whether these are basic educational competencies, occupational competencies of intrapersonal competencies. The competency approach thus provides individuals and their helpers with clear guidelines as to what to do next. Another potential benefit is the generation of the concept of complementarity to supplement the concept of competitiveness so prevalent in modern society. Competencies represent a completely different way of structuring our perceptions of others. The more competencies other people have the better for each of us, and it is essential for the functioning of complex society that individuals develop different repertoires of competencies (pp. 104–105).

The adaptive competency approach to needs analysis is based upon Kolb's (1984) Experiential Learning Theory (ELT) which allows one to view the person (employee) and job in commensurate terms. The cornerstone of this approach is that learning, adaptation, and problem-solving processes are similar and that all jobs involve each of these processes. Therefore, if one describes both the person's adaptive skills and job requirements in learning terms, then one can identify and describe the adaptive or interactive processes that occur in the work setting.

ELT conceptualizes the learning process in such a way that differences in learner styles and corresponding learning environments can be identified. The application of the adaptive competency approach accepts the premise that typical needs analysis at the employee level portrays jobs in one set of terms (i.e., job specifications), and employees are thought of in another set of terms (person-trait characteristics). To achieve a commensurate means of assessing training needs at the employee and job interaction level two critical assumptions underlie the adaptive competency approach: (1) that the person or employee be viewed as an adult learner, and (2) that the job context be viewed as a learning environment in which job performance necessitates some type of cycling through the ELT process (Fry, 1978; Sims, 1981, 1983).

The adaptive competency needs analysis approach measures the employee's learning styles and the requirements of the job and arranges them around the generic learning competencies of Kolb's learning cycle in what is called a competency circle. As Figure 3.3 depicts for the job of an engineering manager, the competency circle portrays a field on which measures of both a person's skills and the job's demands are plotted. Training needs are determined by the degree of match or mismatch between the job demands and the necessary skills to successfully perform the job of engineering manager. In this framework it is not assumed that a match of the job demands and the skills of an employee (engineering manager) is always the goal of the organization. The learning styles described in ELT (learning styles will be discussed in detail in Chapters 5 and 8) are perceived as learning competencies that facilitate the development of a generic class of more specific skills. This generic class of skills is required for effective performance on different tasks. Each job and task requires a corresponding set of learned KSAs for effective performance. The effective matching or mismatching of task demands and these personal attributes results in a performance competency.

In the adaptive competency approach, performance competencies become a vehicle for assessing employee characteristics and job demands in commensurate terms. Thus the performance competencies required for a specific job can be compared to an employee's inventory of performance competencies to determine the degree of match and areas in need of development (training needs).

Nominal Group Process for Training Needs Analysis. HRM specialists are constantly faced with the problem of where to start in defining training

Figure 3.3
Comparison of Job Demands and Skills for Engineering Manager

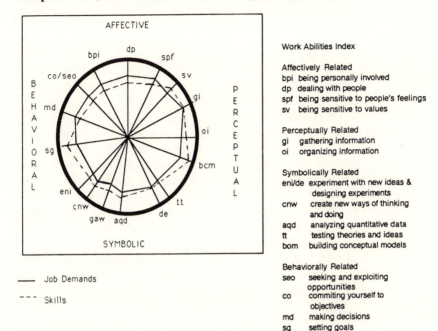

Work Abilities Index

Affectively Related
bpi being personally involved
dp   dealing with people
spf being sensitive to people's feelings
sv   being sensitive to values

Perceptually Related
gi   gathering information
oi   organizing information

Symbolically Related
eni/de experiment with new ideas &
         designing experiments
cnw   create new ways of thinking
         and doing
aqd   analyzing quantitative data
tt   testing theories and ideas
bcm   building conceptual models

Behaviorally Related
seo   seeking and exploiting
        opportunities
co   commiting yourself to
        objectives
md   making decisions
sg   setting goals

——— Job Demands

- - - Skills

needs. In some situations the broad goals of an organization have already been established. The task of the HRM specialists is to bring those goals into closer focus, that is, to determine important training needs. In trying to address this problem trainers wish to avoid two traps into which training commonly falls.

The first of these may be called "topicism." This trap is characterized by a training needs analysis that gathers responses to a preordained menu of topics. A typical approach is a structured questionnaire that asks respondents to rate the value of certain topics—for example, "How much do you (or others) need management training? (A great deal/a lot/some/ not at all)." Alternatively, respondents might be asked to select cards from a topic pack and arrange them in order of importance. These mainstream training needs analysis approaches suffer from the basic problem that they arise from the HRM specialists' constructs or their need to categorize data into training needs or topics. Typical outcomes yield a list of topics arranged in descending order of importance like the following:

1. How to plan and conduct meetings
2. How to process long-range planning results
3. How to counsel employees

4. How to conduct performance appraisals

5. How to select human resources to maximize efficiency

6. How to prepare a personal career development plan

7. Etc.

The second trap may be called "trainerism," for want of a better term. This presumes that the point of departure for assessment of training needs is the expertise or interests of the individual members of staff, and the ultimate product is a judicious mix of these elements. This trap is typically rationalized in such phrases as, "Like all managers, what they (employees) really need is . . . ," or "Since we were recruited to do the training, the assumption surely is we know what is best." The traps here are obvious enough if one is trying to build a program based on needs of the organization. Note that typically both of these traps also assume that the shortfall in employee performance is a function of the ability of individual employees, and that the central thrust of training is to "fix up" the employee by developing skills or expert knowledge.

The nominal group process for training needs analysis provides a useful approach to determining the kinds of training needs in an organization, and determining what must be done.

Phase One—Problem Identification

Step 1: Using a representative group an open question is posed, such as, "What barriers inhibit the performance of managers in your department (or in the service)?"

Step 2: Individuals freely cite barriers. All offers are taken. Concise statements are recorded on butcher paper or blackboard or by similar method. Every attempt should be made to obtain specific rather than vague statements. For example, "poor communication," if clarified, might yield "relations between head office and branch offices are poor," which is a more definable situation. Repeat statements should not be posted.

Step 3: When the group runs out of statements—or after a preset time—the next step is to bring like problems together under a reasonable (say seven to twelve) number of logical and seemingly useful headings. This basketing process allows for the reduction of the statements to a workable list. Statements should not be forced under headings—some may stand alone, while several may be grouped.

Step 4: Draw a chart on a board and list the problem headings; then ask each member to distribute one hundred points among the headings in such a way as to show the relative importance of the problem (or its priority for resolution, if you prefer). There are no restrictions on how points are allocated, except that each column is checked, then summed horizontally. The summed scores give the priority ranking of each of the problem areas as seen by the group. The process provides an easy way of producing a forced consensus, and allows the group to begin work quickly on the listed problem areas.

Step 5: The group now beings to work on the three top-priority problem areas. If time permits, lower-priority problems may be worked on in later rounds.

Phase Two—Problem Analysis

The whole group now divides into three smaller sets and begins three rounds of work. The problem being worked on in each set is different in each round, and each group works on each problem. This ingenious arrangement allows everyone to contribute to the discussion of each problem, but limits the effects of any one individual dominating the discussion.

Times for each round need to be allocated and managed according to the total time available. It is suggested that a minimum time is thirty minutes for each round, and ten minutes for each plenary. Specific tasks are allocated for each round and plenary as follows.

Round 1: Sets are asked to make a concise operational definition of the problem. This may come from perusal of the "barrier" statements listed under the problem heading. For example, a heading of "Organizational Culture" may come to be defined as, "The organization has a culture that prevents people from allowing conflicts to surface, hence interpersonal relations are dishonest, and important operational problems are not faced." Sets may work more productively if people are invited to join the set that is to work on the problem area in which they have most interest.

Plenary: The assembled large group hears each set's Round 1 report in turn, and is invited to comment on the operational definitions of the problem areas. Modifications should be incorporated if there is sufficient agreement.

Round 2: Sets switch problems and the task now is to isolate elements of the problem. The questions "How?" and "Why?" should yield lists of the major elements perceived to contribute to the problem situation. Specifics are needed rather than generalists.

Plenary: Sets report again and the large group is once again invited to comment on or add to the elements listed in Round 2.

Round 3: Some variation in the task is possible at this stage dependent on what precise outcomes are sought. Useful tasks are addressing, "What attributes need to be developed in employees, supervisors, managers to overcome these barriers?" and/or "In what ways can training and development help?"

Plenary: Finally sets report on Round 3 and once again the assembled large group is invited to comment on or add to the work of each set.

This ends the nominal group process. If the process is properly managed it produces: (1) a detailed and generalized list of observed barriers to effective management; (2) an agreed-upon operational definition of each problem area; (3) agreement on what attributes need to be developed among employees to overcome these barriers, and how training might help. The nominal group process for training needs analysis is an alternative to conventional training needs analysis; it also has wide application as a problem- and consensus-finding tool for prioritizing training needs or selecting training methods.

Selecting a Training Needs Assessment Method

A wide variety of training needs methods are available, and several criteria may be used in selecting a needs-assessment method (Newstrom and Lilyquist, 1979). First, employee involvement is important because a feeling of participation in the assessment process enhances employee motivation to undergo training. Employee perceptions about a training program before it begins can affect the effectiveness of training. When employees are provided a realistic preview of training programs and have some choice of which program (or training method) they enter, the outcome of the training is improved. Employees given a preview of programs and some choice will generally make a stronger commitment to attend the program, learn more from the training, and are more satisfied with the program. Why? Perhaps employees who have chosen a particular program because they desire the training are more motivated to learn (Hicks and Klimoski, 1987).

Second, management involvement is important because supervisors generally have accurate information about their employees' performance and are in a prime position to assess the need for training within the work group. Third, the time required is always important in considering any form of data collection, and needs assessment is no exception. And since time is generally a scarce commodity, trainers often favor methods that do not involve large investments of time. Fourth, the cost of the assessment method, in terms of personnel and materials involved, is an important consideration. Training budgets rarely afford the selection of training processes and activities without financial consideration. Fifth, the needs assessment information must be relevant and quantifiable. Vague or subjective opinions about training needs will do little to generate the support from top management essential for a successful training program.

As described earlier in this chapter there is no one best method, and each method has its own strengths and weaknesses. In selecting a particular needs assessment method or combination of methods, HRM specialists must carefully consider the merits and drawbacks of each and make their selections in light of the conditions and constraints within their own organizations.

Changes in Needs Assessment Methods. Training programs are said to be serving company needs more effectively as a result of such factors as an emphasis on "needs-driven" training. Among the many firms reporting a major reorientation toward needs-driven education and training within the past few years are companies like IBM, GE, and Xerox—all of which have long been regarded as leaders and exemplars in the field (The Conference Board, 1985). Participants of the College Board Study suggest that needs-driven training entails a number of closely linked steps—assessing individual and group needs, defining training objectives, selecting participants, designing courses and instructional methods, providing for feedback, and evaluation. In addition, the greater emphasis upon methods of assessing training needs appears in three forms.

First, job-description and performance-appraisal processes are being used more widely, and with greater sophistication, to ascertain the training needs of key personnel. Typically included are individuals judged to hold special promise for advancement to future leadership, and those likely to succeed present managerial incumbents. "Individual contributors," specialists in a variety of professional and technical areas, may also be brought into these processes.

Second, training executives in many companies are working more closely with managers to help them to: (1) interpret the training implications not only of performance appraisals, but of new technological and operating systems, and (2) judge the role of training in improving unit performance. In the process, training goals are being spelled out with greater specificity.

A third factor in the improvement companies report in their needs-assessment process is that training personnel in different parts of the company are exchanging information and judgments to an increasing extent, usually under the auspices of the corporate department (The Conference Board, 1985).

Texas Instruments provides a recent example of how organizations are putting more emphasis on the assessment of training needs before moving into training. Texas Instruments' human resources people knew they had to assess rather than assume they knew the training needs of the staff (Wircenski, Sullivan, and Moore, 1989). Human resources development departments were faced with a dilemma: how to assess the training needed to turn technical talent into instructional expertise—and how to do the assessment quickly. As a result of this dilemma, and with top management approval and data analysis, the human resources department specialist team developed a five-step model that comprised: (1) an initial list of typical tasks, (2) a staff survey to validate those tasks, (3) classroom observations of teaching, (4) structured interviews with instructors, and (5) a final report with recommendations to assess the training needs of the engineer instructors. Figure 3.4 presents the five-step needs-assessment model (Wircenski, Sullivan, and Moore, 1989).

The major strengths of the five-step needs-assessment model are its comprehensiveness and its potential application by other organizations. The model included input from management and training personnel from each of the functional branches of the human resources development department. The approach was quickly accepted by training personnel because of the staff interviews and the rigorous identification of tasks.

Figure 3.4
The Five-Step Needs-Assessment Model

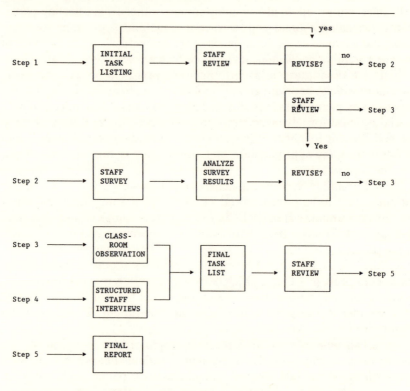

Source: J. L. Wircenski, R. L. Sullivan, and P. Moore, "Assessing Training Needs at Texas Instruments," Copyright 1989, Training and Development Journal, April 1989, p. 61. American Society for Training and Development. Reprinted with permission.

Managers actively participated in developing each of the model stages. Managers were instrumental in giving feedback to the training personnel involved in the details of the needs-assessment survey, staff observations, and staff interviews.

HRM specialists and training departments can learn from Texas Instruments' example of avoiding the temptation to conduct training before conducting a thorough analysis of their own needs. Other organizations can apply the Texas Instruments model to ensure a comprehensive needs assessment to identify and rank their own actual training needs.

Prioritizing Training Needs

Because training seldom is an unlimited-budget item and there are multiple training needs in the organization, it is important for HRM specialists to prioritize needs. Ideally, training needs are ranked in importance on the basis of organizational objectives, with the training that is most needed to improve the health of the organization done first. However, other considerations including the following, may enter into the decision: upper management choices, time involved, HRM specialists' abilities and motivation, money, and the likelihood of tangible results.

An example of successful needs analysis occurred at CMDC Corporation, a middle-sized wholesaler in Denver, Colorado. The company was experiencing a very high error rate in its shipping records, which were prepared by a group of twenty-three clerical employees. The needs assessment consisted of checking all shipping records for one week and tabulating errors for each clerk. Five people accounted for 90 percent of the errors. These five people were then observed for four hours each until a clear pattern of the source of the errors was identified. It turned out that these people did not understand four of the twenty-five basic shipping transactions. A two-hour training session for those five employees reduced the error rate by 95 percent (Mathis and Jackson, 1985).

SUMMARY

Training is an expensive investment for any organization. The cost of obtaining internal training staff or external consultants is high, but the greatest cost is the time lost from productive work by the trainees themselves. Every hour in a training course is an hour of lost productivity. To provide an adequate return on investment, a training program must produce results that exceed its costs. The potential for such a return on investment begins with careful and informed preparation. This preparation begins with an analysis of the need for training.

HRM specialists must ensure that there is only one right reason for doing training: to improve employee performance and further organizational goals by increasing employees' job-related knowledge, skills, and abilities. Training for the right reasons and determining training needs can be enhanced by conducting the three basic analyses. They are organizational analysis, employee analysis, and job analysis.

The potential for an adequate return on investment is improved when those responsible for training make appropriate use of the variety of methods available for assessing training needs. Establishing the need for training can lead to properly designed and implemented training programs and thereby ensure training effectiveness.

The information generated by three basic analyses of training needs is very useful in the preparation of training programs. Although alternatives for systematic needs assessment abound, in reality they are only rarely used. At first glance, however, the amount of time and effort involved in these analyses may appear great. Few organizations conduct these three analyses thoroughly before planning and conducting training programs, even though much of this information is routinely collected and readily available. Organizational and departmental goals are often set by line managers, job descriptions and job specifications are established for recruiting and selection purposes, and employee performance is periodically evaluated as part of the performance appraisal process. Therefore, training needs analysis can begin with information that already has been compiled. Then, additional information not routinely collected (e.g., tests of specific knowledge, skills, and abilities) can be gathered with a reasonable amount of time and effort.

A second major consideration is that a clear deficiency in performance, as established in a training needs analysis, may not necessarily indicate the need for training. The key here is the difference between symptoms and causes. The discrepancy between actual and desired performance of a number of employees is a symptom that may be caused by lack of employee knowledge, skill, or ability. If so, training would be advisable. But employee's performance often suffers for reasons other than their own capabilities. For example, the employees may be poorly supervised, and a training program for the supervisors, not the employees, may be necessary. Still other causes of poor employee performance are totally unrelated to training, such as unclear job responsibilities and performance standards or unfair organizational pay policies.

The organization analysis is necessary to identify potential causes of poor employee performance that cannot be addressed via training. It must always be remembered that training changes only the trainee, not the work situation. For example, no amount of training in motivation and team spirit will raise the morale of employees who are unfairly paid.

Competent training needs analysis not only provides information about the nature of the organizational system, but is also helpful in designing and introducing training action alternatives for correcting possible problems. The training needs analysis affirms the need for training and the benefits of possible training to the organization. Therefore, the analysis of training needs should be comprehensive and thorough. Only then can organizations determine when training is really needed.

4

Collecting and Analyzing Data on Jobs: The Role of Job Analysis in Training

INTRODUCTION

Job analysis represents a fundamental starting point for training as well as other HRM activities. Organizations can use job analysis information to specify the training employees require for effective performance on their current jobs. In addition, complete job analysis information can reveal if new employees need additional training in certain areas to complete their jobs successfully. This can usually be discerned by comparing the employees' past work histories and training to the tasks specified in the job analysis. Job analysis can provide a thorough definition of what constitutes a job, enabling the supervisor to explain the boundaries of the employee's unit of work to a new employee. In any work situation it is difficult for an employee to perform well if there is confusion about what the job is and what is supposed to be done. Examination of the skills required for a job can assist the organization in better training and promoting its employees.

For training programs to provide an adequate return on investment, they must be job-relevant. That is, the learning experiences provided for trainees in the training program must be directly and explicitly related to the duties, tasks, knowledge, skills and abilities (KSAs) they will be required to perform in their job assignments. In addition, training programs must be constructed to meet organizational needs. Job analysis can provide information allowing efficient use of the millions of training dollars spent each year. For organizations to reap the benefits of training programs, the programs must be based upon sound data. The source of valid and reliable job data is job analysis. The extent to which employee training programs are effective and efficient is largely dependent upon the accuracy of job analysis information.

Defining Job Analysis

What is meant by the term *job analysis*? It has been observed that there are probably as many differing definitions of job analysis as there are writings on the topic (Gatewood and Feild, 1987). Some authors refer to job analysis as "a method by which management systematically investigates the tasks, duties, and responsibilities of an organization's jobs" (Carrell, Kuzmits, and Elbert, 1989, p. 42). Others have described job analysis as the collection and analysis of just about any type of job-related information by almost any method for any purpose (Tiffin and McCormick, 1965). Still others have given us definitions which display a philosophical bent, characterizing job analysis as a way of analyzing reality (Levine, 1983). In this book the author prefers a comprehensive definition which views job analysis as a systematic process for collecting, analyzing, and interpreting job-related information (Veres, Locklear, and Sims, 1990). In any event, the term *job analysis* seems to conjure up many different pictures for people interested in it. Attempting to define job analysis, exploring how it is used, and describing methods of collecting data on jobs is the purpose of this chapter.

At least part of the difficulty in defining job analysis stems from a confusion over the term *job*. Most of us seem to mean something fairly specific when we talk about a job. Ordinarily, we mean the job we do on a day-to-day basis—the activity which results in a paycheck. Experts in HRM or training do not use the term in the same way. The collection of duties a given individual performs is usually referred to as a *position*. A position has been defined as a "group of related job functions performed by a single person . . . because each position is staffed by a unique person, it is different from any other position, even those bearing the same job title in the organization" (Lopez, 1988, p. 881). The same author defines a job as "a group of positions whose functions are so similar that their satisfactory performance requires an identical set of incumbent traits" (Lopez, 1988, p. 881). This distinction is an important one because, in order to understand what is meant by job analysis, we must first understand that we are talking about groups of positions whenever we use the term *job* in later discussions.

Having discussed briefly what the concept of a job entails, it seems appropriate to examine the term *analysis*. To many the term implies the separation of a whole into its component parts in order to examine and interpret those parts. Similarly, training specialists describe what is done in a job analysis as breaking down the component parts of a job so that we can achieve some better understanding of it. There are many approaches available to HRM specialists to analyze jobs. Before describing these approaches, one might well ask the question: Why bother conducting job analyses in the first place?

The Importance of Conducting Job Analysis

Job analysis has been described as a fundamental starting point for HRM (Ghorparde and Atchison, 1980) and training (Mathis and Jackson, 1988; Goldstein, 1986; Heneman, Schwab, Fossum, and Dyer, 1989). Two major forces have contributed to this somewhat exalted description: competition and equal employment opportunity concerns (Holley and Jennings, 1983). American employers, faced with increased foreign and domestic competition, have a considerable interest in ensuring that their employees are working in an efficient manner. Technology has changed, and continues to change, the way in which American workers perform their jobs. Eliminating jobs that have outlived their usefulness can streamline organizational functioning. Jobs that have changed in response to new technology create a somewhat different problem. Individuals must be found, trained, or retrained with the requisite KSAs to adequately perform the activities required by their new or altered jobs. Job analysis provides information that can help identify these individuals, by either insuring a competent pool of talent or identifying the training needs for an organization.

Bemis, Belenky, and Soder (1983) summarized how job analysis information can be utilized in each phase of the HRM cycle. Their listing includes job design, job classification and evaluation, recruitment, selection, performance appraisal, performance management, and training. In the area of training, job analysis information can be utilized in the identification of competencies needed for more successful job performance, identification of organization-based competencies, and the development of relevant curricula for classroom and on-the-job training. Others have categorized the application of job analysis techniques somewhat differently. Ash and Levine (1980) identified six major uses of job analysis information that contribute significantly to organizational functioning. These are: (1) job description, (2) job requirements/specifications, (3) job classification, (4) job evaluation, (5) job design/restructuring, and (6) performance appraisal. Many of these areas have important implications for training.

Job Analysis and Training

Job analysis information provides training specialists with detailed information about each job in the organization: what it consists of, how and why it is performed, how it relates to other jobs, the conditions under which it is performed, the standards of acceptable performance, the frequency and criticality of specific tasks, and the equipment, materials, and other work aids used. These data are used in determining the training needs, including objectives, content, sequence, emphasis, and methods. They also provide a means of planning, designing, conducting, and evaluating training systems. More specifically, some of the ways information gained from job analyses can be used in training systems include:

1. Determining training needs, objectives and standards for training
2. Identifying the knowledge, skills, and abilities required for jobs in the organization
3. Establishing prerequisites for participation in various training programs
4. Serving as the basis for the design of effective performance measures used in training programs

Job analysis is *the* critical step in the development of a training system. The data collected by job analysts provide the foundation on which the training system is built. Regardless of how well the subsequent steps in training system design, development, and validation are carried out, if job analysis data are not complete, valid, and reliable, the resulting training system can fail to produce employees who are capable of performing their duties at an acceptable level of competency.

COLLECTING DATA FROM JOBS

As noted above, job analysis is a systematic process for collecting, analyzing, and interpreting job-related information. Information involving job content, work method and approach, and expected outcome is collected and analyzed. In addition, the KSAs required by workers to perform their jobs may also be identified and analyzed. The individuals responsible for collecting job analysis information ultimately influence the accuracy, thoroughness, and cost of gathering such information. The individuals who collect, analyze and interpret job data are generally referred to by the term *job analysts*. Opinions differ on the ideal background and training of job analysts, but the role is unquestionably a critical one. Regardless of intelligence, background, or experience, no one is born a job analyst. All job analysts should complete a formal training program before they are allowed to participate in a job analysis. Sims and Veres (1985) and Siegel (1987) have emphasized the importance of training job analysts and made specific recommendations on a desired curriculum. Briefly, some of their recommendations are:

1. Studying documents relating to the mission, functions, organization, products, and services of the organizational units to be surveyed
2. Studying current job descriptions and specifications for the jobs to be analyzed
3. Preparing and rehearsing analysis of jobs

4. Preparing the forms they will use in collecting job data
5. Developing a schedule for the conduct of the analysts

Sources of Data on Jobs

In performing a comprehensive job survey, job analysts may consult a number of different sources. These include documents such as technical manuals, organization studies, and training materials. Additional sources of information are individuals such as job incumbents, supervisors, managers, engineers, and technical experts who can provide information about the jobs being studied. The term *job agent* is generally used to refer to individuals who provide or collect the desired job information. In addition, the term *subject matter expert (SME)* is sometimes used to refer to job agents other than analysts. Job agents are chosen due to their familiarity with the target job or the possession of special expertise that is relevant to job activities. There are three classes of job agents typically employed to collect job analysis information: (1) job analysts, (2) job incumbents, and (3) job supervisors (McCormick, 1979).

1. *Job analysts.* As noted above, job analysts are specially trained individuals whose mission is to collect and process job information. Formally trained job analysts should require less orientation to the job under study and less time to analyze it, since they are already well-versed in the method of job analysis being used (Gatewood and Feild, 1987). Gatewood and Feild also note that job analysts should provide more objective, reliable, and accurate job data. However, there are some drawbacks associated with their use as job agents. Certain nuances and subtleties of a job may escape them, since job analysts are perforce less familiar with specific jobs than incumbents or supervisors.

2. *Job incumbents.* Employees performing a job should generally be in the best position to describe it. Incumbents are often best able to detail "what is actually done, rather than what *should* be done" (Gatewood & Feild, 1987, p. 187). Also, large numbers of employees may be available, allowing job analysts to obtain differing perspectives on a given job. However, it should be noted that incumbents may have a vested interest in not portraying their jobs accurately. Rather, they may paint an inflated picture of their jobs, if they believe it beneficial to do so (McCormick, 1979; Smith and Hakel, 1979). Another concern in utilizing incumbents is adequacy of verbal skills, since they must convey their impressions to job analysts in written or oral form.

3. *Job supervisors.* Individuals who supervise incumbents performing the job under study should, in theory, provide accurate job data, since they can observe the work being performed. Gatewood and Feild (1987) note that supervisory assessments assume that supervisors have worked closely enough with incumbents to possess "complete information about employ-

ees' jobs," an assumption that may not be warranted. Researchers have observed a tendency for supervisors to describe subordinates' jobs based on what *should* be done rather than what was done in actuality (Sparks, 1979, 1981). Despite this limitation, supervisors *can* provide the analyst with another perspective on a given job. This perspective can be especially important when incumbents' verbal skills are limited.

Cornelius (1988) recently reviewed the research pertaining to the choice of job agent and summarized the major conclusions of that literature. Among his conclusions were:

1. Supervisors and incumbents agree more about the tasks performed than they do about the personal characteristics necessary for job performance
2. Incumbents and supervisors may provide higher ratings than analysts on job elements that are high in social desirability
3. Supervisors and incumbents attach different meanings to various descriptions of work and may organize work activities differently
4. Trained observers (i.e., job analysts) can give similar estimates of job characteristics to those given by job incumbents (p. 51)

Based on these findings, Cornelius recommends that both supervisors and incumbents be used to collect data on job activities, but that trained job analysts should be used to collect data regarding the knowledge, skills, abilities, or other characteristics necessary to perform the job. Moreover, he suggests that the tendency of supervisors and incumbents to inflate their ratings on job characteristics high in social desirability prohibits their use as job agents in situations where job analysis data will be used to make certain decisions—for example, salary decisions.

While job incumbents and supervisors are typically the prime sources of job analysis data, a good analyst will consult with multiple sources in order to collect the information necessary to (1) understand the job in question, and (2) carry out the purpose of the job analysis (Bemis, Belenky, and Soder, 1983). In choosing the source(s) of job data, a job analyst should be familiar with the research on the optimum source for obtaining job data. In some cases, it may be wise to add technical experts (e.g., production engineers, scientists) as job agents if job processes are extremely complex.

There are both advantages and disadvantages of using trained analysts, supervisors, and job incumbents in collecting job analysis information (Leap and Crino, 1989). The advantages and disadvantages of using trained analysts to collect job analysis data are: advantages (objectivity is maximized, consistent reporting of information, and expertise in job analysis method used); disadvantages (expensive and may overlook certain intangible aspects or lack familiarity). The advantages and disadvantages of using supervisors to collect job analysis data are: advantages (familiarity with jobs being analyzed—greater depth of information and familiarity with intangible aspects of a job—and possibly fast data collection); disadvantages (need to train supervisors for effective job analysis, severe time burden imposed on supervisor, objectivity may be a problem—especially if the supervisor feels that current employees are overworked—and less standardization of information). The advantages and disadvantages of using the job incumbent to collect job analysis data are: advantages (greater familiarity with job, fast data collection, less expensive—unless each employee receives job analysis training); disadvantages (problems with response patterns due to ambiguity in job analysis questionnaire, employee may neglect to report certain job duties, very poor standardization of data, and restrictive job sample—unless other employees in the same job also analyze the job).

In essence, certain trade-offs must be made regarding time, cost, and accuracy when selecting individuals to collect job analysis information. Trained analysts generally offer the greatest objectivity and standardization, an important point when job specifications are being designed to withstand scrutiny by the Equal Employment Opportunity Commission (EEOC) or the courts for job-relatedness. However, supervisors and job incumbents may be able to provide more in-depth information at less cost, although bias and poor standardization are more likely. All three types of agents should be used as sources of job information and cross-checking data to ensure accuracy.

Techniques for Collecting Data

Numerous techniques exist for collecting job information from the sources delineated above. HRM specialists tend to prefer various approaches in different situations. Jobs possessing substantial physical components demand different data collection techniques from those that are primarily mental in nature. Some jobs provide extensive documentation of task completion in the form of a detailed paper trail, while other do not. Job characteristics play an important role in selecting a specific technique from among those described below.

Background Research. This technique involves a review of job-relevant documents and should be the first step in any job analysis process. Initially, a review of the job analysis literature should be conducted to identify job analyses or studies performed on the job in question. A literature review might include past job analysis efforts within an organization or similar organizations; the *Dictionary of Occupational Titles* (U.S. Department of Labor, 1977); Volume II of Sidney Gael's *Job Analysis Handbook for Business, Industry and Government* (1988); and professional publications such as the *Journal of Applied Psychology*, *Personnel Psychology*, and *Public Personnel Management*. This initial research serves to familiarize the analyst with: (1) the data collection and analytic techniques used by others, (2) the problems they encountered, and (3) their results (Gatewood and Feild, 1987). Familiarity with past research aids analysts in choosing the most effective techniques for their efforts. Analysts should follow up their review of the professional literature by examining organization documents such as existing job descriptions, technical manuals, training materials, organization charts, and previous job analyses.

Job Performance. Actual job performance may be an effective data collection technique when the job involves primarily physical tasks that can be learned readily, or involves psychomotor skills. Performance-related data may prove very useful in those cases in which no substitute exists for actually performing the job. The operation of equipment that demands hand-eye coordination of fine motor skills may require performing the task for full understanding. Due to time constraints, it is generally more efficient to rely on observation and/or interview techniques than to expend effort in training an analyst to perform the job. However, for some jobs there may be no good substitute for actually performing the required tasks.

Site Observations. Visiting incumbents at their work sites allows the job analyst to observe the specifics of task performance and determine the degree to which tasks are interrelated. Direct observation can familiarize the job analyst with the materials and/or equipment used on the job, the conditions under which work is performed, and the factors triggering the performance of a given job task. The entire work cycle involved in jobs may, in some cases, be observed in a short time. Also, while the job analysts observe the work, they can clarify any issues not fully understood (Holley and Jennings, 1983). To minimize distortions, the analyst should explain the reasons for the visit and take care to be unobtrusive. Future job analysts should note that site observations may not be appropriate for jobs that involve primarily mental operations such as those of upper level managers.

Individual Interviews. The interview is the simplest but least controlled job analysis method (Holley and Jennings, 1983), yet is probably the most commonly used technique for collecting job data (Cascio, 1987; Van De Voort and Stalder, 1988). Job analysts can question experienced job incumbents or supervisors to determine the tasks performed on the job, as well as the worker requirements necessary to carry out those tasks. Interviews may be structured or unstructured. Structure is usually desirable, however, to ensure that analysts obtain the needed information. Interviews are sometimes conducted concurrently with the site visit so that the performance of job activities can be observed and discussed simultaneously. The results of interviews are usually limited to use in the preparation of job descriptions and job specifications, the planning of career objectives, and the setting of performance objectives.

The Group Interview Session. In the group interview technique subject matter experts (SMEs) are convened to discuss the job in question. Typically, job incumbents and/or supervisors serve as SMEs, but technical experts (such as design engineers or top management) may be used to identify tasks when creating a new job or updating an existing one. As with individual interviews, group sessions may be structured or unstructured; typically, the job analyst directs the session and imposes structure upon the discussion in order to elicit the necessary information in the desired format. Brainstorming is one technique commonly applied in the group interview setting (Osborn, 1963).

The Questionnaire. Questionnaires present a list of items that are assumed to be job-related and ask SMEs to rate each item on its relevance to the job in question. SMEs identify those tasks listed on the inventory that job incumbents perform and rate each task on such factors as the importance to successful job performance or the frequency with which the task is performed. In addition, some questionnaires require SMEs to identify the knowledge, skills, and abilities (KSAs) required to perform the job and rate each KSA on factors such as its importance to acceptable job performance or the extent to which possession of the KSA distinguishes between superior and adequate job performance. Questionnaires are commercially available or can be tailor-made to the job of interest. The items that comprise tailor-made questionnaires can be developed using information derived from background research, job performance, site observations, individual interviews, and/or group interviews.

Job Analysis Methods

Job analysts commonly use several methods of obtaining job information in order to achieve a comprehensive picture of the job in question. Most existing job analysis approaches mix and match various job data sources and data collection techniques. The specific job analysis methods presented in this section offer systematic ways of formally applying the data collection techniques. *Formal* means that the collection procedure as well as the end product is standardized. For example, in the individual interview, job analysts are consistent in the questions they ask of different subject matter experts. Furthermore, the data that emerge from the interview are generally structured into precise job statements that would be understandable to someone who is unfamiliar with the job. *Systematic* means that data collection techniques proceed in a set pattern. For example, several current approaches to job analysis progress from background research to individual interviews or observation, group interviews, and ultimately, questionnaire administration.

As noted above, a variety of systems have evolved for conducting job analyses and collecting job-related information. Not surprisingly, a number of systems for classifying job analysis methodology have also been suggested. This chapter will adopt the distinction that is most commonly encountered: the distinction between work-oriented and worker-oriented methods. Work-oriented job analysis focuses on a description of the work activities performed on a job. Emphasis is on what is accomplished, including a description of the tasks undertaken and the products or outcomes of those tasks. For example, a work-oriented analysis of a secretarial position might generate observable tasks such as "types letters" or "files documents." Other names for this approach include task-oriented and activity-based job analysis.

Among the more notable work-oriented job analysis methods is Functional Job Analysis (FJA; Fine and Wiley, 1971). The two most prominent features of FJA are its formal task statement (Fine, Holt, and Hutchinson, 1974) and its worker function scales. These scales identify differing levels of complexity in three areas of task performance: things, data, and people. The worker function scales have been popularized by their adoption in the *Dictionary of Occupational Titles* (U.S. Department of Labor, 1977). Other well-known work-oriented job analysis methods include the Critical Incident Technique (CIT; Flanagan, 1954), which has been successfully applied to training issues (Bownas and Bernardin, 1988) and the Task Inventory/ Comprehensive Occupational Data Analysis Program (TI/CODAP; Christal, 1974).

Worker-oriented analyses tend to examine the attributes or characteristics required of the worker to perform job tasks. The primary product of work-oriented methods are the KSAs and other characteristics required for effective job performance, whereas a worker-oriented analysis of a secretarial position might generate worker characteristics such as "skill in typing" or "knowledge of the organization's filing system." Commonly encountered worker-oriented job analysis methods include the Position Analysis Questionnaire (PAQ; McCormick, Jeanneret, and Mecham, 1972), the Job Element Method (JEM; Primoff, 1975) and the Threshold Traits Analysis System (TTAS; Lopez, 1986). Until relatively recently, worker-oriented approaches dominated the field, so much so that one author, in a 1976 publication, describes worker-oriented methods as "conventional job analysis procedures" (McCormick, 1976).

The distinction between work- and worker-oriented approaches to job analysis has been blurred in recent years as researchers and practitioners have recognized the utility of collecting both types of information (Guion, 1978; McCormick, 1979; Prien, 1977). This development led to recommendations for the use of multiple job analysis systems. Primoff, for example, integrated elements of JEM with FJA and CIT to meet emerging content-validation requirements (Bemis, Belenky, and Soder, 1983). New systems were also developed that attempted to meet a variety of HRM needs. These so-called multimethod approaches employ data collection techniques that obtain both work- and worker-oriented information.

The Iowa Merit Employment System (IMES; Menne, McCarthy, and Menne, 1976) was an early attempt to incorporate both work- and worker-oriented job analysis data. Other multimethod approaches include the Behavioral Consistency Method (Schmidt et al., 1979), the Versatile Job Analysis System (Bemis, Belenky, and Soder, 1983), the Guidelines Oriented Job Analysis (Biddle, 1976), the Health Services Mobility Study Method (Gilpatrick, 1977), and the Integrated Job Analysis (Buckly, 1986).

Evaluation of Job Analysis Methods

Several factors have given rise to an increased preference for multimethod approaches to job analysis. Veres, Lahey, and Buckly (1987) enumerate some of the factors contributing to a rise in multimethod approaches, including level of task specificity, communicability, and the requirements of the "Uniform Guidelines on Employee Selection Procedures," adopted in 1978 by the Equal Employment Opportunity Commission, Civil Service Commission, Department of Labor, and Department of Justice (hereafter cited as *Guidelines*). The Guidelines require that validity studies include a job analysis that generates the "important work behavior(s) required for successful performance" (p. 38302). At this point, it may be helpful to consider the Guidelines' definition of a selection procedure: "any measure, combination of measures, or procedure used as a basis for *any* employment decision" (p. 38308). Given this definition, the Guidelines cover any measure or procedure that is used as the basis for an HRM decision (for example, training). Thus, human resource professionals must consider the approach to job analysis that is used to construct each procedure—and worker-oriented techniques clearly do not conform with the Guidelines.

In addition, the courts have supported the Guidelines by endorsing a multimethod approach to job analysis. Courts have determined that a job analysis without task-oriented information does not comply with regulatory guidance and Title VII (Thompson and Thompson, 1982). They have also required demonstration of the ties between work behaviors (or tasks) and their companion KSAs (*United States* versus *State of New York*, 1978)—a goal that can only be achieved when both types of job information are collected.

Unfortunately, no research-based answer is available on the question of a "best" job analysis system (Bernardin and Beatty, 1984). Since research provides no definitive guidance on what system to use, the Guidelines' requirements and court opinions merit considerable weight. As mentioned previously, legal considerations would seem to favor multimethod approaches. Also, a number of researchers have advanced conceptual and measurement-oriented arguments for adopting multimethod approaches to job analysis (Guion, 1978; Prien, 1977). Others have argued that multimethod approaches should be preferred on more pragmatic grounds (Veres, Lahey and Buckly, 1987). In any case, multimethod approaches seem to be gaining more acceptance. These systems will probably dominate job analysis practice in the future, a circumstance that should lead to better data upon which to build training programs.

A CASE STUDY OF HOW JOB ANALYSIS FITS INTO PLANS FOR TRAINING PROGRAMS: THE MULTIMETHOD APPROACH IN ACTION

In the preceding pages, the process of job analysis was examined in some detail, however, the discussion did not consider job analysis in context. A good way to provide the reader with a feel for job analysis in the "real world" is with a brief case study illustrating how job analysis fits into plans for training employees for new managerial jobs that would result in training within several departments in the organization. This case vividly illustrates the steps used during job analysis that led to training needs determination and the prioritization of training.

Job analysis studies were undertaken as a first step in the determination of training needs as part of the development of a training program. The method used to analyze these ranks is an outgrowth of job analysis methods such as FJA (Fine and Wiley, 1971), IMES (Menne, McCarthy, and Menne, 1976), IJA (Buckly, 1980, 1986), the Alabama Merit System Method (Elliot et al., 1980) and VERJAS (Bemis, Belenky, and Soder, 1983). The approach used defines both the work performed (in the form of work behaviors) and the attributes of the workers performing that work (in the form of KSAs). In this case, data were collected from incumbents, supervisors, and upper-level management using a variety of techniques including observation, individual interviews, group interviews, technical conferences, and a structured job analysis questionnaire. The method consisted of six operational phases: (1) review of background information, (2) site observations and individual interviews, (3) group interviews, (4) technical review and editing, (5) questionnaire administration and data analysis, and (6) final technical review for determination of training needs and prioritization of training.

Phase One—Review of Background Information

During Phase One of the job analysis process, the job analysts (JAs) began by familiarizing themselves with the organization's operations through the review of written materials such as organizational charts and existing job descriptions. In addition, the results of previous job analysis efforts were examined to obtain more specific information regarding the job duties of the jobs being studied.

Phase Two—Site Observations and Individual Job-Incumbent Interviews

In Phase Two and prior to the formal group interview sessions, the JAs conducted site observations at the work sites of job incumbents. Considerable time was spent talking with and observing job incumbents. (Typically, incumbents assigned to different jobs are interviewed and observed.)

Site observations were used to become familiar with the work environment and the job content domain prior to the group interview sessions. In addition, the questions asked of incumbents during on-site interviews were designed to acquaint the JAs with the KSAs that incumbents believed were important for successful job performance. The locations visited for on-site observations were selected in cooperation with the members of the organization, in an effort to expose the JAs to incumbents in a variety of assignments and provide a comprehensive picture of the organization's operations. For example, the JAs observed a manager supervising the training of several new employees and followed other managers from different parts of the organization on different shifts.

Phase Three—Group Interview Sessions

During the group interview sessions, the job content domain was developed and defined by the pooled judgments of job incumbents working under the supervision of the job analysts. As mentioned earlier in this chapter, job incumbents who participate in the job analysis effort are called subject matter experts (SMEs) due to their familiarity with the target job. The organization selected twelve SMEs for each managerial job in accordance with the JAs' policy for selection of group interview participants. The practice was to select SMEs (1) that were representative by gender, race, shift and duties performed, of the job classification population; (2) with at least six months' experience in the job classification under review; and (3) whose performance in that classification was considered satisfactory by the organization.

Development of Work Behavior Statements. A group interview session was held for each of the two ranks under consideration. Both sessions began with SMEs "brainstorming" to provide an exhaustive listing of *all* job-related activities performed by the managers in their position in short (two- to three-word) phrases. In one session, SMEs provided phrases such as "attends meetings," "trains subordinates," and "develops budgets." SMEs generated *work behaviors* (which described, in broad terms, the major work activities of the job) and *tasks* (which described the specific actions associated with the work behaviors). After brainstorming, the SMEs (managers) were asked to group task statements under the broader work-behavior statements. The purpose of this step was to specify the actions involved in each major work activity. For example, SMEs were asked to identify those actions from the brainstorming list involved in a broad work activity such as performing hands-on management activities; they told the JAs that the tasks "supervises subordinates," "evaluates employees," and "counsels employees" were specific activities that they engaged in to accomplish the broad duty of "performing hands-on managerial activities."

After the SMEs grouped the appropriate task statements under a work behavior statement, they were asked to define the work behavior by telling the JAs necessary details about each of the tasks composing that work behavior. Thus, task statements were expanded to include: (a) what the worker does (an action verb describing a specific observable action); (b) to what or to whom it is done (the object of the verb); (c) how it is done (list of procedures, materials, tools, equipment used, following what instructions); and (d) why it is done (the reason for the task—the expected result, output, or product).

Development of Knowledge, Skill and Ability Statements. After the work behavior statements were developed, the JAs asked the SMEs to brainstorm for the KSAs needed to perform their job duties. As in work-behavior brainstorming, each KSA was described in short (two- or three-word) phrases. For example, one group of SMEs generated the KSAs "knowledge of supervisory techniques," "ability to counsel employees," and "knowledge of human behavior." To ensure the identification of all KSAs, the JAs compiled a brainstorming list by reviewing each work-behavior statement and having SMEs name all the KSAs needed in order to perform the work behavior. Next, once identified, SMEs expanded the KSA statements to describe (1) the extent to which each was needed by employees in the rank under study, and (2) why it was needed. KSA statements were written in the following form:

—skill in _____to/with a score of _____as needed to _____
—knowledge of _____to include _____as needed to _____
—ability to _____to include (such as) _____as needed to _____

For example, the expanded KSA statement for "ability to counsel employees" was: "Ability to counsel employees (K, S, or A of what) on performance problems with the aid of organization policies (extent to which K, S, or A is needed) as needed to complete and review semiannual performance appraisal reviews for pay and promotion purposes (why K, S, or A is needed).

Phase Four—Technical Review and Editing

Following the group interviews, the JAs edited the work-behavior and KSA lists to ensure clarity and completeness. In other words, they corrected grammatical errors, changed the wording in some statements, and reorganized the list to ensure the meaningful organization of job content and job requirements. The work-behavior and KSA lists were then reviewed by a Technical Advisory Committee consisting of five senior top managers. This committee was set up in order to review the JAs' lists and inform them if the SMEs had omitted an important work behavior or KSA. The committee's feedback was incorporated into the final version of the work-behavior and KSA lists.

Phase Five—Questionnaire Administration and Data Analysis

The job analysis phases described above provided the JAs with a comprehensive picture of the managerial jobs under study. This picture, however, did not incorporate any information concerning the relative importance or frequency of the work behaviors, nor did it distinguish between those elements of the job that must be performed competently upon job entry and those that may be learned later. These questions were of great importance because the job analysis results would be used to develop a job-related training program for managers. In designing a training program it is important to determine the KSAs employees needs to perform their respective work activities. Therefore, a structured Job Analysis Questionnaire (JAQ) was administered to determine (1) the critical aspects of the jobs performed by the incumbents, and (2) the KSAs essential to the performance of those critical job activities. All available incumbents completed the questionnaire.

Prior to completing the questionnaire, incumbents were given a copy of the list of work behaviors and asked to determine those work behaviors they performed on their individual jobs. Participants were instructed to read each of the work behaviors (and the tasks comprising that behavior) and cross out the task statements they did *not* perform on their job. The JAQ was then completed by the incumbents to describe how the work behaviors and KSAs related to their individual jobs. It was emphasized that the appropriate frame of reference for a rater was his or her current job—not a hypothetical "typical" incumbent's job.

The four questions about work behaviors asked of the SMEs were:

1. To what degree are you responsible for performance of the work behavior?
2. Indicate the percentage of time you spend performing this work behavior.
3. How important is it that you perform this work behavior successfully?
4. Is it necessary that newly promoted employees be able to perform this work behavior upon entry to the job?

The three questions concerning KSAs asked of SMEs were:

1. How important is this KSA for acceptable job performance?

2. Is it necessary that new employees possess this KSA upon entry to the job?

3. To what extent does possession of this KSA distinguish between superior and adequate performance of employees?

The single question concerning the relationship between work behaviors and KSAs was: to what extent is each KSA needed in performing each work behavior?

Following questionnaire administration, responses from incumbents to each question concerning the work behaviors and KSAs were computer-analyzed and summarized to determine the critical components of the job-content domain.

Phase Six—Final Technical Review

The organization's Technical Advisory Committee (TAC) met for a second time following data analysis, to review the outcomes of questionnaire administration and discuss the implications of the job-analysis outcomes for future training. The TAC supported the results of the job analysis and expressed the belief that the critical work behaviors and KSAs identified by the incumbents did, indeed, accurately reflect the jobs currently performed by incumbents. The information obtained from the job analysis described in this short case *feeds* into, and helped form the basis for, the managerial training program.

SUMMARY

This chapter has attempted to convey a general idea of the practice of job analysis and its use in training systems. A key to determining training needs is job analysis. There is a variety of methods available to training specialists and others given the responsibility for determining training needs. Most of those methods help ensure that the training program is job-relevant and should demonstrate, to both the organization and individual trainees, the relationship between the actual training and the back-home work (job) situation. Multimethod approaches that include competently trained job analysts are an important key to the potential success of any training effort and must be addressed by training personnel.

Job analysis is a key ingredient in the development of a training system. It is important in determining training needs, evaluating prerequisites to training, and evaluating training systems and specific programs. If job analyses are poor, subsequent steps in the training effort will probably be poor also. It is therefore important that the HRM specialist understand the importance of conducting a thorough job analysis if appropriate training needs are to be identified and a successful training program is to be implemented.

5

Designing Training Programs to Develop Pivotal Skills and Competency Levels

INTRODUCTION

A training program is a planned system of goals and objectives based on a needs assessment (for example, completing a thorough job analysis), program content, learning principles, division of labor (trainer-trainee), a definable set of training activities or experiences to include specific training methods and aids, and procedures for evaluation of the training program. The extent to which these systemic elements can be structured in an orderly and rational manner will have much to do with the training program's eventual success.

Planning is perhaps the key word. A training program without a plan is impossible to prepare for and impossible to evaluate. Good planning ensures that a training program will not exhaust its budget too soon, will effectively schedule the various training program components, and will bring the right mix of resources, trainers, and trainees together at the right place and the right time.

This chapter will present the importance of good training design by discussing some of the principles that should be included in the design of training programs, will introduce the concepts of pivotal skill and competency development, and will review Kolb's Experiential Learning Model (ELM) (1984a) and corresponding learning styles as key variables in the design of training programs.

PRINCIPLES OF GOOD TRAINING DESIGN

The following principles adapted from Havelock and Havelock (1973) should be taken into consideration by those responsible for designing a training program: structure, relevance, specificity, generality, reinforcement, in-process evaluation and feedback, openness and flexibility, linkage, involvement, cost effectiveness, redundancy, synergy, training for psychological wholeness of learning, and training for transferability and compatibility.

1. *Structure*. Several important aspects of structuring design include: (1) planning, (2) defining goals, (3) specifying learning that should meet objectives, and (4) specifying the sequence of training activities that should lead to the desired learning. The training program's components should be planned, structured, and flexible. With skillful program planning, program objectives can be evaluated and changed, consciously and deliberately. Another important aspect of structuring is sequencing, the arrangement of individual activities in a step-by-step series that logically leads to the program's goals.

2. *Relevance*. A training program should be relevant to the objectives; the objectives should be relevant to some organizational need and to the trainees' back-home situations; the training should be relevant to the needs, wishes, and background of the trainee. In the actual design of training activities, experiential involvement and realism are important factors in success: "The more similar the conditions of the training setting to the back-home setting, the more likely will be the application of new knowledge, skill, abilities, and orientations back home. This is a major rationale for the use of simulation technique in training" (Jung, 1970).

3. *Specificity*. Related to both structure and relevance is the principle of specificity. Goals, learning, and training activities should be specified as much as possible and, where appropriate, stated in behavioral terms. Without some specification, it is impossible to plan meaningful programs, assess relevance of particular elements, and evaluate outcomes. Specificity also facilitates flexibility and conscious choice among alternative elements. It may also allow program simplification, since many elements with different rationales often turn out to have similar or identical behavioral or operational specifics.

4. *Generality*. The task of translating program concepts into "usable form" actually requires both generalization (from specific training experiences) and specification (back-home application from the training program's generalizations). Learning is effectively internalized when the trainee is able to go from the specific to the general and back to the specific with ease.

Generality is an important design principle in another sense. Trainees will have very diverse backgrounds regardless of how carefully they are selected, and they will in some situations be returning to very diverse work settings. Therefore, training content must be general enough in its applicability to benefit a range of people, learning styles, and situations.

5. *Reinforcement*. Training designers should be continuously conscious of the principle of reinforcement and should look for times, places, and situations in

which effective positive reinforcements can be applied. Specific experiences and the training event as a whole should be seen by the trainee as beneficial, worthwhile, and to some extent enjoyable.

6. *In-Process evaluation and feedback*. Good planning, specification, and structuring of training activities allow the evaluation of program elements while the training is still going on. HRM specialists need knowledge on whether to go ahead, "repeat, or reorganize parts of the training program." This "knowledge of results" is a crucial reinforcement for the HRM specialist and trainee and is the basis for rational decision making. However, to be most effective, feedback must be immediate. Training activities should also be designed to include longer term (summative) evaluations to help designers of training programs make future training events more effective.

7. *Openness and flexibility*. While a training program should be planned and structured in advance, it should also be continuously responsive to the unanticipated needs of individual trainees and to unanticipated circumstances. Recognition and some accommodation to the initial expectations and contributions of trainees and HRM specialists is especially important in setting the tone of the training program. Training program designers should be open to—and actively seek out—the experiences of others who have designed and participated in similar events in the past, so that past mistakes can be avoided.

8. *Linkage*. The linkage concept applies to the content of the training itself. It is important that there be linkage of the here-and-now experiences on the training site to the back-home realities that must be faced later, as well as between objectives and training elements, specifics and general learning, and the training of the trainee.

9. *Involvement*. The training program should have the power to capture and hold the attention of the trainees. This usually means that the trainees need to participate actively in the utilization of a variety of training methods, experiences, and so forth during the training program.

10. *Cost-effectiveness*. Training designs should generally aim at providing the greatest benefit to the largest number of trainees at the minimum cost. Although there is no rigid formula for balancing costs and benefits, realism and pragmatism are important in considering the budget, the number and quality of HRM specialists and trainees that can be involved, and the time available for training. It is also important to build transferability (see below) into as many aspects of training as possible.

11. *Redundancy*. Any effective communication has a great deal of redundancy built into it, and this principle applies doubly to a complex communication activity such as a training program. Summarization is one obvious and important way to apply the redundancy principle. Trainees should be given previews of what they are about to experience, and later should be reminded and encouraged to recall what they have learned as it becomes relevant and timely.

12. *Synergy*. Learning seems to take place most forcefully when a number of inputs or stimuli from different sources converge on one point. This is the principle of synergy. In a sense, the implication is that training programs should not rely primarily or exclusively on any one medium or communication device. Several

media should be employed, preferably in concert: these may include simulations, role plays, and small and large group discussions where appropriate and feasible.

13. *Train for psychological wholeness and learning.* Knowledge, skills, abilities, and attitudes need to come together (a kind of synergy) if the learning is to be adequately internalized. Inclusion of all four aspects of learning is an important principle in training program design.

14. *Train for transferability.* Jung (1970) notes the importance of this principle in training program design: "Unless there is some chance for trying out and practicing behavior under back-home conditions, literally or by simulation training, an individual who may show change at the training site will not be likely to transfer it to their [trainees] back-home setting."

15. *Compatibility.* Training should be compatible with the trainee's learning style, expectations, and probable future work situation. It is not very easy to follow the compatibility principle without having a great deal of background and diagnostic information about individual trainees and their circumstances.

16. *Evaluation.* A training program design should include a formal and specified procedure for evaluation. Such evaluation is important and useful in a number of ways. First, it requires training program designers to plan and think clearly about what they want to achieve and how they can do it. Second, it provides information to sponsors and top managers or training policy planners on whether or not such programs should be continued, repeated, terminated, or modified. Third, if it is so designed that the trainer can receive feedback during training, it can allow for in-process training program improvement. Finally, it can give the trainees feedback and reinforcement on their own behavior.

HRM specialists should be cognizant of these principles when designing training programs. In addition, the training design should incorporate a framework that allows for the development of specific pivotal skills and competencies (levels). The next section will discuss such a framework.

DESIGNING TRAINING PROGRAMS TO DEVELOP PIVOTAL SKILLS AND COMPETENCIES IN TRAINEES

HRM specialists must constantly delve deeply into the nature of what is competent employee performance in jobs and must relate that to the design of training programs. The work of the occasional insightful HRM specialist has shown concern with how complex and diverse pivotal skills are learned and developed. Designing training programs that develop pivotal skills is the most challenging aspect of the HRM specialist's role. With the vast increase in knowledge, technology, and complexity in organizations, the HRM specialist must respond to constant demands for training programs that result in competent trainees or graduates.

A well-designed training program ensures the professional growth of an organization's work force. And because implementation of such programs can be viewed as an investment in human resources, employee morale is likely to improve as employees see themselves as valuable members of the organization. This will likely result in increased productivity.

Thorough job analysis, which defines the KSAs required by various positions within an organization, provides the information needed to accurately assess both an employee's and an organization's training needs. Such assessments aid in the design of an effective, viable training program. Once designed, the implementation of the program is in the hands of the HRM specialist. This section provides a tried and tested design for training programs that develop pivotal employee skills and competency levels.

Nature of Pivotal Skills

A number of training program designs and instructional strategies have been proposed and described in the training literature in the last twenty years. Each of these designs and methods was intended to increase the effectiveness of trainees' learning. While evidence does show that variables such as organization and presentation of material can induce a difference in trainees' learning, each training design must relate to a greater goal: training in pivotal skills. The challenge for today's HRM specialist is to select pivotal, rather than peripheral, skills and to design a functional training program. A prerequisite to developing a pivotal skill is a sound operational definition of the skill in question.

Different job requirements attach differing amounts of importance to different skills as noted in Chapter 4. Pivotal skills are not only central but necessary for successful completion of the job. Peripheral skills are those that an employee may possess, but that have no extraordinary—or perhaps even significant—impact on job performance. Therefore, training program designs must emphasize proficiency and competency in pivotal skills of various jobs.

Why Train for Competence?

The responsibility associated with designing training programs that focus on pivotal skill development or competency-levels cannot be understated. Inadequate design or implementation of a training program, or implementation of a program not tailored to an organization's needs, can often lead to capital losses in the form of retraining employees, employee benefits paid to separated personnel, and constant restructuring or designing of a less-than-adequate training program.

While the design of an effective training program is an integral part of implementing a successful training program, the training program design is of little consequence unless the content of such training appropriately corresponds to the organization's needs and goals as discussed in Chapter 3. Thus, program designers must determine the very specific qualifications dictated by the various positions within an organization, identify evaluation indicators, and finally, develop a functional training system (McAshton, 1979).

Determining the qualifications or competencies appropriate for a given position involves more than simple identification of the KSAs required by that position. Butler (1978) defined competence as "the ability to meet or surpass prevailing standards of adequacy for a particular activity" (p. 7). This definition can be expanded to include an individual's values, critical-thinking patterns, judgment, and processes of attitude formulation and integration of theory from the humanities and sciences into various organizational roles. With this in mind, it becomes evident that a well-designed training program is one that prepares its participants to apply integrated knowledge in a practical and job-related manner. In Chapter 4 it was emphasized that the content of a training program can be best determined through a thorough job analysis that identifies the qualifications or competencies of a particular position. To ensure that the focus of the program is on outcome rather than simply on the development of knowledge, an evaluation process must be developed to measure the extent to which the training goal has been achieved (Hayenga and Isaacsen, 1980).

Competence in a pivotal skill is the ability to meet or surpass prevailing standards of adequacy for a particular activity. It includes job-related skills. Pivotal skill-based training is derived from the identification of pivotal skills and provides instruction designed to develop and enhance those skills. The evaluation process must measure the extent to which development and enhancement of pivotal skills have been achieved. All training processes must also focus on outcome, not merely on the acquisition of knowledge. Pivotal skill-based training should include the following characteristics:

1. Pivotal skills must guide the planning of the training program. Each pivotal skill should describe a desired behavioral outcome, and through this description it should guide the planning, the implementation of learning experiences, and the prescription of criteria and methods of evaluation.

2. Pivotal skills should be derived from roles and should emphasize performance rather than just knowledge. Pivotal skills emphasize how the trainees will use their acquired knowledge. Learning these pivotal skills does not end with simple recall. The pivotal skill is always stated in such a manner as to answer the question, "How will the trainee utilize the pivotal skill?"

3. Pivotal skills emphasize judgment, not merely psychomotor ability. Pivotal-skill development encompasses more than simple performance. It includes making some judgment about the accuracy and appropriateness of the skill, and it implies a standard of excellence. The focus on pivotal skill directs and ensures learning in the higher levels of the cognitive, affective, and psychomotor domains.

4. Pivotal skills state the conditions under which a trainee performs, the actions or behaviors, and the standard performance. Examples of a pivotal-skill statement might include:

—based on the principles of organization design and structure, managers will be able to analyze critically an organization chart and determine the applicability of the chart to the organization it represents

—given a coworker experiencing stress (condition), the trainee will be able to assess and intervene (action) so that the co-worker can more effectively cope with the stress (standard of performance)

A major goal of pivotal-skill training is to enable trainees to achieve levels of competent performance in identified and designated skills. The pivotal skills must be achieved in the training program, field experiences, or other situations. Because pivotal skills prescribe instruction and evaluation, it is evident that lectures, demonstrations, or discussion methods alone will not enable trainees to develop the pivotal skills. Efforts toward the design of training programs that develop pivotal skills would be greatly facilitated by application of a clear model of pivotal skill-based and competency level-oriented training design. Kolb's (1984a) ELM provides such a framework from which to draw ideas.

HRM specialists must also understand that the development of pivotal skills is dependent upon several conditions, each of which implies a principle that should be incorporated into the design of the training program if pivotal-skill development is to result. These principles will be presented following a brief discussion of Kolb's ELM.

KOLB'S EXPERIENTIAL LEARNING MODEL AND LEARNING STYLES

Kolb's ELM is a simple model that summarizes important elements of learning as a problem-solving approach and shows learning as a four-stage, cyclical process. Figure 5.1 shows that learning can begin with any of the four stages shown in the figure. One stage in the Kolb model is the concrete experience. As individuals encounter new experiences, they begin the process of learning from those events. The experience may then be followed by observation and reflection. During this time, individuals try to make sense of what has happened. Of course, they can observe and reflect on experiences of other people. This stage then leads into the formation of abstract concepts and generalizations. Here, they try to compare the current experience to previous experiences. The focus here is on the modification of those past experiences to take into account the new concrete experience. This stage can involve the use of written material (e.g., books) as a basis for comparison between theory and their experience. The next stage is the testing of hypotheses in future situations, which leads them back to new concrete experiences. According to Kolb the learning process requires orientations that are polar opposites: active and reflective, concrete and abstract. Shifting from one orientation to another results in four

Figure 5.1
The Experiential Learning Model

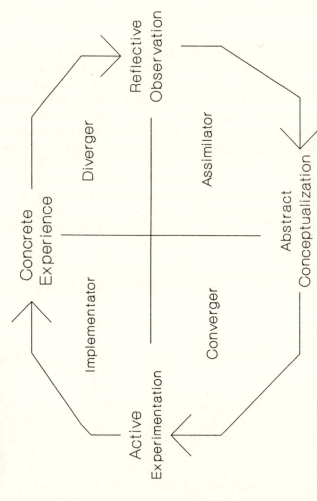

David A. Kolb, EXPERIENTAL LEARNING, c 1984, p. 21.
Reprinted by permission of Prentice-Hall, Inc. Englewood Cliffs, New Jersey.

separate types of activities, each of which is required at some stage of the learning process.

Several aspects of this model are important to note for those designing training programs. First, the model shows learning to be more than a stimulus-response process. Thinking and analysis occur during reflection and generalization, as well as in the testing of hypotheses. Second, the learning cycle is continuous. Previous learning influences current learning, and current learning influences future learning in a developmental or training process.

Forgetting can also be explained by this model of learning. Forgetting is caused not merely by the passage of time, but rather by the events that occur after the initial learning experience (Manis, 1966). After the learning cycle is completed, an individual begins a new learning cycle. Perhaps the new learning invalidates the old learning or just consumes the person, not allowing practice of the previously learned behavior. In the design of training programs, if HRM specialists expect a person to remember something he or she has just learned, they must allow the person to continue to repeat it, so that forgetting does not occur. It also does not hurt to continue to reward desired behavior. Withholding a reward can cause extinction of behavior, which is much like forgetting.

The third point about Kolb's model is that since the learning process is cyclical, it is possible to begin new learning at any stage of the process. For example, a person may read about a new theory of management before going out to experiment with this new information. Here, the person enters at the abstract conceptualization stage and then progresses to the hypothesis-testing stage. Where a person starts and the direction his or her learning takes depend on the individual's goals and needs as well as on previous learning and the stage that has been rewarded in the past.

The three preceding points suggest the final point: learning is a highly individualized process. It is also difficult for others to observe, since it is an internal process. People have different styles of learning. HRM specialists must be cognizant of the four styles or activities—divergence, assimilation, convergence, and implementation (a term the author prefers to "accommodation" as used by Kolb, which implies passivity and compromise)—when designing training programs and how they might use this information in understanding and training employees. For example, should a training program have people of similar learning styles, or would it better to have a variety of styles? With a variety of pivotal skills or competency levels introduced in a training program, what combination of styles should be mixed? How can HRM specialists give different training to people with different learning styles?

Kolb's Four Basic Learning Styles

1. *Divergence.* An orientation toward concrete experience focuses on being involved in experiences and dealing with immediate human situations

in a personal way. It emphasizes feeling as opposed to thinking; a concern with the uniqueness and complexity of present reality, as opposed to theories and generalizations; an intuitive, "artistic" approach as opposed to the systematic, scientific approach to problems. People with a concrete-experience orientation enjoy and are good at relating to others. They are often good intuitive decision makers and function well in unstructured situations. People with this orientation value relating to people, being involved in real situations, and having an open-minded approach to life and learning.

This kind of activity is required to seek background information and sense opportunities, investigate new patterns, recognize discrepancies and problems, and generate alternatives. Persons strong in divergence excel in situations that call for imaginative ability and "brainstorming." People with this learning-style preference are best at viewing concrete situations from many different points of view. Their approach to situations is to observe rather than take action.

2. *Assimilation*. An orientation toward reflective observation focuses on understanding the meaning of ideas and situations by carefully observing and impartially describing them. It emphasizes understanding as opposed to practical application; a concern with what is true or how things happen as opposed to what is practical; an emphasis on reflection as opposed to action. People with a reflective orientation enjoy thinking about the meaning of situations and ideas—and are good at seeing their implications. They are good at looking at things from different perspectives and at appreciating different points of view. They like to rely on their own thoughts and feelings to form opinions. People with this orientation value patience, impartiality, consideration, and thoughtful judgment.

This kind of activity is required to develop theory, compare alternatives, establish criteria, formulate plans and hypotheses, and define problems. Strengths associated with this activity include abilities to observe, analyze, and conceptualize. Persons with highly developed assimilation skills excel in reasoning and are less interested in people than in abstract concepts. People with this preferred learning style are best at understanding a wide range of information and putting it into concise, logical form. They find it more important that a theory have a logical soundness than practical value.

3. *Convergence*. An orientation toward abstract conceptualization focuses on using logical ideas and concepts. It emphasizes thinking as opposed to feeling; a concern with building general theories as opposed to intuitively understanding unique, specific areas; a scientific as opposed to an artistic approach to problems. A person with an abstract conceptual orientation enjoys and is good at systematic planning, manipulation of abstract symbols, and quantitative analysis. People with this orientation value precision, the rigor and discipline of analyzing ideas, and the aesthetic quality of a neat, conceptual system.

This kind of activity is required to select among alternatives, focus efforts, evaluate plans and programs, test hypotheses, and make decisions. The learning strengths lie in the application of ideas and the ability to theorize and experiment. Individuals with this preferred learning style would rather deal with technical tasks and problems than with social and interpersonal issues.

4. *Implementation.* An orientation toward active experimentation focuses on actively influencing people and changing situations. It emphasizes practical applications as opposed to reflective understanding; a pragmatic concern with what works as opposed to what is absolute truth; an emphasis on doing as opposed to observing. People with an active-experimentation orientation enjoy and are good at getting things accomplished. They are willing to take some risk to achieve their objectives. They also value having an impact and influence on the environment around them—and like to see results.

This kind of activity is required to advocate positions or ideas, set objectives, commit to schedules, commit resources, and implement decisions. The learning strengths lie in the tendency toward risk-taking and the enjoyment of carrying out plans involving new experiences. People with this learning-style preference have a tendency to act on "gut" feelings rather than on logical analysis.

Capabilities for performing tasks at an appropriate skill level vary according to each individual in each learning and performing stage. Predictable weaknesses are associated with either an excess or a deficiency in any state. As mentioned earlier in this section, Kolb's ELM incorporates the conditions of adult learning into a framework that can be applied to the design of training programs that emphasize the development of pivotal skills and competency by trainees. Principles that HRM specialists should take into consideration when designing training programs will be discussed in the next section.

Key Principles for Enhancing Pivotal Skill and Competency Development

The development of pivotal skills and attainment of competency levels by trainees is dependent on several conditions, each of which implies a principle that must be incorporated into the design of training programs. These principles are discussed in detail below:

1. *Developing pivotal skills and attainment of competency levels require a high tolerance for eclecticism, due to the frequency with which trainees face new situations and problems.* Tolerance for eclecticism—the acceptance of and ability to deal with varying points of view—can be expanded through experience and social support. The prospective trainee needs prototypes for adjusting to a wide variety of organizational and job settings.

Equally important is the learning of pivotal skills so that the trainee will learn to adapt rapidly to the realities of particular job situations. While a high tolerance for eclecticism may appear easy to acquire at first glance, it is in reality exceedingly difficult to accomplish. This is so because people, in fundamental ways, differ from each other, and often view the differences—in skill level, performance, race, age, education or socioeconomic position—to be good or bad, right or wrong, appropriate or inappropriate, and so forth. It is fairly obvious that judgmental dichotomous attitudes are problematic. Even more problematic is the fact that people are different in terms of personality and temperament. As a result of these very fundamental differences, people have different motives, different purposes and aims, different values, different needs, different drives, different impulses, different urges, and different learning styles. These, in turn, cause people to perceive, cognize, think, conceptualize, understand, believe, and learn differently from each other (Wolfe, 1980).

Innately "knowing," of course, that whatever one is, is "correct" or the way people "should be," one is quick to perceive those who differ as fundamentally afflicted, flawed, stupid, lazy, bad, sick, or any combination thereof. Fortunately, our tendency to wish those near us to be just as we are is seldom granted; we are all richer for that. The point is this: people are fundamentally different, and designers of training programs must constantly be aware of this difference. HRM specialists cannot erase the fundamental differences between people, but they *can* develop a high tolerance for people (trainees) who are different. That tolerance can grow into respect for their differences, which are then viewed as neither good nor bad but merely as different. When this happens, tolerance has become a training tool, replacing the detriment of intolerance that previously existed. The HRM specialist (indeed, any individual in an organization) who has not developed the pivotal skill of exercising a high degree of tolerance is decidedly at a disadvantage when compared with trainers and individuals who have. In essence there is a strong need for the presence—and, therefore, for the development—of flexibility and adaptability in those responsible for designing training programs.

2. *The development of pivotal skills and attainment of competency levels require an emphasis on both practice and application.* An emphasis on experiential learning and active practice in training programs requires a clear understanding of the organization and jobs in which the trainees work. This understanding includes knowledge about the organization's training and employee's training needs, the internal or external forces that maintain or change them both, and the possibilities for further training or development.

Assisting trainees in obtaining pivotal skills and competency levels also requires that training program designers prepare trainees to understand the importance and use of a variety of pivotal skills. These skills should help the trainees to see clearly what their training needs are and what opportunities exist for further development. Training for the development of pivotal skills and attainment of competency levels should emphasize the importance of application and designs that are most appropriate to learning. Such a training design allows the trainee the opportunity to practice pivotal skills in situations that are as close to the back-home work environment as possible.

3. *Direct experience in settings similar to those in which the trainee will perform after the training program is necessary for the development of pivotal skills and attainment of competency levels.* The attainment of pivotal skills and competency levels comes, in part, from a cognitive understanding of the role, but primarily from practice—through exercising skills, making a critique of the consequences (intended and otherwise) of performance, and exploring and understanding other ways of performing. Active experimentation, observation, and reflection are all necessary components of pivotal-skill and competency development. Therefore, trainees need to identify and understand the objectives of particular organizational roles, methods, and pivotal skills. In addition, they need to know which situations call for particular pivotal skills and the required competency levels, and under what conditions these skills have the best likelihood of producing desired results. In fact, the trainees must understand how these skills produce any results at all. In short, designers of training programs must understand that there are analytical tasks involved in learning different pivotal skills.

Prospective trainees also learn pivotal skills by seeing them applied, and by watching skilled personnel as they demonstrate their work. As an apprentice learns at the side of the master craftsman, so too must trainees observe others in action and talk with them about their work. The greater the number of exposures to role models, the better the chance that trainees will understand and acquire pivotal skills and the requisite competency levels. Whether in real-life situations or simulations, trainees need to try out the particular pivotal skills involved in producing desired effects. Trainees also need to engage with others in a working capacity—responding to expectations, handling problems, and facing the consequences. The use of experiential exercises and the case-study method is one way of representing such real life situations.

4. *The development of pivotal skills and attainment of appropriate competency levels require assessment using valid, reliable techniques that measure the attainment of training, pivotal-skill outputs or competency level.* The assessment of competence in pivotal skills takes place in a context. Usual testing or assessment procedures and contexts assess trainees in situations unlike those experienced in a true work environment. HRM specialists must not focus only on those trainees who are highly competent at performing a task during a training program, yet do not know what to do

when confronted with real back-home work problems. In the design of some training programs, the development of pivotal skills by trainees does not occur during the training program because the training program emphasized the wrong setting or context for demonstrating their competencies. According to Wolfe (1980), "However objective and controlled typical assessment procedures are, their validity for measuring competence is in doubt." Relevant assessments (or the data for them) must be generated in a variety of experiential settings, such as experiences or situations that closely simulate the back-home work setting. The assessment center approach (Moses and Byham, 1977; Peterson and Stakenas, 1981), which includes written tests as well as such techniques as in-basket exercises and simulations, appears to be a promising way to measure performance in a more suitable context.

Peterson and Stakenas (1981) state the following important characteristics of assessment procedures that would be appropriate for inclusion in the design of training programs and measurement of pivotal skills:

—they should call for the integration of subskills into "generic" skills;
—they should take place in real-life or simulated real-life settings to enhance the predictability of the behavior occurring in subsequent adult (job) roles in society;
—they should be technically sound and practical to use;
—they should specify generic skills, their subskills, and content.

5. *The development of pivotal skills and attainment of competency levels require useful feedback.* During the design and implementation of training programs, HRM specialists should ensure the availability of feedback about the impact of trainees' performance. HRM specialists face a dilemma: as those responsible for the training effort they must encourage the realization of full potential, and as evaluators they must hold trainees to high standards of excellence and give valid feedback about the adequacy of performance. An important factor of training program design is the creation of a genuine feedback process. For purposes of learning, feedback is required frequently and soon after performance. More importantly, it must be *descriptive* of the consequences of performance, *not evaluative* in tone. Direct attention to the development of genuine feedback processes is essential, and trainees and HRM specialists alike need to be clear when the process is feedback and when it is assessment for organizational decisions (i.e., raises, performance appraisals, promotions, and opportunities for future training).

In addition to trying out acquired methods and pivotal skills in practical situations, trainees must practice critical reflection on the consequences produced by these actions. In this book, the term *feedback* refers to direct observation of the real consequences of one's act—genuine feedback.

Learning progresses much more directly when trainees are required to examine and experience. If possible, the results of their decision deliver quick feedback in respect to consequences or probable consequences. This type of feedback allows trainees to learn how to detect outcomes and match them against stated objectives. Trainees can also decide if the task is finished, whether they need to do something more, or to accomplish the task by some different means, or if they must increase their competency, proficiency, or efficiency in order to improve their performance. Reflecting on genuine feedback stimulates a search for alternative responses—and which of them might be more appropriate the next time the problem is encountered. The next cycle of feedback should reinforce improvement and eliminate error.

6. *The development of pivotal skills and attainment of competency levels are dependent upon increased self-knowledge.* HRM specialists must avoid the tendency to treat pivotal skills and attainment of competency levels as a combination of knowledge and skills that can be taught to the trainee. The designers of training programs must also recognize the special importance of personal growth and self-knowledge. The trainee needs to learn to focus inward, toward greater self-insight and mastery, as well as outward. Trainees must be taught to understand how their needs, expectations, fears, biases, personalities, and learning styles influence their use of pivotal skills in various situations. Therefore, one responsibility of those who design training programs is to assist trainees in understanding that these factors are a part of the pivotal-skill development equation and that they must be identified and understood. A knowledge of self assists trainees in realizing what things they can or cannot do, and in developing an identity that integrates KSAs, values, propensities, and personal learning strengths. It also provides them with the insight needed to lessen the effects of, or to eliminate, perceived personal inadequacies (such as weaknesses in certain learning areas).

7. *Reflection and consolidation are essential final steps in the development of pivotal skills and attainment of competency levels.* At some point it becomes appropriate to step back, reflect on one's experiences, and consolidate the skills one has learned. Reflection time is needed for both trainees and HRM specialists to ascertain the acquisition of the KSAs that are to be acknowledged through the completion of the training program, as well as the movement of the trainee to higher levels of competency and skill requirements or promotion. An assessment or reward for completing the training program, if it is to be meaningful, should be based on achievement of knowledge and demonstration of designated pivotal skills and attainment of competency levels, and should provide for trainees, HRM specialists, and eventually managers a review of the actual pivotal skills developed, competency levels attained, and any new behaviors. At this

point, trainees should be prepared to move on into the work place with the ability to perform well and further to develop pivotal skills and higher competency levels relevant to their work roles.

Responsibilities of HRM Specialists in Program Design

In designing training programs that focus on pivotal-skill development and the attainment of competency levels, the responsibility of HRM specialists is much broader than merely imparting knowledge. The tasks facing those who wish to revamp the design of training programs in order to increase development of pivotal skills and attainment of competency levels are:

—identifying the kinds and levels of skills required for survival and excellence in roles in organizations;

—developing and maintaining structures, conditions, and climates for learning;

—generating and providing resources—including, of course, their own knowledge and investigative, evaluative, and documentary skills regarding training program design;

—identifying and providing access to off-the-job as well as on-the-job training or learning environments and resources;

—providing individual assistance and feedback on various dimensions of the trainees' performance in specific pivotal skill areas;

—serving as role models and mentors by guiding and advising trainees as they pursue the mastery of pivotal skills and achievement of competency levels;

—developing alternative but efficient training processes that take into account individual learning styles, abilities, and work and life circumstances.

A significant ideological barrier, which must be overcome if training program designs are to be successfully implemented, is the pervasive content orientation of many HRM specialists. One consequence of this orientation is a preoccupation with the covering of content material rather than mastering pivotal skills and achieving competency levels. An exclusive preoccupation with knowledge acquisition may foster the implicit (and unwarranted) assumption that such knowledge will "transfer" readily into the skills needed to meet the demands of life beyond the training program. However, in training programs that emphasize development of pivotal skills and attainment of competency levels, content is viewed as a means for engendering the capabilities required for survival and excellence. This ideological conversion requires thorough consideration not only of how to train, but of how trainees are to learn and apply their knowledge.

In too many training situations, HRM specialists are, by and large, left to their own devices to determine not only the content to be covered in their courses, but also how well trainees are expected to master it. In training programs that stress development of pivotal skills and attainment of competency levels, the results of training—namely, growth in the mastery of pivotal skills—can be observed and used to evaluate training effectiveness. When HRM specialists and trainees know what is to be learned, they can work together to achieve the required standards.

The kinds of complex skills required by members of today's organization cannot be developed through only one learning process. A training program based on only one training or learning design will, at best, make only an inadequate contribution to pivotal-skill and competency development. Abstract conceptualization (which tends to be the medium of many training programs) is extremely important, but it provides only the first layer of training. Although the first layer is basic, because it is theoretical in nature, it provides only a concrete foundation upon which specific skills, the bricks and mortar and thus the visible portion of the training effort, are built.

Concrete experience, reflective observation, and abstract conceptualization—three different learning processes—in combination provide a basis for understanding the problems one must deal with in work life. A fourth generic learning process—active experimentation—is a further requirement for the development of pivotal skills and competency. Only when HRM specialists commit themselves to including these four processes in the design of training programs will training programs based on pivotal skill and competency become more realistic.

Both the environment and the process of training must be well planned and well managed because of their special contributions to competence. Those aspiring to the higher levels of effective and efficient organizations need to learn how to function effectively in several learning modes and in various environments. Kolb's ELM (1984a) provides a framework for matching each pivotal skill with the type of training most likely to instill that skill. As the trainee moves through each phase of the model, each skill can be taught using the principles that best facilitate the development of pivotal, as opposed to peripheral, skills.

Optimally, the trainee and HRM specialist join in a collaborative venture in which both aspire to a common objective: the development of pivotal skills and competency in the trainee. Both seek and create a wide variety of pivotal-skill and competency-based learning experience, and both track the course of development. When designers of training programs plan and design a training program to meet trainees' needs, and when HRM specialists and trainees know what is to be learned, then they can work together to achieve the desired standards as effectively and efficiently as possible.

From the author's own experiences in training others to conduct job analyses, produce improved performance ratings, and develop employee counseling skills, it has been concluded that trainees going through the four-phase model are able to test and put into action several different pivotal skills and competency levels. The first phase of the model aids the trainee in identification and articulation of the particular qualifications and characteristics he/she wishes to develop during the training program. It should be remembered that the qualifications to be developed during training are initially identified and agreed upon through organizational, employee performance appraisals, and job analysis. The second phase, which involves reflection, focuses on the actual application of what has been learned and thus enables the trainee to develop a clear understanding of what the pivotal skills and different competency levels actually entail.

Having identified the particular characteristics desired, and reflected on their actual application, the trainee must then integrate these pivotal skills into his or her own conceptual framework in order to test these ideas/impressions against the reality of the work environment. (How will the pivotal skills be applied or used in real-life situations? What are the potential alternative reactions or approaches to implementing them?)

The fourth phase requires the trainees to develop their own implementation plans. This way, each trainee must predict how the different competencies are used in the performance of his or her job. The implementation plan focuses attention on the basic purpose of pivotal-skill development and attainment of competency levels in training programs: application or implementation—and eventual evaluation of the effectiveness of the pivotal skill in use. Implementation plans developed by the trainee can be stated in the form of rules of thumb, or action resolutions, and should be based on the original qualifications identified during Phase 1 of the training needs analysis. Again, these are pivotal skills that can be directly tied to specific jobs.

Kolb's ELM is cyclical. Once a trainee integrates new characteristics into his or her behavioral repertoire, future job performance will require dependence on the enhanced or new competency level achieved. This interaction sometimes involves modification of the use of the different pivotal skills, thereby becoming the source for new learning needs. Thus, the trainee's learning process is continuous and is shaped by the requirements of future training programs.

Kolb's model has also been used by the author to provide training to HRM specialists in the design and implementation of a training program for supervisors. The HRM specialists were trained to identify pivotal skills (e.g., interviewing, listening, and self-expression) and competency levels needed by supervisors to counsel their employees. In another instance, HRM specialists were trained to provide instruction to supervisors in conducting performance appraisals. The goal of this training was to improve the quality of supervisory performance ratings. Specific objectives of the training program were identification of objective measures of performance and reporting judgments without error or bias. Both training situations resulted in a positive reaction from trainees, an improvement in their interpersonal skills, and an improvement in the trainees' performance levels.

In each situation, trainees were trained in using Kolb's ELM to design training programs and to assist others in identifying their specific learning needs, sharing those needs with other participants, and practicing problem-identification or analysis directly related to their work experiences. For example, during the employee-counseling-skills training program, trainees identified a particular counseling situation they had experienced in a work situation and role-played that experience for the rest of the trainees. Individual feedback was provided to all participants on their interviewing techniques, listening skills, and self-expression, by going through the four phases of Kolb's ELM.

SUMMARY

HRM specialists can make use of Kolb's ELM in developing and designing training programs that focus on work-related skills and competencies, by ensuring that the training program requires the trainees to reflect on the pivotal skill being learned, by examining possible solutions or alternative ways of using the pivotal skill, and finally by constructing a strategy for attaining the necessary competency level. This procedure/process leads back to the first stage of the model, and the cyclical process begins again.

The fundamental assumption in the application of Kolb's ELM is that learning should be based on experience. HRM specialists can make use of the ELM to design training programs that emphasize the development of pivotal skills and competency in particular areas by focusing on work-related problems or situations and requiring the trainee (learner) to (1) reflect on the experience or skill being learned, (2) examining possible solutions or alternative approaches for using the skill, and (3) constructing a strategy for implementing the skill.

6

Establishing Training Objectives and Determining Program Content

INTRODUCTION

In spite of sizable budgets, good intentions, and real needs, many training programs fail to achieve lasting results. Why? Too often, it is because the purported goals of the training are vague. If we don't know where we're going, we can't tell if we got there. Nor can we tell if it's where we wanted to be.

This chapter deals with selecting, writing, and organizing training objectives, and determining program content. While training course outlines, programs of instruction, or training guidelines may be available to the HRM specialist, most of these documents are of limited help in planning tailored training activities. Furthermore, as emphasized in Chapter 4, a valid source of training objectives is systematically collected through the use of objective job or task data. The effectiveness of the training system depends on the efficiency of the human resource management staff in selecting and writing meaningful training objectives.

STATEMENT OF TRAINING OBJECTIVES

The selection of training objectives is a judgmental procedure that involves close scrutiny by qualified organizational personnel of the full range of job duties, tasks, and elements performed by employees in a particular job and detailed in job analyses. The criteria used by the HRM specialist as a basis for selection must ensure that the skills that are appropriate for formal training are formulated as objectives for specific training programs.

Job analyses detail the full dimensions of a particular job with all its variations, caused by the organization in its efforts to achieve overall strategies and goals. It would be unrealistic and extravagant, in terms of time, personnel, money and other resources, to provide the amount and kind of training required to equip every graduate of a training program to perform and execute a job task (pivotal or peripheral) associated with a particular occupation or skill in any position anywhere. For the same reason, it is often impractical to train employees to the level of proficiency required in some positions; however, the attempt must be made. Some training is more realistically and more practically conducted on the job. Consequently, it is essential for the HRM specialist to select from the total list of job performances those for which formal training is most appropriate and feasible and to decide what standards or level of proficiency will be required for successful training program completion.

Training priorities for specific job duties and tasks (pivotal skills) must also be assigned to ensure that the most critical skills are taught even if reductions in the length and or cost of the training program are necessary. That is, if business or other conditions require the implementation of an austerity program, training in pivotal skills will still be possible without revamping the entire training program. The cut can come at the end of a specified segment of the program, and whatever is left over can become the sum and substance of the on-the-job training program. These requirements can be easily passed on to supervisors of operating activities in a form that will tell them precisely how much of the needed training has been provided and what remains for them to accomplish.

Part of the waste that occurs in training is directly due to the fact that objectives, even if valid, have not been stated in terms that permit the development of optimally effective training programs. Too often, the objectives of training have been stated vaguely. Typically, statements of objectives have been worded in such ways as "to provide the trainee with a general knowledge of . . . ," "as a working knowledge . . . ," "an understanding and appreciation of . . . ," or "to develop the ability to . . . " Statements like these are ambiguous; they can be, and inevitably are, interpreted differently by the HRM staff and trainees. They are imprecise; they do not provide the direction and guidance needed to select valid evaluation instruments and devices.

Objectives must be understood by both the HRM specialists and trainees; therefore, if precise and efficient training is to be provided, objectives must be stated in behavioral terms. This means that they must describe clearly and unambiguously what the trainee must be able to do, the conditions under which he or she must be able to perform, and the standard or criterion of acceptable performance—both at critical points during the development of pivotal job skills and at the end of the training program.

The idea is to state the objectives so that the success or failure of the training program can be evaluated by referring to the objectives (Pierce and Wentorf, 1970; Campbell, 1980). For skills training, this is straightforward; for example, the successful trainee will be expected to type fifty-five words per minute with two or fewer errors per page. But behavioral objectives can be more difficult to state. Contrast the objective "to understand that each employee is an individual" with "the supervisor develops profiles on each employee listing personnel data and comments on the specific examples of performance and reviews the employee's profile prior to any developmental meetings with the employee" (McGehee, 1979).

There is no way to judge if the first objective has occurred. The second objective contains verifiable statements that provide a basis for evaluating whether or not the program was successful. The formulation of behavioral objectives is a difficult task. Yet, if training objectives are not stated in the manner of the second objective above, the likelihood of achieving the purposes of the training is extremely small. Unquestionably, even with vaguely stated objectives the trainee will learn something; but what he or she learns may bear little resemblance to what was intended.

Uses of Training Objectives

The objectives of the training program must be directly related to the needs determined during the needs assessment phase, or the program developer's understanding of the trainees' jobs (as determined perhaps through job analysis), or the subject matter at hand. The content of programs, the techniques used, and even the trainees and HRM specialists chosen depend on the objectives of the training program. Is the training for management or computer programming? Are the trainees experienced? How important is this training to the organization? How much time and money are we willing to invest in it? Which payoffs can we anticipate from the training? The importance and relationship of these objectives to the organization's strategies determine the level of resources committed to training efforts. There *must* be a link between the training objectives and the organization's objectives. To take a simple case:

—sales trainers have the objective of trying to impart new product knowledge and the techniques for using it in selling;

—sales personnel attending the training will have the objective of learning something that will help them to get orders for the new products;

—sales managers will have the objectives of reaching targets and obtaining new sales;

—the organization will have the intention of obtaining sales volume that matches the potential product volume and that will maintain or increase its share of the market.

Training objectives provide the basis for all the remaining steps in the development of a training program system. As mentioned earlier, they guide the selection of program content, and to some extent guide selection of methods and techniques. They also serve as the criteria against which a program can be evaluated when it is over (a point to be discussed in more detail in Chapter 11). Training objectives constitute the real heart of a training program. The quality of other training decisions rests heavily on the adequacy of statements of training objectives. In addition, training objectives serve certain administrative purposes. Some of the more important uses of training objectives follow:

Consistency in the Design of the Training System. As depicted in Chapter 1, training systems are composed of several interacting and integrated subsystems. There are the human elements—the HRM specialists and trainees. There are the material elements—the equipment, training aids, texts, handouts, and the like. And there are the organizational and strategy elements—the methods, techniques, systems of trainee and HRM specialist organization, and media. To make sure that all these elements dovetail and support each other, they must be selected and used on the basis of a set of objectives that are common to all subsystems.

Effective Communication. The main function of statements of objectives in training is communication. Training objectives that are sent clearly by the sender and received ungarbled by the receiver are more likely to be achieved than objectives that are not clearly communicated. In short, with clearly stated objectives, HRM specialists can do a better job of training, and trainees can do a better job of learning. The HRM specialists know precisely what they are attempting to do, and trainees know what is expected of them in terms of behavior of performance as a result of training. Statements of training objectives are therefore useful to the HRM specialist to develop means of checking on their own and the trainees' performance. The HRM specialists may also use objectives to inform their colleagues, substitute trainers, department heads, training supervisors, managers, and executives about the content of their program and to tell them how trainees will be able to perform when, they have completed the training system.

Selecting Appropriate Training Program Content. Well-stated training objectives provide a clear description of job requirements. Because training objectives can be written in a fashion that avoids equivocation and ambiguity, the process of selecting the optimum method, medium, and system of organization is greatly simplified. The HRM specialist who knows precisely what the trainee must be able to do upon completion of the training block or unit can be more objective about selecting the training strategy that will accomplish the goal.

Umambiguous HRM Specialist and Trainee Goals. Training objectives permit both the HRM specialist and trainees to know precisely what is required of the trainee at the end of any training unit or complete training program. This knowledge provides the trainees with a sense of direction, and enables them to determine for themselves what progress they are making toward the attainment of the goal. Such knowledge is, in itself, a strong motivating factor. Knowledge of goals helps the HRM specialist to avoid gaps and unnecessary duplication in training. In short, well-stated training objectives make learning more effective and more efficient.

Basis for Developing Criterion Measures. Training objectives are essential to the construction of valid and reliable criterion tests. Criterion measures are specialized tests that provide the training system designer with another means of determining whether the training system is appropriate and effective. Valid tests are difficult to construct under any conditions, but without well-stated training objectives to serve as a foundation, the validity of criterion tests and measures is likely to be questionable.

Objective Evaluation of Training. With well-stated training objectives both the HRM specialist and other program evaluators know what the outcome of the training should be. This permits objective evaluation of the training program in action—and acceptance by the HRM specialist of the validity of the comments of the evaluator.

Requirements for On-the-Job Training Programs. With well-stated training objectives available to them, supervisors have a clear picture of the knowledge and skills that graduates of a training program will bring to the job. This facilitates the development of realistic on-the-job training programs that dovetail with the formal training program.

Establishing Requirements for Contract (External) Training. Last, precisely stated training objectives can be used to define training requirements to contracted HRM specialists if the training is to be conducted either in-house with external trainers or out-of-house. Behaviorally stated training objectives make it possible to communicate to contractors exactly what the output of the training must be. Such a step means not only that there will be a better chance of getting the required training product, but also that the danger of wasting funds will be minimized. In short, with behavioral objectives, the external trainer's performance is more easily monitored.

Setting Training Objectives

Complete training objectives contain three elements: (1) a statement of desired performance, (2) an indication of any important conditions under which the desired performance is to occur, and (3) a criterion of acceptable performance that is suitable, if possible, for measurement (Mager, 1984). They can take one or more of the following forms:

Table 6.1
Examples of Instructional Objectives

Type of Objective	Examples
Knowledge	All trainees will understand, and be able to attain, a grade of 80 or better on a test designed to measure the principles of performance appraisal, including types, uses, assessment procedures, errors and their avoidance, providing feedback, and EEO issues.
Attitudes	All trainees will believe that performance appraisal is important to effective management and that every employee has a right to receive an accurate appraisal annually. To be judged by their statements in class and their behavior on the job.
Skills	All trainees will be able to accurately appraise three videotaped examples of employee performance. All trainees will be able to provide high-quality feedback to their "subordinates" in role playing.
Job behavior	All trainees will provide all of their subordinates with high-quality appraisals within six months after completion of training.
Organizational results	All trainees' work groups will improve their performance levels by 5 percent during the first year following training.

1. Knowledge objectives refer to the material that participants are expected to know when the program is over
2. Attitudinal objectives state the beliefs and convictions that participants are expected to hold as a result of the program
3. Skill objectives describe the kinds of behaviors participants should be able to demonstrate under learning conditions
4. Job behavior objectives indicate the desired responses of participants once they are back on the job
5. Organizational result objectives state changes in profitability, sales, service, efficiency, costs, employee turnover, and the like that should result from the program

Table 6.1 shows how each type of objective might be stated for a training program on performance appraisal. As the table shows, a given training program may have multiple training objectives. Generally, short-run training objectives are stated in terms of knowledge, attitudes, or skills, with job behaviors (abilities) relating to a more intermediate time span, and organizational results being the range objectives (Heneman, Schwab, Fossum, and Dyer, 1989). In many cases, the link between a training program and improved organizational results is so tenuous that it is unrealistic to set such objectives. Rather, it must be assumed that if trainees change their job behavior, the results will be beneficial to the organization.

Criteria for Selection of Training Objectives. The following criteria are offered as guides for the selection of appropriate objectives for training. It is not essential for all criteria to be met in order for any single item to be included in the list of training objectives of a training program. In some cases, the meeting of one criterion alone may be sufficient justification for the inclusion of a knowledge, skill, or ability in a list of training objectives.

1. *Universality.* The criterion of universality asks the questions: Where is this knowledge, skill, or ability (KSA) used? In which jobs? Does it have wide or narrow application? Is it so unique that it is infrequently found in the job descriptions of incumbents of positions with this title? If it is truly unique, the likelihood is that the skill should be taught on the job, rather than as a part of a formal training program.

2. *Difficulty.* The difficulty criterion asks the trainer the questions: Is the knowledge, skill, or ability difficult to acquire? Are people likely to learn this skill on their own and with minimum danger to themselves, to equipment, or to materials? If the answer to either question is "no," and if the item meets at least one other criterion, it probably should be included in the list of training objectives.

3. *Cruciality.* The criterion of cruciality asks the questions: How important is the skill when practice of it is called for? What happens if the job incumbent does not possess the knowledge or pivotal skill? What is the impact of this deficiency on the product or service, or the image of the organization?

4. *Frequency.* The criterion of frequency asks the questions: How often must the employee perform this task? Is there a known best way of handling it? Can a standard way of handling this task be taught? Is there any real benefit in teaching it in training?

5. *Practicability.* The criterion of practicability asks the questions: Will the investment in training yield proportional increases in skill? Is a formally trained person a measurably better performer than someone who has learned the skill on his own or on the job?

6. *Achievability.* The criterion of achievability asks the questions: Can the majority of trainees meet the standard described in the objective? Do they have the aptitude, the intelligence, the maturity, the motivation, and the educational and experience background required to deal with the training content and to attain the desired standard?

7. *Quality.* This criterion asks the questions: Are the skills acquired most useful to average-acceptable workers? Does the program result in either overtraining or undertraining?

8. *Deficiency.* This criterion asks the questions: What is it that people in this job frequently do poorly or not at all? What aspects of the job need to be emphasized because a sizable number of job incumbents make mistakes or display an unacceptable level of proficiency? This information is often obtained by way of the performance discrepancy or performance analysis as discussed in Chapter 3 in the section on needs assessment.

9. *Retainability*. The criterion of retainability asks the questions: How long will it be before the trainee uses this skill on the job? How susceptible to deterioration is this skill or knowledge? Does it require maintenance training to retain it? What level of accomplishment is required at the conclusion of initial training to ensure a sufficient residue of the skill to handle tasks involving it some time later on the job?

10. *Follow-on training*. The criterion of follow-on training asks the questions: What level of proficiency is needed for a graduate of this training program to undertake a program of advanced or on-the-job training? What should the planner of subsequent training be able to count on in the way of prior knowledge and level of skill or competence?

Procedures for Selecting Objectives. The final job analysis report provides a basis for decisions with regard to whether a specific KSA will be taught and the level of training required. Although the data indicate such facts as the percentage of job incumbents performing each duty and task, the frequency with which they are performed, and an index of their criticality, other important criteria require the application of judgment of qualified personnel (subject matter experts). Such judgments must be made by fully qualified personnel using a standard rating scale to arrive at decisions on training objectives and their priorities.

The following procedures for selecting training objectives have been recommended by Tracey (1984).

Step 1: On the Training Objectives Worksheet shown in Figure 6.1, list all the duties and tasks contained in the final job analysis report in Chapter 4.

Step 2: Rate each of the items in the list of duties and tasks in terms of each of the ten criteria discussed earlier. Values for each criterion are described in the Criterion Scoring Guide in Table 6.2.

Step 3: Sum the scores for each duty and task, and enter the total in column 12 of the Training Objectives Worksheet.

Step 4: Establish the training priority for each task. Indicate this priority by assigning a priority number in column 13 of the Training Objectives Worksheet. A range of scores for each priority is included at the bottom of the worksheet.

The meanings of the priorities are as follows:

0 The task will not be taught at all.

1 Complete and thorough training will be provided; all trainees must demonstrate mastery of the task; they must be able to perform at the level of competency required on the job.

2 Some training will be provided all trainees; trainees must demonstrate that they can perform the task, but not with the competency required on the job.

Figure 6.1
Training Objectives Worksheet

Tasks	Criteria											
	Universality	Difficulty	Cruciality	Frequency	Practicability	Achievability	Quality	Deficiency	Retainability	Follow-up training	Total score	Priority
1	2	3	4	5	6	7	8	9	10	11	12	13

Total score   Priority
0 - 10   0
11 - 20   4
21 - 30   3
31 - 40   2
41 - 50   1

Table 6.2
Criterion Scoring Guide

Criterion	Score					
	0	1	2	3	4	5
	0-10	11-25	26-50	51-75	76-90	91-100
Universality: What percentage of incumbents perform the task?						
Difficulty: Can the task be learned on the job?	Very easily	practical	Minor problems	Many problems	Major problems	Practically impossible
Cruciality: Is the task Critical to job performance?	Not critical	Rarely critical	Sometimes critical	Often critical	Very often critical	Always very critical
Frequency: How often is the task performed?	Less than quarterly	Quarterly	Monthly	Weekly	Daily	Several times per day
Practicability: How does the proficiency of a formally trained man compare with those who learned on the job?	Much less proficient	Somewhat less proficient	About the same	Somewhat higher	Much higher	Very much higher
Achievability: Can the task be learned to the degree required in a reasonable time frame?	Practically impossible	Minor problems	Many problems	Minor problems	Practical	Very easily
Quality: To which type of incumbent is the skill most useful?	Poor performer	Outstanding performer		Below average performer	Above average performer	Average performer
Deficiency: How frequently are deficiencies noted in job incumbents?	Never	Rarely	Sometimes	Often	Very often	Always
Retainability: What is the time interval between training and use of the skill?	Used Immediately	Used within first month	Used within 1-3 months	Used within 4-6 months	Used within 7-12 months	Used after 12 months
Follow-on training: What type of training is given on the skill following initial formal training?	Immediate advanced formal training	Thorough and complete on-the-job training	Some formal on-the-job training		Occasional informal on-the-job training	No additional training

3 All trainees will be introduced to the task; they will not be expected to be able to perform the task upon completion of training, but it has been described and demonstrated to them.

4 If time permits, trainees will be introduced to the task, but they will not be expected to be able to perform the task upon completion of training.

Final Selection of Objectives. The completed Training Objectives Worksheet should be submitted to at least three qualified subject matter experts for review of task ratings and priorities. Reviewers should have the final job analysis report when making this review. When the forms have been reviewed, all interested parties should meet face-to-face to iron out differences in the ratings and assignment of priorities. The objective of the meeting is to reach a consensus on the inclusion of specific duties and tasks in the training system and their respective priorities.

Writing Training Objectives

Good objectives are half the battle and the general rules for good expository writing apply to the writing of objectives. The overriding consideration is to be certain that the objectives state the desired behavior and the conditions under which it is to occur and serve as the standard against which individual performance can be measured and the training program evaluated. The written training objectives include plain, generally understood English, since the basic purpose is to communicate the training intent.

To communicate clearly and get ideas across correctly, these five rules should be followed:

1. Avoid unfamiliar words. Consider the reader's comfort, interest, and capacity to understand. Unfamiliar words make no mental impression, so use only words which you are certain the reader of the objectives will understand.

2. Do not confuse or misuse words. It is easy to make mistakes in usage, but errors can be avoided if you develop a writing conscience. An old admonition that applies is: "When in doubt, look it up or leave it out."

3. Be terse. Brevity makes written communication easier to understand. Long and involved sentences make it difficult to comprehend the intended meaning. Use only one idea in a sentence.

4. Seek simplicity. Use simple, short words, phrases, and sentences to keep the "fog count" down. Economize on adjectives and language flourishes. Make every word count.

Table 6.3

Standards for Checking Adequacy of Training Objectives

1. **General.**

    a. Are the statements free from grammatical, spelling, and typographical errors?
    b. Has the writer avoided the use of unfamiliar words?
    c. Is the sentence structure clear, concise, simple, and straight forward?
    d. Is the use of punctuation, abbreviations, and hyphenation correct and uniform?
    e. Do the statements avoid ambiguity?

2. **Behavior.**

    a. Does the statement clearly and precisely describe what the trainees will be doing when they demonstrate what they have learned?
    b. Does the statement avoid the use of "loaded words"?
    c. Does the statement describe a complete action?
    d. Does the statement begin with an action verb?
    e. Does the statement describe a meaningful unit of performance?
    f. Is the behavior clearly relevant to the job or task?

3. **Conditions.**

    a. Does the statement clearly and completely describe the conditions under which the trainee must demonstrate the required behavior?
    b. Does the statement begin with the word "given"?
    c. Does the statement identify what the trainee will be given to do the job or task (tools, equipment, job aids, or materials)?
    d. Does the statement describe the physical environment (space, climatic conditions, and the like) when these are significant?
    e. Does the statement describe the assistance the trainee will receive (if any)?
    f. Does the statement describe the amount and kind of supervision (if any) the trainee will receive during job performance?

4. **Criterion.**

    a. Does the statement clearly describe how well the trainee must perform?
    b. Is the minimum level for acceptable performance clearly defined?
    c. Is the quality of the work products or services defined in terms of standards of accuracy, completeness, format, sequence, clarity, neatness, tolerances, or number of errors permitted?
    d. Is the quantity of the work products or services defined in terms of the number of units to be completed per unit of time or in terms of the total number of units required?
    e. Are time standards clearly defined in terms of performance, speed of performance, or total time allowed for performance?
    f. Are the standards realistic and attainable?
    g. Are the standards relevant to the job or task?
    h. Are the standards measurable?
    i. Do the standards avoid the use of such imprecise words as "effective," "acceptable," "proper," and "average"?

5. Read what you write. After following all the preceding rules in writing objectives, there is more to be done. You must read the objectives to ascertain whether the words you have used are the right ones, saying what you wish to convey. The first word that occurred to you in drafting your objectives may not be the best one. Find the one that says what you want to say.

In writing behaviorally based performance training objectives, draft objectives should be subjected to a final, rigid check prior to their publication, distribution, and use. The items listed in Table 6.3 are some of the most important standards to apply in checking the adequacy of training objectives (Tracey, 1984).

Stating and writing measurable training objectives is particularly important so that the content of the training programs and training methods can be addressed specifically to expected results. It should be remembered that a well-written training objective will have three parts: (1) a statement of terminal behavior, that is, what the learner will be able to do upon completion of training; (2) a description of the conditions under which terminal behavior is expected to occur; (3) a statement of the minimum level of achievement or competence that will be accepted as evidence that the learner has accomplished what was required.

Useful sources of reference on the writing and use of objectives are Mager's classic work on behavioral objectives (1962), Bloom's writing on cognitive objectives ((1956), Hamblin on the use of objectives to control and evaluate different kinds of training (1974), Rackham and Morgan on using behavioral objectives to set goals for interpersonal training (1977), and Tracey's (1971, 1984) and Mager's (1962, 1984) works on selecting and writing training objectives. Decisions on content, potential trainees, and training method flow logically from these behavioral objectives.

Determining Training Program Content

Training program content refers to the material to be covered and to the general sequence in which it will be presented. Two primary determinants of training program content are training objectives and the information base that is available on the subject. When training objectives are specific to a particular job, job descriptions and specifications can serve as the information base. (This information is derived from the job analysis.) When they relate more to a broad field, general "theory" must be relied on. Sometimes both can be used. For the training program in Table 6.1, for example, the designer might first study the managers' jobs to determine how performance appraisal is to be used and then selectively choose from among the theoretical materials available on performance appraisal.

Training program content should match job content inasmuch as possible, for both practical and legal reason. Practically, the greater the content validity, the more effective and efficient training can be—since no essential material is omitted, and no irrelevant material is included. Also, it helps to foster the transfer of training back to the job. Content validity is also a legal necessity, since training is often a prerequisite to job selection or assignment, and in this context falls under Title VII of the Civil Rights Act as well as the *Uniform Guidelines on Employee Selection Procedures* (Russell, 1984). In recent years, systematic processes have been developed that enable "subject matter experts" to translate the behavioral content and the knowledge and skill requirements of jobs into training program content (Wexley, 1984).

In addition to job content, potential training participants also influence training program content. Most material can and should be adjusted in level of difficulty and rate of presentation to be consistent with the participants' current state of understanding and their abilities to learn. This is one reason it is so important to assess trainability when employee development needs are determined.

A final determinant concerns the designer's beliefs about learning. One key issue involves whole-versus-part learning—that is, whether material is to be presented all at once and then repeated in total, or is to be broken into smaller elements, each to be mastered before the next is tackled. Generally, part learning is preferable, particularly when the material is complex (Wexley and Latham, 1981). Also, it is generally agreed that the transfer of training problems is lessened if material is presented in the same sequence in which it will be used on the job (Wexley and Latham, 1981). This is why it is important for designers to conduct job analyses and to study job descriptions and the actual work performance of trainees.

Outlining Training Program Content. To effectively outline training program content the usual procedure is to prepare a rough draft of the outline, indicating the major subject-matter areas to be covered, and then gradually expanding the outline until a detailed statement of training content is produced. Some training program designers prepare a two-dimensional matrix in which training objectives are listed on one axis and the training content categories are listed on the other axis. In the resulting cells the specific facts, concepts, principles, and skills needed to achieve the objectives are inserted.

Avoiding Pitfalls in Determining Training Program Content. In developing training program content outlines, care must be taken to avoid the following: (1) leaving out important parts of the subject matter, (2) overemphasizing topics that do not merit detailed treatment, and (3) allowing unnecessary duplication or overlapping in the material presented.

These pitfalls can be avoided by consulting with subject matter experts and by studying documentary materials. Periodic review of outlines during development will also help to indicate omissions, duplication, and overlap.

Helpful Steps in Training Program Content Selection. The following steps should be followed in selecting training program content:

Step 1: Examine training objectives and develop separate topical outlines for each task.

Step 2: Submit the topical outline to subject matter experts for a check of completeness and accuracy. The purpose of this step is not to review detail, but rather to ensure that major items of content required for competent performance have been included and that nonessential content has been omitted.

Step 3: Revise the topical outline in accordance with the recommendations of the subject matter experts.

Step 4: Develop a detailed outline for each segment of the topical outline or training objective. Each item in the preliminary topical outline should be analyzed, and the teaching points should be formulated in declarative statements, using appropriate references.

Step 5: Eliminate unnecessary duplication within the detailed points to be taught. If a training point essential to the development of a KSA later in the sequence duplicates a training point developed earlier, identify it as a review item of training content.

Step 6: Submit the detailed content outlines to subject matter experts for final review.

Step 7: Revise the training content outlines as indicated by the reports of the reviewers.

From the analysis of training needs and translation of them into behavioral objectives, the HRM specialists derive the content of the training program. Since there are well over 20,000 jobs listed in the *Dictionary of Occupational Titles*, the number of skills to be developed can be quite unique. For example, communication, leadership, and budgeting skills are frequent subjects of training programs (Rothwell, 1983). The ones to be taught are derived from the training needs analysis, which in turn leads to setting the objectives of the training program. They can vary from improving typing skills to learning a new computer language to effective use of a new machine.

SUMMARY

Objectives are essential to systematic training. Effective goal setting and objectives form the basis for effective training systems, and are therefore just as essential as setting objectives in other functional areas of the organization (financial, marketing, and production to name a few). Moreover, objectives and training program content go hand in hand—the objectives determine how activities are planned, implemented and evaluated, and the evaluative information determines how objectives are set and modified. Although the real-world task of setting objectives and determining training program content is complex and subject to rational and irrational influences, systematically considering their development, implementation and evaluation is not only possible, but essential.

The content of training programs, the techniques used, and even the trainees chosen depend on the objectives of the training program. Is the training program for management or word processing? Are the trainees experienced? How important is this training to the organization? How much time and money is the organization willing to invest in it? Which payoffs can the organization anticipate from the training? The importance and relationship of these objectives to the organization's strategies and the training program cannot be underestimated. Therefore, once the training program objectives are established, HRM specialists are then able to turn to specific program content and other details to design the training program. These other details will be described in the next chapter.

Training Program Design and Selection of Training Methods

INTRODUCTION

This chapter examines issues in the design of training programs and establishes criteria for the selection of the optimum method, technique, or medium to achieve training objectives. Toward this end the chapter will discuss the importance of someone assuming responsibility for training programs, the legal aspects designers of training programs must be cognizant of, maximizing trainees' learning, understanding individual differences, the transfer of training, and the selection of training methods.

Responsibility for Training

If training is so essential to organizations, it must be done effectively. This requires that someone assume responsibility for these programs from preassessment through final evaluation. In some situations the failure of training programs results from the failure to adhere to the principle that it is the responsibility of all line managers to develop and utilize their own units' human resources to get the results for which they are held directly accountable—and that staff (HRM specialists) can/should really only assist them in this (Hagedorn, 1984; Taylor, 1974). HRM specialists can help line managers serve the training and development needs of their employees by (1) holding interviews with employees and gathering performance data, (2) analyzing performance requirements for each position, (3) comparing employee skill and performance levels with those requirements, (4) recommending and designing training programs to improve employee skill levels to reduce any unfavorable deficiencies, and (5) conducting training programs where appropriate.

The success of any training program requires that employees take a role in their own training as well. After all, training cannot occur unless the employee has a real desire for it. This does not suggest, however, that all individuals should be limited by the extent to which a worker is able to take the lead in the training effort.

Top-level managers have traditionally been able to exercise the most initiative in their own training. At lower levels, the supervisor and the organization become increasingly responsible for the design and implementation of training programs. Although employee responsibility is not eliminated entirely, there may be a shift from the employee being responsible for initiating training to the employee being responsible for using and applying available training programs. The exception to this, however, may be the top manager, who, although not actually initiating specific training programs, must provide support and commitment to the effort. Often this support and commitment are initially provided by an organization's training policy and then reinforced with the actions of top executives.

For training to be effective, employees *must* see top management supporting it in an open manner, both personally and financially. As mentioned earlier, like many staff functions, responsibility for training is shared between line management and the HRM staff. One breakdown of the roles and responsibilities of line management (operations manager) and HRM staff (HRM management) during specific training activities follows:

1. Determination of training needs and objectives is approved by operations manager (OM) and done by HRM staff
2. Development of training criteria is approved by OM and done by HRM
3. Trainers are jointly chosen or nominated by OM and approved by HRM
4. Development of training materials is approved by OM and done by HRM
5. Planning and implementation of the training program is done by HRM
6. Doing the training is occasionally done by OM, but normally done by HRM
7. In the evaluation of the training, the OM reviews the results and the evaluation is done by HRM (Ivancevich and Glueck, 1989)

Effective training design and implementation require that line and staff are able to work closely together on all phases of the training process, and that both parties understand and recognize their shared authority (Michalak and Yager, 1979). HRM specialists or line managers unwilling to approach the training process cooperatively find that training does not help their organizations. Although the responsibility for training will differ from organization to organization, certain responsibilities are usually reserved for either line managers or staff personnel.

The HRM staff often serves as an expert source of training assistance and coordination to (1) perform actual needs analysis, (2) design tools that may be used to survey needs, (3) determine personnel who need training, (4) write training objectives, (5) determine the type of training program and training techniques, (6) perform the training program evaluation, and (7) present the findings to line management. The HRM unit often has a more long-range view of employee careers and of the importance of developing the entire organization than do individual operating managers. This difference is especially true at lower levels in the organization.

On the other hand, line managers are likely to be the best source of the technical information used in skill training. In addition, line managers (1) supply training staff with necessary performance data, (2) review and approve needs analysis and training objectives, (3) review and approve training program and techniques, (4) if applicable, perform on-the-job training (or supervise it if conducted by a nonsupervisory employee), and (5) review results. Line managers are also in a better position to decide when employees need training or retraining (Carrell, Kuzmits, and Elbert, 1989; Mathis and Jackson, 1988). Because of the close and continual interaction they have with their employees, managers determine and discuss employees' career potentials and plans. Again, training efforts will fail without active managerial participation and involvement. If the organization is small, managers may have to handle the activities normally performed by HRM specialists in larger organizations.

Occasionally, more than the HRM specialists and operating managers are involved in designing the training effort. For example, at General Telephone of Florida, the training, labor relations, and public affairs departments combined forces to prepare video training programs to train managers to handle grievances and arbitration. Community theater actors performed the roles, to show participants how to perform while on the job (Ivancevich and Glueck, 1989). The determination of who is responsible for the training effort is a key issue that must be addressed early in the design phase of a training program. Legal issues are also important considerations in the design of a training program. The next section will discuss how Equal Employment Opportunity Commission guidelines affect the design of training programs.

Legal Issues and Equal Employment Opportunity

Legal considerations are relevant to several aspects of training. One aspect is the determination of the training needs of an applicant for a job. For example, an applicant cannot be eliminated from the selection pool for lack of a skill that can be learned in eight hours. Thus, it is important to determine what pivotal skills an individual needs to perform a job, what skills an applicant possesses, which training programs can remove any deficiencies, and the time necessary to complete these programs.

The Civil Rights Act forbids discrimination in any term or condition of employment because of race, color, religion, sex, age, or national origin. The act covers training activities, just as it does any other HRM activity. Anyone involved in training employees must understand how EEOC guidelines apply (Bartlett, 1978). The federal "Uniform Guidelines on Employee Selection Procedures" affect five areas of training (Wexley and Latham, 1981): job entry, training program admission, the training process itself, career decisions, and affirmative action plans.

Training Required to Obtain a Job or a Promotion Must Be Job Related. Job entry training may be necessary before a person can be considered for entry to a job—for example, passing a pole-climbing course prior to being considered for a job as a telephone installer or repairer. Legal problems may arise in instances where women or minorities are less likely to pass the training course than white males (that is, when "adverse impact" exists" *and* the company has no proof that the training requirements are related to job proficiency). To avoid such difficulties, all trainees must be given an equal chance to complete the training successfully. And, of course, the validity of the training requirements must be demonstrated. The company must be able to show that people with the training perform their jobs better than those without the training.

Selecting Employees for a Training or Development Program Must Not Be Done in a Discriminatory Manner. As noted above, legally, Title VII of the 1964 Civil Rights Act prohibits discrimination against individuals on the basis of their race, sex, age, religion, or national origin in admission to apprenticeship or other training programs. When discriminatory practices have been uncovered and brought to court, the courts have made decisions effecting far-reaching changes in how organizations select employees for training and development programs (Norton, 1987).

The Training Process Itself Must Not Be Discriminatory. The training process itself may have an adverse impact on women and minorities. For example, physical equipment for training may be designed primarily for men, thereby making it difficult for some women to use because of their generally shorter legs and arm reach (Redesign of the equipment might eliminate this problem). In an organization-specific example, to comply with federal legislation, AT&T redesigned pole climbing so that women could successfully complete the pole-climbing training course (Smith, 1978). The vocabulary level in training manuals may require a reading ability far higher than is necessary to perform the job itself, thus eliminating those with less education. In short, if the training process itself consistently results in inferior performance by women and minorities, the program may have to be redesigned unless such inferior training performance is reflected in corresponding inferior job performance.

If Career Decisions Are Made by Management on the Basis of Success during Training, It Should Be Shown that the Training Was Job-Related. Career decisions, such as retention in the training program or preferential job assignment, are sometimes made on the basis of measures collected during training. Again, if women and minorities consistently perform poorly in training, the performance measures themselves must be validated to show that performance in training reflects later performance on the job (a correlation between training success and subsequent job success should be shown). Sound HRM practice dictates that this be done anyway to assess whether training dollars are being spent well.

Preferential Treatment for Training Minorities Is Legal if an Affirmative Action Program Exists. Affirmative action plans commonly specify preferential goals for the recruitment, selection, and training of women and minorities. Such treatment was supported in the Supreme Court case *United Steelworkers* v. *Weber* in 1978. The Supreme Court ruled that affirmative action programs involving training are legal where evidence of racial imbalance exists. The court also upheld the use of dual seniority systems for admitting employees into training (Ledvinka, 1982). In the biggest consent degree ever, General Motors agreed (with the EEOC) to spend $42.5 million over six years to hire, train, and promote more women and minorities. GM agreed to establish companywide hiring goals for women and minorities in eight job categories, including apprentices, supervisors, security officers, and sales managers. The company also agreed to spend over $21 million on training this target group for higher-level positions and to provide an additional $15 million educational package of endowments and scholarships for more than 100,000 employed and laid-off women and minorities and their families (Lienert, 1983).

Specific discriminatory training practices can often be determined by the responses to the following questions:

1. Are minorities and/or women given the same training opportunities as white males?

2. Are requirements for entry into a training program (i.e., tests, education, or experience) job-related, or are they arbitrary?

3. Are nearly all machine functions or other specialized duties that require training performed by white or male workers?

4. Does one class of trainees tend to get more challenging assignments or other special training opportunities?

5. Do supervisors know what constitutes training? (It could be almost any learning experience from how to fit a drill bit to a two-week seminar on complex sales procedures.)

6. Who evaluates the results of instruction or training—only white males?

7. Are all trainees given equal facilities for instruction? Are they segregated in any way?

8. Do a disproportionate number of females and/or minorities fail to pass training courses? (If so, find out if it is because they receive inferior instruction.)

To defend against charges of discrimination, organizations—and, specifically, designers of training programs—can provide a reasonable defense by showing that the training programs were conceived and administered without bias. This, however, will be exceedingly difficult to demonstrate unless companies have the foresight to document their training practices. Therefore, they should follow these guidelines:

1. Register affirmative action training and apprenticeship programs with the Department of Labor. They are required to be in writing. Include the goals, timetables, and criteria for selection and evaluation of trainees. Such a record will help prove job-relatedness and the absence of any intent to discriminate. It can also be valuable in proving that an organization's training program was not used as a pretext to discriminate.

2. Keep a record of all employees who wish to enroll in your training program. Detail how each trainee was selected. Keep application forms, tests, questionnaires, records of preliminary interviews, and anything else that bears on an employee's selection or rejection for at least two years or as long as training continues.

3. Document all management decisions and actions that relate to the administration of training policies.

4. Monitor each trainee's progress. Provide progress evaluations and make sure counseling is available. Continue to evaluate the results even after completion of training.

Clearly, the legal aspects of training programs should not be underestimated. However, neither should they preoccupy HRM specialists to the point of not considering other, equally critical, aspects of training design and implementation, such as individual differences, maximizing trainees' learning, transfer of training, and selecting training methods.

Individual Differences

Individual differences are important in the design and eventual implementation of a training program. Individual differences should be glaringly obvious in the training environment. Some trainees are fast learners, some are slow learners, some begin at higher initial states than others, some are capable of higher terminal states than others, and some improve very little despite continuous practice. (Chapter 8 discusses in detail the importance of individual differences in the training process.) These variations in learning patterns are the result of differences in ability, motivation, and learning styles among trainees.

HRM specialists need to be flexible enough to modify their training strategies to accommodate these differences (e.g., through optional additional practice sessions, more detailed explanations and demonstrations, and the selection of a variety of training methods). The extent to which designers of training programs are flexible in responding to individual differences and selecting training methods should result in more effective and meaningful training programs. Once individual differences are identified and acknowledged, it becomes important to focus on another issue in the design of training programs: maximizing trainees' learning.

Maximizing Trainees' Learning: Trainability

Organizations should provide training to those who are most likely to profit from it; individuals prefer to be trained in the things that interest them and in which they can improve. To provide instruction for trainees in areas in which they have no aptitude or interest is a result of poor training program design, which will not benefit them and will certainly not benefit the organization.

From a cost-benefit perspective the largest component of training is the cost of paying the trainee during the training period (Chapter 12 discusses the cost-benefit concept in more detail.) Hence, cost savings are possible if training time can be reduced. Perhaps the easiest way to do this is by identifying and training only those employees who clearly are "trainable." The term *trainability* refers to how well a person can acquire the skills, knowledge, and behaviors necessary to perform a job, achieving its specified outcome within a given time (Robertson and Downs, 1979). It is a combination of an individual's ability, motivation, and learning preferences.

The design of training programs must make efforts to identify those trainees most likely to profit from training. Trainees most likely to profit from training can be identified reasonably accurately as depicted in the following example. One study showed that current methods for assigning enlisted Navy personnel to specific jobs could be improved by using a concept called "miniature training and evaluation testing" (Siegel, 1983). Using this approach, a recruit is trained (and then subsequently tested) on a sample of the tasks he or she will be expected to perform on the job. The approach is based on the premise that a recruit who demonstrates that he or she can learn to perform a *sample* of the tasks of a Navy job will be able to learn and to perform satisfactorily *all* of the tasks of that job, given appropriate on-the-job training. In fact, a battery of nine training-evaluation situations derived from a job analysis of typical entry-level tasks for various naval occupations—such as sailor, fire fighter, and air crew member—was able to improve substantially the accuracy of prediction of job performance over that obtained with standard tests.

Trainees most likely to profit from training can be identified reasonably accurately when measures such as the one in the above example are combined with two other kinds of information: (1) the extent of each potential trainee's job involvement and career planning (Noe and Schmitt, 1986; Noe, 1986), and (2) each employee's choice to select the training in question. Once these trainees have been identified, HRM specialists can then design the training program for maximum learning. Attention can then be given to the transfer of training.

Transfer of Training

The best-designed training programs are of little benefit to the organization or the individual if the training cannot be, or is not, transferred to the back-home work situation. *Transfer* refers to the extent to which KSAs or other characteristics learned in training can be applied on the job (Cascio, 1989). Transfer may be positive (i.e., it enhances job performance), negative (i.e., it hampers job performance), or neutral. Long-term training or retraining probably includes segments that contain all three of these conditions. Training that results in negative transfer is costly in two ways—the cost of training (which proved to be useless) and the cost of hampered performance.

To facilitate the transfer from learning to doing, designers of training programs should consider the following (Goldstein, 1986; Wexley and Latham, 1981):

1. Maximize the similarity between the training situation and the job situation.

2. Provided as much experience as possible with the task being taught (so that the trainees can deal with situations that do not exactly fit textbook examples).

3. Provide for a variety of examples when teaching concepts or skills.

4. Label or identify important features of a task.

5. Make sure that general principles are well understood (particularly in jobs that require the application of principles to solve problems, such as engineering, investment analysis, or computer programming.

6. Ensure that what is learned in training is rewarded on the job. Immediate supervisors or top management, by their example or words, must support what was learned in training if the training is to have much impact on job behavior.

7. Design the training so that trainees can see its applicability to their jobs ("What you learn today, you'll use on the job tomorrow").

8. Use questions to guide the trainee's attention.

9. Either assign behavioral goals for applying what was learned in training, or allow the trainees to generate their own. Have the trainees discuss their intentions and activities for attaining these goals with other trainees, rate their progress subsequently (e.g., in one month), return their ratings to the trainer, and attend a later group session (Wexley & Baldwin, 1986).

A final issue that is important in the design of training programs is the selection and use of training methods. The selection and use of training methods will be the focus of the next section.

Selecting and Using Training Methods

Lecture, conference, demonstration, and performance methods have been used in training from the beginning. New training methods appear every year. While some are well founded in learning theory or models of behavior change (e.g., behavior modeling), others result more from technological than from theoretical developments (e.g., videotapes, computer-based business games). The decision to use one strategy or another must be made on the basis of careful analysis of the training situation from several standpoints: training objectives, training program content, trainee population, training staff, space, facilities, equipment, training materials, time, and costs.

One of the ways training methods can be classified is into three categories: information presentation, simulation methods, and on-the-job training (Campbell, Dunnette, Lawler, and Weick, 1970):

1. *Information presentation techniques.* These include lectures, conference methods, correspondence courses, motion pictures, reading lists, closed-circuit TV and videotapes, behavior modeling and systematic observation, programmed instruction, computer-assisted instruction, sensitivity training, and organization development.

2. *Simulation methods.* The case method, role playing, programmed group exercises, the in-basket technique, and business games fall into this classification.

3. *On the job training methods.* These include orientation training, apprenticeships, on-the-job training, near-the-job training (using identical equipment but away from the job itself), job rotation, committee assignments (or junior executive boards), on-the-job coaching, and performance appraisal.

Training methods can also be divided into two broad classifications of methods: on-the-job and off-the-job techniques. Normally, a tradeoff exists between off- and on-the job training techniques. Off-the-job training is relatively efficient from the standpoint of learning, but relatively inefficient in transferring learning from the classroom to the job. On-the-job techniques present few transfer-of-training problems. However, on-the-job training may be particularly inefficient.

On-the-Job Training. On-the-job training (OJT) refers to methods that are applied in the workplace, while the employee is actually working. The Bureau of National Affairs reports that 90 percent or more of all training is performed on the job (Bureau of National Affairs, 1975). On-the-job training may involve learning how to run a machine, to complete forms and paperwork, to drive a vehicle, to conduct an interview, or to sell the company's product. Both new and existing employees at all job levels—unskilled, skilled, clerical, management, and staff—are often trained on the job. Some common on-the-job training techniques include job orientation, job-instruction training, apprentice training, internships and assistantships, job rotation, programmed learning, and computer-assisted instruction.

The widespread use of OJT is, no doubt, due to the many benefits it offers. Among the potential assets of this type of training are (Carrell, Kuzmits, and Elbert, 1989):

1. The employee is doing the actual work, not hypothetical or simulated tasks.
2. The employee receives instructions from an experienced employee or supervisor who has successfully performed the task.
3. The training is performed in the actual work environment under normal working conditions and requires no special training facilities.
4. The training is informal, relatively inexpensive, and easy to schedule.
5. The training may build cooperative relationships between the employee and the trainer.

Among the potential liabilities of OJT are (Goldstein, 1974):

1. The trainer may not be motivated to train or to accept the responsibility for training; thus, training may be haphazard.
2. The trainer may perform the job well but lack the ability to teach others how to do so.
3. The trainer may not have the time to train and may omit important elements of the training process. While the employee is learning on the job, resources will be inefficiently used, performance (at least initially) will be low, and costly errors may be made.

The idea in OJT is that individuals are trained on the same machines, while doing the same work that will be expected of them when they are fully trained employees. The idea is that OJT will result in positive transfer (participation in the training programs leads to improved performance) because many of the conditions for positive transfer are present. For one, the similarity between the training situation and the actual workplace is high. Further, trainees are aware of the relationship between their performance in the training program and their success on the job. Unfortunately, on-the-job training is often haphazardly conducted. Someone is singled out as a trainer and told to show the trainee "the ropes." Often the training program is not well planned and systematically conducted by the employee trainer, whose teaching skills may also not be adequate to the task. When the employees selected as trainers are not performing the job as it should be performed, their bad habits become the training model. In addition, a poorly conducted OJT program may create safety hazards, result in damaged products or materials, and place unnecessary stress on trainees.

Perhaps the greatest problem is one of motivation to conduct the training. Not all employees are anxious to teach, nor to be responsible for teaching someone the job. This is especially true when time taken out of an employee's workday to train someone is perceived to cost the trainer in terms of his or her own work performance and possible rewards. A story is told, for example, about chicken catchers who work in nine-person crews and who are paid on a group incentive plan according to the number of birds they catch and crate. These employees deeply resent the introduction of trainees on their crews because the training task detracts from the catching task, and everyone's pay goes down (Wexley and Latham, 1981).

Off-the-Job Training. Off-the-job training is any form of training performed away from the employee's work area. Off-the-job techniques take place in classrooms or meeting rooms away from the workplace. Two broad forms of off-the-job training programs exist: (1) in-house programs are coordinated by the employee's organization and conducted within a company training facility; (2) off-site programs are held away from the organization and sponsored by a professional association, educational institution, or independent training firm. A wide variety of training methods are employed to train employees off the job; these range from lecturing to using relatively new techniques that involve expensive and sophisticated audiovisual techniques.

Organizations with the biggest training programs often use off-the-job training. The majority of the 50,000 trainers in the United States and the $200 billion spent on training are in off-the-job training. A survey of training directors in Fortune 500 companies examined their views of which off-the-job training techniques were the most effective for specific objectives. The training directors indicated that if knowledge acquisition were the objective, it would be best to use programmed instruction. On the other hand, if the training was intended to improve the problem-solving skills of participants, then it would be better to use the case method of training— that is, having participants analyze job-related cases (Carroll, Paine, and

Ivancevich, 1972). The most frequently used methods for off-the-job training are the conference/discussion, programmed instruction, computer-assisted, and simulation approaches (Goldstein, 1986).

Among the potential assets of off-the-job training are (Wexley and Latham, 1981):

1. Training is cost-efficient, because groups rather than individuals are usually trained.
2. Trainers, usually full-time instructors or training personnel, are likely to be more competent trainers than on-the-job trainers, who normally spend only a fraction of their time training.
3. More planning and organization often go into off-the-job training than into on-the-job training.
4. Off-site courses and seminars enable small companies with limited resources to train employees without the formidable expenses of a large training staff and training facilities.

Among the potential liabilities of off-the-job training are:

1. Employees attending off-the-job training are not performing their jobs. This is an added expense of training, though training benefits should exceed costs in the long run.
2. Off-the-job training often has problems of transfer of learning. Sometimes off-the-job training is of limited practical value to the trainee—particularly when the training is conducted away from the organization. Because it is impossible for the HRM specialist to customize a course for each participant, off-the-job programs normally contain limited applications for a trainee's specific problems and situations. This is the greatest potential drawback to off-the-job training.

Selecting a Training Method

Although no single training method is by nature superior to any other, the goals or objectives of a particular program may be better served by one method than another. In recent studies, lectures were the most commonly used training method. Films, case studies, and role playing were also among the more commonly used techniques of both technical skills training and management development (*Wall Street Journal*, 1986; American Society for Training and Development, 1986). Not all of the materials available to training programs were represented in the survey upon which this information is based (American Society for Training and Development, 1986). In a more recent study by *Training* magazine (*Training*, 1989) lectures and videotapes were the most frequently used methods. While case studies and role playing were the least commonly used techniques.

Training magazine's 1989 Industry Report (*Training*, 1989) showed that the popularity of instructional methods had changed little since 1986. In 1987, videotapes were the most common vehicle, barely beating out lectures. In the succeeding two years, videotape instruction held its narrow edge, indicating that its first-place ranking in 1986 was no fluke.

It would be naive to suggest that either on-the-job or off-the-job training methods will always be the most effective type of training to use. A wide variety of methods are available for use in training employees. The one to use in a given case depends on both the nature of the training and what the training department wishes to accomplish; in many situations, it may be appropriate to use a combination of two or more of the recognized methods. Some methods mentioned above involve actual job performance; others use classroom-type instruction. The nature of the material to be presented, the number of persons to be trained, the background and ability of the trainees, the kind and amount of equipment available, the length of time that can be devoted to training, and the results to be achieved must all be considered when determining the best method for a particular training program.

To the extent possible, it is desirable to use the methods that involve the trainee actively in the learning process. This is essential to ensure "gluing in" of what is taught. Training efforts that have an over-reliance on passive, one-way methods of communication produce few lasting results (and much boredom), indicating in effect selection of training methods. Because each organization has its own set of assets and liabilities, selection of a particular training method should be made after closely examining the organization's specific training environment (McGehee and Thayer, 1961).

To choose the training method (or combination of methods) that best fits a given situation, what is to be taught must first be defined carefully (that is the purpose of the needs assessment phase). Training needs and objectives must be considered. If the trainee's job contains relatively uncomplicated tasks, and if immediate production by the employee is an important objective, then on-the-job training may be preferable. On the other hand, if employees need exposure to new concepts, tools, and techniques, then off-the-job training may be preferable.

Second, resources often play an important role in choosing between on- and off-the-job programs. Managers of organizations that have few or no training resources—facilities, equipment, and qualified on-the-job trainers—often have little choice but to look to off-site programs for training employees.

Third, the money available for training significantly determines training activities. On-the-job training becomes increasingly attractive as training budgets shrink. Many administrators are simply unable to afford off-the-job training offered by professional associations and private training groups, because the cost per participant of a three-day seminar, including travel, food, lodging, and seminar fee, may run well into four figures. For the small, financially strapped organization, on-the-job training and low-cost off-the-job programs (such as university and government-sponsored courses) are often the only economically feasible training alternatives.

Only after the above issues are understood can the method be chosen that best fits these requirements. To be useful, the chosen method should meet the minimal conditions needed for effective learning to take place; that is, the training method should:

1. Motivate the trainee to improve his or her performance
2. Clearly illustrate desired skills
3. Provide for active participation by the trainee
4. Provide an opportunity to practice
5. Provide timely feedback on the trainee's performance
6. Provide some means for reinforcement while the trainee learns
7. Be structured from simple to complex tasks
8. Be adaptable to specific problems
9. Encourage positive transfer from the training to the job

SUMMARY

Regardless of whether training is job-related or developmental in nature, a particular training method must be chosen by training program designers. Some methods involve the use of visual aids to enhance the learning experience, while others are strictly dependent on a lecture format. The decision to use one or more particular training methods must be given clear attention to improve the design and potential success of the training program.

Those responsible for designing training programs have to understand the importance of assigning responsibilities during the training effort. The HRM specialist can serve as an expert source of training assistance and coordination. On the other hand, managers can also make an important contribution to a training program, especially as a source of technical information used in skill training. The HRM specialist, manager, and trainee must all share responsibility for the design of the training program.

Because of the implications of training for trainees and organizations, training program designers must be cognizant of how legal considerations impact training in organizations. The federal "Uniform Guidelines on Employee Selection Procedures" affect five areas of training: job entry, training program admission, the training itself, career decisions, and affirmative action plans. However, as emphasized in this chapter, training program designers should not preoccupy themselves to the point of not considering other, equally critical, aspects of training design, such as maximizing trainees' learning.

In conclusion, effective training programs require someone assuming responsibility for the programs prior to their implementation (during the preassessment phase). Both the organization's line and staff functions should assume joint responsibility for completing a preassessment, a training needs analysis, and the design of the training effort. In addition, they must be cognizant of the legal issues that can have a direct impact on the training program.

The potential success of any training effort is also dependent on the extent to which KSAs or other characteristics learned in training can be applied to the back-home work situation. Finally, those responsible for designing training programs should take care in selecting and using training methods. Once the design issues discussed in this chapter are addressed, the designers of training programs can move on to selecting trainees and trainers, as well as to other training issues. Other issues to which training program designers must be attuned are discussed in the next chapter.

Selecting Trainees: Understanding Individual Differences, Learning, and Learning Styles

INTRODUCTION

The selection of trainees who will participate in the training program is an important factor. Often this is obvious; the training program may have been designed to train particular new employees in certain skills. In some cases, the training program is designed to help with EEO goals; in others it is to help employees find better jobs elsewhere when layoffs are necessary or to retrain older employees. Techniques similar to the selection procedures for training methods may be used to select trainees, especially when those who attend the program may be promoted or receive higher wages or salaries as a result. However, regardless of the trainees that are selected to attend a training program, understanding the importance of learning, learning principles, and the individual differences (learning styles) of trainees is a key to the potential success of the training effort.

Perhaps the most challenging thing about training is that there are no two individuals exactly alike, and no two training programs exactly alike. Individual differences are glaringly obvious in the training environment. Trainees differ from one another in looks, interests, likes and dislikes, understanding, and rate of learning. Variations in learning patterns are the result of differences in ability and motivation among trainees. Therefore, in planning learning activities that provide the optimum motivation, the HRM specialist needs to recognize that individual differences stand out as a critical factor.

Individual trainees vary in their reactions. Therefore, the HRM specialist must study each member of the training program so that the training program will secure favorable reaction from the greatest number—all of them, if possible. The greatest single factor in considering training program content is that individual differences must be recognized and compensated for during implementation of the program. HRM specialists have not always recognized this factor or have been unable to develop a concept to cope with it. Increased understanding of the learning process and principles of learning can enhance the potential success of the training effort.

LEARNING—A DEVELOPMENTAL PROCESS

Learning, the unique domain of humankind, has always been a major area of research attention for many researchers interested in understanding the process of learning and its implications for educators—and more recently trainers—in selecting appropriate pedagogical methods in order to improve classroom instruction. Learning is one of the most important individual processes that occurs in organizations and, of course, in training programs. For purposes of this book, *learning* is defined as *a relatively permanent changer in an attitude or behavior that occurs as a result of repeated experience* (Kimble and Garmezy, 1963). The next section explores the importance of understanding adult-learning theory and principles of learning in the training effort.

Whether training takes place on or off the job, employees are expected to learn and apply new KSAs to benefit both the organization and its employees. Because training is a type of learning, HRM specialists can benefit from understanding and applying certain principles of learning when designing and implementing training programs (Schneier, 1974; Hess and Sperry, 1973). Also, because neglect or misapplication of principles of learning could easily result in training that fails to achieve results, it is important that HRM specialists become familiar with principles of learning and the basics of adult-learning theory (Wexley and Latham, 1981).

Knowles (1984) says that adults will learn "no matter what." Learning is as natural as rest or play. With or without books, visual aids, inspiring trainers, or classrooms, adults will manage to learn. HRM specialists can, however, make a difference in *what* people learn and in *how well* they learn it. If adults (and, many believe, children as well) know *why* they are learning, and if the reason fits their needs as they perceive them (the "so what?"), they will learn quickly and deeply.

Adult-Learning Theory

Among the major theories of learning, behaviorism is fairly well defined, and most HRM specialists in the United States associate the term and the theory with its leading contemporary proponent, B.F. Skinner. This is not the case with adult-learning theory. There have been many adult-learning theorists, researchers, and practitioners, each contributing an element to its development (see, for example, Kolb, 1984a, discussed in Chapter 5; Tough, 1979, 1982; Kidd, 1973; Houle, 1961). Malcolm Knowles's theory on adult learning has been used effectively in training in business and industry. Knowles (1980; Knowles and Associates, 1984) has postulated his adult-learning principles and practices under the banner of "andraogy." A brief discussion of Knowles's adult-learning theory will help the reader understand its usefulness to training efforts.

As commonly understood in the world of training and human resources management, adherence to adult-learning theory would call for the design of training activities to be based on the learners' needs and interests so as to create opportunities for the learners to analyze their experience and its application to their work and life situations. The role of the HRM specialist is to assist in a process of inquiry, analysis, and decision making with learners rather than to transmit knowledge.

In the context of adult-learning practices, the learner exercises greater autonomy in matching his or her preferred modes of learning to the specified learning objectives and also has more say about what the outcomes of the learning process are intended to be. The emphasis on methods that encourage insight and discovery makes it a familiar approach, close to the "natural" way many people have acquired new knowledge or developed new skills since reaching maturity.

Knowles says he originally defined andragogy as "the art and science of helping adults learn, in contrast to pedagogy as the art and science of teaching children" (1980, p. 43). Later he came to see andragogy as "simply another model of assumptions used alongside the pedagogical model . . . most useful when seen not as dichotomous but rather as two ends of a spectrum" (p. 43).

The principles and practices that fall under the umbrella of andragogy are based on several crucial assumptions about how adult learners are different from children. Margolis and Bell (1984) give us a useful summary of those assumptions, distilled from Knowles's major works (1980, p. 17; Knowles and Associates, 1984):

1. Adults are motivated to learn as they develop needs and interests that learning will satisfy. Therefore, learners' needs and interests are the appropriate starting points for organizing adult learning activities.

2. Adult orientation to learning is life- or work-centered. Therefore, the appropriate frameworks for organizing adult learning are life- or work-related situations, not academic or theoretical subjects.

3. Experience is the richest resource for adult learning. Therefore, the core methodology for adult-learning programs involves active participation in a planned

series of experiences, the analysis of those experiences, and their application to work and life situations.

4. Adults have a deep need to be self-directing. Therefore, the role of the HRM specialist is to engage in a process of inquiry, analysis, and decision making with learners.

5. Individual differences among adult learners increase with age and experience. Therefore, adult-learning programs must make optimum provision for differences in style, time, place, and pace of learning.

Until recently, there was growing evidence that use of the andragogical framework could make a difference in the way adult-learning (training) programs were organized and operated as well as in the way trainers and human resources managers saw their role in helping adults learn (Knowles and Associates, 1984).

Principles of Learning

Principles of learning are the guidelines to the ways in which people learn most effectively. The more the principles are included in training, the more effective training is likely to be. The principles are motivation, goal setting, behavior modeling, participation, feedback, organization, repetition or practice, reinforcement, and application. The following is a brief summary of the way learning principles can be applied to job training (Hilgard and Bower, 1966; Ivancevich and Glueck, 1989; Carrell, Kuzmits, and Elbert, 1989; Cascio, 1989).

Motivation. In order to learn, a person must want to learn. In the context of training, motivation influences a person's enthusiasm for training, keeps attention focused on the training activities, and reinforces what is learned. Motivation is influenced by the belief and perceptions of the trainee as displayed in Figure 8.1 (Cascio, 1987). Four important factors including the work environment and three beliefs are portrayed in Figure 8.1. To the extent that these factors are present, the motivation to learn is likely to be high. If these motivational factors are missing, an HRM specialist may leave a training program with nothing at all accomplished.

When employees are motivated to change and acquire different behavior, training should be easier and more successful. Sometimes the need for training is not clear to employees. They may consider training a waste of time and resist being taken away from their jobs. One effective way to motivate trainees is to show them how training will help accomplish organizational and personal goals (Latham and Locke, 1979). These goals may include improved job performance and increased opportunities for promotion. HRM specialists should not automatically assume that all employees want to be trained, and therefore, should make employees aware of how they will benefit from training.

Figure 8.1
Factors that Affect Motivation in Training Programs

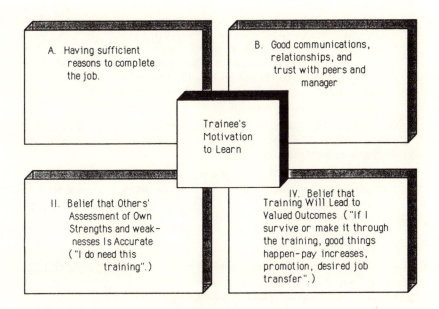

I. Favorable Work Environment

A. Having sufficient reasons to complete the job.

B. Good communications, relationships, and trust with peers and manager

Trainee's Motivation to Learn

II. Belief that Others' Assessment of Own Strengths and weaknesses Is Accurate ("I do need this training".)

IV. Belief that Training Will Lead to Valued Outcomes ("If I survive or make it through the training, good things happen-pay increases, promotion, desired job transfer".)

III. Belief in Own Ability to Master Training Content ("I can definitely do this well".)

Wayne F. Cascio, APPLIED PSYCHOLOGY IN PERSONNEL MANAGEMENT, 3e, © 1987, p. 367. Reprinted by permission of Prentice-Hall, Inc., Englewood Cliffs, New Jersey.

Goal Setting. It appears from evidence that the most effective way to raise a trainee's motivation is by setting goals. Goal setting has a proven track record of success in improving employee performance in a variety of settings and cultures (Matsui, Kakuyama, and Onglatco, 1987; Mento, Steel, and Karren, 1987). On average, goal setting leads to a 10 percent improvement in productivity, and it works best with task of low complexity (Wood, Mento, and Locke, 1987).

Goal theory is founded on the premise that an individual's conscious goals or intentions regulate her or his behavior (Locke, 1968). Research indicates that once a goal is accepted, difficult but attainable goals result in higher levels of performance than do easy goals or a generalized goal such as "do your best." These findings have three important implications for motivating trainees:

1. The objectives of the training program should be made clear at the outset (as described in Chapter 6). Each objective should describe the desired behavior, the conditions under which it should occur, and the success criteria by which the behavior will be judged (Mager, 1962). For example: In a four-hour performance test at the end of one month of training (conditions), you will be able to reupholster an armchair, a couch, and a hassock, demonstrating the correct procedures at each step in the process (desired behavior). All steps must be executed in the correct order and must meet standards of fit and trim specified in the textbook (success criteria).

2. Goals should be challenging and difficult enough that the trainees can derive personal satisfaction from achieving them, but not so difficult that they are perceived as impossible to reach.

3. The ultimate goal of "finishing the program" should be supplemented with subgoals during training—such as trainer evaluations, work-sample tests, and periodic quizzes. As each hurdle is cleared successfully, trainees' confidence about attaining the ultimate goal increases.

Behavior Modeling. Much of what we learn is acquired by observing others. We will imitate other peoples' actions when they lead to desirable outcomes for those involved (e.g., promotions, increased sales, or more accurate tennis serves). The models' actions serve as cues to what constitutes appropriate behavior (Bandura, 1986). A model is someone who is seen as competent, powerful, friendly, and having high status within an organization. We try to identify with this model because her or his behavior is seen as desirable and appropriate. Modeling tends to increase when the model is rewarded for behavior and when the rewards (e.g., influence, pay) are things the imitator would like to have. In the context of training (or coaching or teaching), we attempt to maximize the trainees' identification with a model. For us to do this well, research suggests that we do the following:

1. Select a model who is similar to the observer in age, sex, and race. If the observer sees little similarity between himself or herself and the model, it is unlikely that the model's behaviors will be imitated.

2. Portray the behaviors to be modeled clearly and in detail. To focus the trainees' attention on specific behaviors to be imitated, provide them with a list of key behaviors to attend to when observing the model, and allow them to express the behaviors in language that is most comfortable for them. For example, when one group of supervisors was being taught how to "coach" employees, the supervisors received a list of the following key behaviors: (a) focus on the problem, not on the person; (b) ask for the employees' suggestions, and get their ideas on how to solve the problem; (c) listen openly; (d) agree on the

steps that each of you will take to solve the problem; and (5) plan a specific follow-up date (Hogan, Hakel, and Decker, 1986).

3. Rank the behaviors to be modeled in a sequence from least- to most-difficult; be sure the trainees observe lots of repetitions of the behaviors being modeled.

4. Finally, have the behaviors portrayed by several models, not just one (Goldstein and Sorcher, 1974; Latham and Saari, 1979).

Behavior modeling overcomes one of the shortcomings of earlier approaches to training: telling instead of showing. For example, trainees used to be *told* to be "good communicators"—a behavior that most people agree is useful and that most trainees were already familiar with prior to the program—but the trainees were never *shown how* to be good communicators (Cascio, 1989). Behavior modeling teaches a desired behavior effectively by:

providing the trainee with numerous, vivid, detailed displays (on film, videotape, or live) of a manager-actor (the model) performing the specific behaviors and skills we wish the viewer to learn (i.e., modeling); giving the trainee considerable guidance in and opportunity and encouragement for behaviorally rehearsing or practicing the behaviors he/she has seen the model perform (i.e., role playing); [and] providing him/her with positive feedback, approval, or reward as the role playing enactments increasingly approximate the behavior of the model (i.e., social reinforcement) . . . (Goldstein and Sorcher, 1974, p. 370).

Participation. Another way to inspire trainees is through their active participation in the training process. Although direct involvement is an integral part of on-the-job training, off-the-job training—especially in the classroom—sometimes fails to consider this important principle of learning. Lecturing is certainly a valuable training technique, but reliance on lecturing alone will result in boredom and apathy. Active participation in the learning process through conferences and discussion enables trainees to become directly involved in the act of learning.

Learning usually is quicker and more long-lasting when the learner can participate actively. Participation improves motivation and apparently engages more senses that help reinforce the learning process. As a result of participation, we learn more quickly and retain that learning longer. For example, most people never forget how to ride a bicycle because they actively participated in the learning process.

Feedback. Feedback is any form of information about one's attempts to improve. Feedback is essential for learning and trainee motivation. Feedback on progress in a training program reduces anxiety and lets trainees know what they must do to improve. Most employees taking part in a training program want to know how they are doing and how their progress compares to training objectives. Giving the employee feedback is usually an informal part of on-the-job training, and close communication between the HRM specialist and trainee helps the feedback process (Ilgen, Fisher, and Taylor, 1982). Feeback in short courses and seminars is usually less frequent, and normally consists of informal comments by the instructor or a discussion of the results of tests. The emphasis should be on when and how the trainee has done something correctly: for example, "You did a good job on that report you turned in yesterday—it was brief and to the heart of the issues." Feedback promotes learning and motivation in three ways:

1. It provides direct information to trainees about the correctness of their re- sponses, thereby allowing them to make adjustments in their subsequent be- havior

2. When somebody who cares about your success is paying close attention to you, be it trainer, coach, or teacher, it makes the learning process more interesting and hence maximizes your willingness to learn

3. Feedback leads to the setting of specific goals for maintaining performance (Erez, 1977; Matsui, Kakuyama, and Onglatco, 1987)

To have the greatest impact, feedback should be provided as soon as possible after the trainee's behavior. It need not be instantaneous, but there should be no confusion regarding exactly what the trainee did and the HRM specialist's reaction to it. Feedback need not always be positive either.

Organization. Training must be presented so that segments of materials build on one another; gaps, contradictions, or ambiguities in the material must be avoided. For example, in organizing a course about the operation and maintenance of a large printing press, the safety precautions that must be taken should be presented first. Next, the major parts of the machine and the functions of each should be explained. Then, a competent operator could be observed running the machine, followed by hands-on experience with several uncomplicated tasks, and so on. The final portion of training may involve preventive maintenance and minor repairs. In this example, each part of training flows into another without inconsistencies or gaps.

Material must be organized to maximize meaningfullness (material that is rich in associations for the trainees and is therefore easily understood). Factual material is learned more easily and remembered better when it is meaningful (McGehee and Thayer, 1961). To structure material to maxi- mize its meaningfulness:

1. Provide trainees with an overview of the material to be presented during the training. Seeing the overall picture helps trainees understand how each unit of the program fits together and how it contributes to the overall training objectives (Wexley and Baldwin, 1986).

2. Present the material by using examples, terms, and concepts that are familiar to the trainees in order to clarify and reinforce key learning points. Such a strategy is essential when training the hard-core unemployed (Gray and Borecki, 1970).

3. Complex intellectual skills are invariably composed of simpler skills, and it is necessary to master these simpler skills before the complex skills can be learned (Gagne, 1977). This is true whether one is learning accounting, computer programming, or x-ray technology.

Thus the basic principles of training design consist of (a) identifying the component tasks of a final performance, (b) ensuring that each of these component tasks is fully achieved, and (c) arranging the total learning situation in a sequence that will ensure a logical connection from one component to another (Gagne, 1962).

Repetition or Practice. Regardless of individual differences and whether a trainee is learning a new skill or acquiring knowledge of a given topic, the person should be given the opportunity to practice what is being taught. Practice is also essential after the individual has been successfully trained. A wealth of behavioral research shows that frequent practice during training helps the learning process. Practice is important whether the skills being learned are technical (e.g., operating a lathe or computer) or behavioral (e.g., communication or interpersonal skills).

Practice has two aspects: active practice and overlearning (Cascio, 1989).

Active practice. During the early stages of learning, the HRM specialist should be available to oversee directly the trainee's practice; if the trainee begins to "get off the track," the inappropriate behaviors can be corrected immediately, before they become ingrained in the trainee's behavior. This is why low trainer-trainee ratios are so desirable.

Overlearning. When trainees are given the opportunity to practice far beyond the point where the task has been performed correctly several times, the task becomes "second nature" and is said to be "overlearned." For some tasks, overlearning is critical. This is true of any task that must be performed infrequently and under great stress: for example, attempting to kick a field goal with only seconds left in a football game. It is less important for types of work where individuals practice their skills on a daily basis (e.g., auto mechanics, electronic technicians, assemblers). Overlearning has several advantages:

—it increases the length of time that the training material will be retained;

—it makes the learning more "reflexive" so that tasks become "automatic" with continued practice;

—the quality of performance is more likely to be retained during periods of emer-
gency or added stress;

—it facilitates the transfer of training to the job situation.

Including practice sessions in technical training is relatively easy, but
practicing interpersonal skills presents challenges to the trainer. Frequently, role-playing techniques are used to practice such skills. It is almost
impossible to find a professional tennis or piano player, for example, who
doesn't practice several hours a day. Practice can be a form of positive
reinforcement.

Reinforcement. To be acquired, modified, and sustained, behavior must
be rewarded, or reinforced (Skinner, 1969). According to the principles
of reinforcement, people will do what is rewarded and avoid doing what
is not rewarded or is punished. The principle of reinforcement also states
that punishment leads only to a temporary suppression of behavior and is
a relatively ineffective influence on learning. Reward says to the learner,
"Good, repeat what you have done." Punishment says, "Stop it, you made
the wrong response." Mild punishment may serve as a warning for the
learner that he or she is getting off the track, but unless the learner is told
immediately what he or she needs to do to get back on the track (corrective
feedback), punishment can be intensely frustrating.

Although learning can be rewarding for its own sake, it is generally
regarded as a difficult and distasteful process that must be rewarded extrinsically to ensure its effectiveness. This fact may be useful for training
programs, because extrinsic rewards are often at the disposal of the organization and the HRM specialists. For example, managers may praise
their employees for learning a new skill, and the organization may provide
promotional opportunities for those who successfully complete a training
program. These extrinsic rewards are said to reinforce individuals' behavior
(for example, learning a new skill) because they are given on the basis of
that behavior. Both rewards and mild punishment can and should be used
in a training situation, but keep in mind that the most powerful rewards
are likely to be those provided by the trainee's immediate supervisor. In
fact, if the supervisor does not reinforce what is learned in training, then
the training will be transferred ineffectively to the job, if at all.

Application. Job training is useless unless learning can be applied at
work. The transfer-of-learning problem is particularly troublesome in off-
the-job instruction. The problem is less severe for technical training because the technology used on the job should be identical to that used during
training.

Minimizing transfer-of-learning problems poses a challenge to trainers.
The HRM specialist must study the job environment of prospective trainees
and create settings that resemble each trainee's own job environment as
much as possible (Baumgartel and Jeanpierre, 1972). When constructing

the training environment, consideration must be given to the physical setting, the technology of the work, intergroup and interpersonal relationships, and supervisory styles. HRM specialists must do their best to make
the training as close to the reality of the job as possible. Thus, when the trainee
returns to the job, the training can be applied immediately (Berke, 1984).

LEARNING STYLES AND LEARNING SKILLS

However superb the analysis of training needs, however clear and job-
related the training objectives, however competent the design of the training program, however careful the process by which the HRM specialist
secures the motivation or commitment of a trainee to their own learning
needs, the HRM specialists will be throwing the provision of learning onto
stony ground if they do not provide the learning in a form congruent with
each trainee's basic learning style and with the skills of learning he or she
possesses.

The HRM specialist needs, in fact, to improve learning efficiency and
productivity by making more effective use of better training program design
and methods. The HRM specialist needs some parallel process to the
improvements made in relevant training program design and method, a
process that helps the trainees define and understand their own learning
processes. To improve learning the HRM specialist needs to be able to
identify more than exciting development in trainees' learning processes.
The HRM specialist certainly needs to say more than, "Nandi learned from
an excellent training program," or "Malroy learned from a seminar," or
"Donald was given excellent help in coaching subordinates." The HRM
specialist must identify ways of distinguishing which processes are going
to help individuals. One way of acquiring this information is by increasing
one's understanding of learning styles.

Knowledge of learning styles will help HRM specialists further understand that trainees have a variety of learning strengths and weaknesses that
are developed through earlier learning experiences, analytical abilities, and
a host of other experiences they bring to a training session. In addition,
knowledge of learning styles will help the HRM specialist understand the
learning difficulties some trainees have in specific aspects of the training
program. Furthermore, this knowledge will help the HRM specialist select
appropriate training strategies and training program designs.

Definition of Learning Styles Revisited

Everyone has a learning style. Observations of trainees within the typical
on-the-job or off-the-job training program provide some understanding of
the diversity of individual characteristics. If a group of trainees were given
fifty minutes to develop a listing of the "Important KSAs for a Particular

Job," many would pursue the task in different ways. Some would work independently, whereas others might cluster in informal peer groups to discuss the topic. Some would require extensive structure before initiating the project and ask about which resources to use, mandated length of the list, or what form the assignment should follow; others might welcome open parameters and creatively develop unusual ways to demonstrate their knowledge. Within one group there would be trainees who were highly motivated to complete the task and others who lacked incentive and readily became bored or lethargic. The astute observer will note additional variations in how trainees concentrate to learn. That uniqueness often classifies them in different types or style of learning.

Although trainees learn continually, they do have preferences about how they learn. David Kolb (1976; 1985a) calls these "learning style" preferences (see Chapter 5 for a detailed discussion of Kolb's accompanying ELT). Some trainees have a receptive, experience-based approach to learning; these individuals rely heavily on feeling-based judgments and learn best from specific examples, involvement, and discussion. Kolb calls these learners Concrete Experiencers. Other trainees have a tentative, impartial, and reflective approach to learning. Such individuals rely heavily on careful observation and learn best from situations that allow impartial observation. Kolb calls these the Reflective Observers. Still other trainees have an analytical and conceptual approach to learning, relying heavily on logical thinking and rational evaluation. These individuals are termed Abstract Conceptualizers and learn best from impersonal situations, from the opportunity to integrate new learning with what is already known from theory.

Finally, there are trainees who are called Active Experimenters. Their approach to learning is pragmatic ("Yes, but will it work?"). They rely heavily on experimentation and learn best from projects, back-home applications, and "trying it out." They must have the answer to the question: "Now that I know all this, what am I going to do with it?"

Significance and Use of Differences in Learning Styles

If learning styles are indeed different, and if it is accepted that a changing of learning styles would be a high-priority training activity in most organizations, some important considerations emerge. It is likely that many trainees are placed in learning situations from which they are currently incapable of learning. It may be right to send employees who come from the Converger or Implementator categories to significant post-experience training programs. It is possible too that an Implementator would benefit; it seems unlikely that a Converger would.

Of course it is the analysis and subsequent discussion of learning styles that is the most useful part of the process, rather than the acquisition of a particular label. Most trainees do not fall entirely into one category.

Therefore, while "talking shorthand" about the use of styles, it should be recognized that a better understanding of the components of the basic approaches to learning possessed by trainees is important to training, rather than arbitrary, black-and-white definitions.

The style classification can be used in the following way:

1. It can help a trainee to understand his or her own likely approach to learning/training opportunities, and perhaps how to use that basic approach better. It may be important to note on this point that the author takes the view that increased self-knowledge is enabling rather than disabling.

2. With less certainty, it may help the trainees increase their range of learning: a desirable goal will be that each trainee shall have a fully integrated range of styles. However, in reality, by the time trainees actually get to a training program it may be too late to aim realistically at this point.

3. It certainly should help advisers to suggest training opportunities that are congruent with learning style instead of antagonistic to it.

4. The HRM specialist should be able to construct learning groups more effectively in the sense of more consciously choosing which trainees to put with which other trainees in learning groups or on a real-time job or work-related activity. The questions that are opened up here are clearer than the answers. Do you put Convergers and Divergers together?

5. Perhaps part of the answer to the last question is derived from the view that a HRM specialist can help trainees understand what they might learn about each other. It may be that with a group that has devoted some attention to analyzing learning styles and their individual differences, trainees within the group, and perhaps the whole group, will be better able to make use of the skills available in it. For example, instead of seeing the Assimilator as a noncontributor, that person may be someone capable of contributing in a particular way. Perhaps more importantly, because more frequently, individuals should be able to assess better potential relationships of style between a supervisor or HRM specialist and a trainee. It is easy to see that an Assimilator will have significant differences in learning from a Diverger. Again reality obtrudes; it is likely that the learning styles reflect basic learning and communication patterns, and the discomfort is likely to arise in many areas other than learning.

6. Trainees can refine and improve their understanding of learning skills. Again this seems to be an area far too little studied. Examples of learning skills are:

   —the ability to establish effectiveness criteria for yourself

   —the ability to measure your effectiveness in different situations

   —the ability to identify your own learning needs

   —the ability to plan personal learning agendas

   —the ability to take advantage of learning opportunities

   —the ability to review your learning processes

   —the ability to listen to others

   —the capacity to accept help

—the ability to face unwelcome information

—the ability to take risks and tolerate anxieties

—the ability to analyze what other successful performers do

—the ability to know yourself

—the ability to share information with others

—the ability to review what has been learned

Clearly the HRM specialist should help trainees improve their skills and should be capable of relating skills to particular learning styles and to particular learning or training opportunities. Learning-style information can be crucial to an HRM specialist's credibility and ability to place a trainee in relevant training experiences. The HRM specialist must continually find a response to the question: How do learning styles and the associated learning skills relate to these training opportunities?

Ways of Describing and Assessing Learning Style

Prior to the mid-1970s, researchers experimented with cognitive style; their definitions were different, but all were concerned with how the mind actually processed information or was affected by individual perceptions (Coop and Brown, 1970; Gardner, et al., 1959; Kagan, Moss and Sigel, 1963; Hill, 1971; Witkin, 1975). In 1971 and 1972, Prentice-Hall published two books about the emerging concept of learning style (Kolb, 1971b; Dunn and Dunn, 1978). Kolb's well-thought-through conceptualization remained entirely in the realm of how the adult mind functioned. The Dunns posed a model that included eighteen environmental, emotional, sociological, and physical characteristics that they had learned to response to in New York classrooms from thirty to thirty-seven students.

The Dunns and Kolb were not the only researchers developing learning style constructs. During the 1970s and 1980s Canfield and Lafferty (1970), Gregorc (1979), Hunt (1979), Ramirez and Castaneda (1974), Schmeck, Ribich, and Ramanaiah (1977), Renzulli and Smith (1978), Reinert (1976), and Honey and Mumford (1982a, 1982b, 1986a, 1986b) all developed varied definitions, models, instruments, and techniques for assessing students' learning characteristics. In some ways those models differed, but many strands revealed essential similarities and were mutually supportive (Dunn, DeBello, Brennan, Murrain, and Krimsky, 1981).

As can be seen in the previous discussion, there are many ways of describing and assessing learning styles—again, that means the typical ways a person behaves, feels, and processes information in learning situations. The essence of the models briefly mentioned thus far is that they described similar phenomena observed from different vantage points—much like the blind men who were explaining an elephant by reporting only certain parts of its body. Thus, learning style is demonstrated in that pattern of behavior and performance by which an individual approaches educational experiences. It is the way in which each person absorbs and retains information and/or skills; regardless of how that process is described, it is dramatically different for each person.

The following researchers' ways of describing and assessing learning styles can be used by the HRM specialist in training programs: Honey and Mumford; Grasha and Reichmann; Murrell; Dunn and Dunn; and Kolb. (See Chapter 5 for a discussion of Kolb's Experiential Learning Theory and Learning Styles.)

Honey and Mumford: Four Learning Styles. Honey and Mumford (1982a, 1982b) have postulated four basic styles of learning found in managers, with fairly full descriptions of each style. In addition, they produced an eighty-item Learning Styles Questionnaire (LSQ), on which respondents are asked to agree or disagree, that may be used as a more objective way of determining which style an individual falls into. The vast majority of these items are behavioral—i.e., they describe an action that someone might or might not take. Occasionally an item probes a preference or belief rather than a manifest behavior. The LSQ is scored by awarding one point for each ticked ("agree") item. The LSQ is designed to probe the relative strengths of four different learning styles (Activist, Reflector, Theorist, Pragmatist).

Activists prefer to learn from immediate experiences and new challenges. They are bored with implementation and longer-term consolidation and are the life and soul of the managerial party. Reflectors prefer observing data before making conclusions. They like to consider possible angles and implications before making a move, so they tend to be cautious. They actually enjoy observing other people in action and often take a back seat at meetings. Theorists adapt and integrate information in an objective manner. They prize rationality and logic, tend to be detached and analytical, and are unhappy with subjective or ambiguous experiences. They assemble disparate facts into coherent theories. They like to make things tidy and fit them into rational schemes. Pragmatists prefer to test ideas and theories in practice. They respond to problems and opportunities "as a challenge" (the Activists probably would not recognize them as problems and opportunities).

Grasha-Reichmann: Three Styles of Learning. Reichmann (1974) classifies three learning styles (Dependent, Collaborative, and Independent) with the Grasha-Reichmann Learning Styles Questionnaire (GRLSQ). The GRLSQ consists of ninety items and has a self-report scale. A person who scores high as a Dependent learner generally prefers a teacher-directed, highly structured course with explicit reading assignments, explicit class assignments, and a predetermined number of tests. The Dependent learner would most likely prefer a straightforward lecture without term papers, but if a term paper is to be assigned, the Dependent learner would want the topic to be assigned by the teacher, with fairly detailed instructions. A person who scores high as a Collaborative learner prefers a discussion class with as much interaction as possible. The Collaborative learner prefers group projects and collective assignments, such as case studies. The person who scores high as an Independent learner likes to have some influence on the content and structure of the course. This type of student would like some role in the determination of the material covered, the number of tests given, and so forth. Independent learners would prefer that the teacher serve as a resource person rather than as a formal lecturer. If a paper is to be assigned, Independent learners would prefer to choose their own topics instead of having the teacher assign a specific topic.

Dunn and Dunn: The Five Elements of Learning Style. Dunn and Dunn (1978) suggest that learning style is based on an individual's response to five categories of "elements" (environmental, emotional, sociological, physical, and psychological). An individual's needs or preferences in each category add up to his or her learning style.

The Dunns' model is a complex, comprehensive picture of the needs and preferences that influence how—or whether—we learn something. It acknowledges that learners differ in their reliance on auditory, visual, tactile, and kinesthetic perception processes; in their orientations of self, peers, and authorities; in the power of their motivation to learn; and in the strength of their sense of responsibility of the results of the process.

It admits that individuals differ in their needs for mobility, their daytime and nighttime energy levels, and their "intake" needs (do you need to smoke, chew gum, or drink something when you are concentrating?) The Dunns' model is unique among the models discussed here in its coverage of various environmental and physical elements of learning style and its recognition that people respond differently to their surroundings in a learning situation, especially if what they are learning is complex or difficult. The Dunns' emphasis on various environmental and physical elements of learning is important for HRM specialists to understand in the design of training programs and training environments most conducive to efficient and effective training.

Responses to one hundred items on a Likert-type scale—the Productivity Environmental Preference Survey, or PEPS (Price, Dunn, and Dunn, 1982)—produce a profile clustered around twenty-one different elements. The PEPS is designed to identify and analyze the conditions that encourage an individual's best performance in such things as solving problems, making decisions, and learning. It is concerned with *how* you prefer to learn, not why, and reveals the pattern of needs and preferences that is your learning style.

Murrell: Four Learning Models for Managers. Murrell's (1987) model was designed exclusively for managers and introduces four domains of learning based on a person's preference for cognitive or affective learning and the person's preference for concrete and abstract experiences. Responses to a twenty-item questionnaire, the Learning Model Instrument, results in four learning domains (Feeling Planner, Participative Implementer, Task Implementer, and Thinking Planner). The Feeling Planner enjoys learning situations that provide for learning with people in concrete situations but has limited opportunity to get close to them. Participative Implementers prefer learning situations that allow them to interact with people and still get their hands dirty. They prefer hands-on experiences and prefer to keep busy. Task Implementers prefer learning situations that are task-focused, where they can focus on details and specifics in a thoughtful manner. The Thinking Planner shows a preference for learning through task-oriented experiences, in an environment that contains primarily abstract things, numbers, or printouts.

Learning-Style Analysis—How Good Is the Instrumentation to Identify Learning Styles?

The purpose of learning-style analysis is to identify trainees strategies for learning and to wed them with training materials, experiences, instruction, and methods that foster a high rate of return—efficient, lasting achievement within a logical amount of time (Corbett and Smith, 1984). A fundamental prerequisite for use of any analytical device in learning-style analysis for training (or research) is the demonstration of a significant level of reliability and validity in the instruments. Ohio State University's National Center for Research in Vocational Education published the results of its two-year study of instruments that purportedly identified learning and cognitive styles (Kirby, 1979), and selected instruments were appraised as having "impressive reliability and face and construct validity" (p. 72). Certainly instruments like those would be the ones most appropriate for HRM specialists to use in choosing learning-style instruments.

Selected learning-style instruments have been well researched and reported extensively in the literature; others are the products of interviews by their developers, clinical applications, or other research studies. Instruments that have been validated through experimental investigations represent a better, more solid foundation. St. John's University's Center for the Study of Learning and Teaching Styles released a report summarizing the known reliability and validity data of many of the better known learning-style instruments (*Learning Styles Network Instrument Assessment Analysis*, 1983). In addition, interested HRM specialists should see Ferrell (1983), Veres, Sims, and Shake (1987) and Sims, Veres, and Locklear (1990) for more recent research on learning-style instruments.

In conclusion, learning styles can be used by the HRM specialist in the following ways:

1. To give feedback to trainees on their own preferred styles of learning and domains of strength;
2. To help a new group of HRM specialists or trainees to learn more about one another in order to work together more effectively; and
3. To provide an overall explanation of the training environment so that participants will receive a conceptual understanding of the experiential approach to learning as suggested by adult-learning theorists (Kolb, 1984a; Knowles, 1984).

One of the ways the author has found helpful in gathering information on learning styles during the first training session is presented in Exhibit 8.1. The introduction of learning styles and individual differences should make for a better training program.

SUMMARY

This chapter emphasized the extreme importance of understanding individual differences, learning principles, factors that affect motivation of trainees in a training program, and the variety of individual learning-style models that trainers can consider in thier training efforts. It should be evident to HRM specialists that the application of a learning-style preference instrument to trainees can provide them with important information. Most important is that each training program will have trainees with disparate learning-style preferences and a variety of learning strengths and weaknesses that have been developed through earlier learning experiences, analytical abilities, and a host of other experiences they bring to the first training session.

The function of training is to enhance organizational performance through individual employee training. With this in mind the HRM specialist must be aware of the mixture of learning styles in a training session and must select the training methods and the trainers that best match the learning strengths of the students in the training program.

HRM specialists must recognize that trainees learn differently, and what may be an optimal training method for one trainee may discourage another trainee. Indeed, HRM specialists should make sure that a variety of training or learning opportunities are presented to trainees for each major knowledge, skill, or ability presented in the training program.

Those responsible for a training effort should also take care in selecting trainers for the training program. Chapter 9 discusses the importance of trainer selection and the internal-external team approach to training.

Exhibit 8.1
Using Learning-Style Data in the First Training Session

The focus on learning styles in training can be very helpful if the first training session (meeting between HRM specialists and trainees) increases the trainees' and HRM specialists' understanding of learning styles in general and sets the tone or climate for the remainder of the training program. Toward this end, the first training session should help the HRM specialists and trainees understand the importance of learning-style preferences and their potential effect on learning during the training experience. In addition, the first training session should also establish a training climate that encourages risk-taking as trainees begin to think about different ways people go about learning, and should introduce trainees to a way of training that requires them to better understand the learning difficulties or weaknesses they may have in different situations.

In a training program, after introducing themselves, the HRM specialist(s), along with the trainees should complete and score Kolb's Learning Style Inventory II (LSI II). Kolb's theory postulates that habits of learning emphasize some aspects of the learning process over others. The HRM specialist should give a lecturette on Kolb's ELM. Once again, Kolb's ELM argues that learning occurs through a process that might begin with a *concrete experience*, which leads to *reflective observation* about the experience. *Abstract conceptualization* follows in which models, paradigms, strategies, and metaphors are applied to the results of the experience. *Active experimentation* concludes the cycle as the concepts are then put into practice, thus generating new concrete experience.

After the lecturette, the trainees and HRM specialist(s) share the results of the LSI II with each other. This sharing experience encourages participation from all trainees and opens discussion on similarities and differences between the trainees and how different people go about learning and problem solving. An interesting aspect of using this approach in the first training session is that trainees will be *acting out* a particular part of the learning process. In other words some will form an *abstract conceptualization* issue—e.g., the validity of the LSI II, Kolb's ELM, or what is the "right or best" way to learn. For others *active experimentation* will focus on issues of pragmatic usefulness—e.g., how Kolb's ELM can be used to help an employee or manager. The *concrete experiencers* are often struggling to deal with the feelings they are having, while the *reflective observers* will be doing just that—being silent and observing.

Trainees should then be placed in groups with other trainees who have the same learning style. Each group of trainees should spend time developing a list of the agreed-upon learning strengths and weaknesses of the group, those training or learning situations with which they have the least amount of difficulty, and those which pose the most learning difficulty for them. Back in the total group each subgroup shares its list, and the concluding discussion focuses on the importance of understanding individual preferences with regard to learning and on the need to develop strengths in all of the learning-style preference areas.

Selecting Trainers

INTRODUCTION

Next to the trainee, the trainer is the most important part of the training system. Great care must be exercised in choosing effective trainers. To some extent, the success of the training program depends on proper selection of the person who performs the training task (Greiner, 1987). Personal characteristics (the ability to speak well, to write convincingly, to organize the work of others, to be inventive, to inspire others to greater achievement, and the trainer's own learning and training style) are important factors in the selection of trainers.

The trainer sets the pace, provides the guidance and assistance, and often furnishes the subject-matter expertise. The trainer also plays an important role in evaluating the training system during the validation phase of training program design. Therefore, the quality of the total training system depends largely on the competence of the training staff. For the foregoing reasons, the task of selecting trainers and establishing standards for their performance represents an important step in the design, implementation, and evaluation of training systems.

The purpose of this chapter, therefore, is to develop a greater understanding of the role of the trainer, discuss some of the more important factors in trainer selection, and identify what makes a good trainer—and then to present some common trainer pitfalls, and describe the issues and benefits of using an internal-external team approach in training programs.

THE HRM SPECIALISTS' ROLE IN TRAINING

There has been an ever-increasing interest and emphasis on the role of trainers involved in training and development programs. Seventy percent of the $44 billion budgeted for training programs in 1989 went toward paying the salaries of staff trainers and support personnel (secretaries, for example) assigned to training departments (*Training,* 1989). In addition, the increasing interest in training as a profession is evidenced by the number of persons belonging to only one of the professional societies involved in these activities. The American Society for Training and Development (ASTD) had 15 members in 1943, 5,000 members in 1967, 9,500 members in 1980, and a little over 26,000 in 1989. Of course, this does not include many persons involved in training activities who may be members of other societies, like the American Psychological Association, the American Educational Research Association, the American Academy of Management, and the American Management Association, to name a few.

In a survey of 3,000 ASTD members to identify which activities were a significant part of their work, Pinto and Walker (1978)) determined that the activities that occupied the greatest part of the training practitioners' work were program design and development, in order to meet specific learning and behavioral needs. Such an analysis provides important information on the kinds of activities that trainers have been traditionally involved in and some of the factors that must be considered when selecting a trainer.

In another analysis of survey results (Clement, Walker, and Pinto, 1979), data were reported about the most important skill or knowledge requirements for the training practitioner. In this instance, members of ASTD were asked, "What is the most important skill or knowledge requirement for success as a training and development professional?" The largest number of responses were for human relations skills, which include developing mutual trust and interpersonal relationships. The responses were especially focused on relationships to managers with whom trainers must work in designing training programs. The next-largest group of responses was related to communication skills needed as part of the training process. The next set of responses emphasized knowledge of the training field, including recent developments, understanding new training technology, and how adults learn. The fourth-ranked item, analytical skills, was related to abilities to analyze performance deficiencies, assess training needs, and so on. Other responses dealt with management skill, referring mainly to items related to managing the training department, and knowledge about the organization, referring to the kind of knowledge that makes it possible to anticipate training needs and understand organizational goals. The activities and the knowledge and skill titles presented above are good illustrations of the complex role of the trainer and many of the factors that must be taken into consideration when selecting trainers.

Factors in Trainer Selection

If training is to be planned and conducted with optimum effectiveness, training personnel must be competent. Only those best-qualified by education, experience, technical knowledge and skill, and pedagogical knowledge and skill should be selected as trainers. In addition, the trainer must have the ability to plan, organize, execute, and evaluate the training program.

To some extent this dependence on trainer skills can be lessened by providing prepackaged materials or a program designed by training experts. However, most organizations depend on their training staffs to design the entire program, from needs assessment to evaluation. Hence, trainers must be aware of how people learn, the most appropriate methods for assessing training needs, how to establish training objectives and integrate them with the diagnosed needs, how to bring together the different training methods to accomplish these objectives, and, perhaps most importantly, how to communicate effectively. There are a number of alternatives available to assist organizations in securing trainers. University programs, private training consultants, and formal programs established by such organizations as the American Management Association—all may provide competent trainers to an organization. The accomplishment of the training mission and the achievement of training objectives hang in the balance on how effective the organization is in selecting its trainers.

For this reason, a carefully selected list of prerequisites for trainer selection must be developed by an organization for each training program. Such a listing will provide a firm basis for identifying potential trainers, interviewing and evaluating a trainers' ability, and making final selection decisions.

Some Criteria for Selecting a Trainer

Criteria for the selection of a trainer can be identified by analyzing the training program from two perspectives: training program content or subject-matter, and training strategy or method. The type, level, and difficulty of the program content determine the kind and amount of expertise the trainer must possess. The training strategy determines the professional knowledge and training skills required of trainers. Therefore, the training objectives, the content of the program, and the training strategies are the source of criteria for selecting a trainer.

A trainer cannot teach what he or she does not know. For this reason, a first consideration in the identification of potential trainers is to locate personnel who possess the knowledge and skills that are required by the training program.

A second consideration is the professional knowledge and experience the trainer has in using the principal of learning and training as they apply to adult learners. Knowing and doing are quite different things, particularly in training. There are many identifiable skills and abilities associated with training duties. Among the most important are the skills needed to select and use a variety of training methods, techniques, and aids; the skill to deal with individual differences (for example, learning styles and skills) among trainees; the ability to motivate and guide trainees; and the ability to construct, use, and interpret evaluative instruments on the effectiveness of the training program and the trainer.

Another criterion is that the trainer must be a good communicator both orally and in writing. Most of the basic methods used in training (lecture, demonstration, conference), many of the techniques of instruction (illustrating, questioning, and explaining), and many of the training aids require good oral communication skills. In addition, effective written communication skills are necessary for such training tasks as writing and preparing lesson plans and writing material on the board or butcher paper.

A final criterion in selecting a trainer is the ability to work with people. Effective interpersonal skills are the cornerstone of facilitating, motivating, and working with trainees in a training program. However, the selection of trainers can be enhanced by deciding on the specific roles, activities, knowledge, and skill requirements the trainer must perform. Some of these roles might be the following: needs analysis and diagnosis; determine appropriate training approach; program design and development; develop material resources (make); manage internal resources (borrow): manage external resources (buy); individual development planning and counseling; job/performance-related training; conduct classroom training; group and organization development; training research; manage working relationships with managers and clients; manage the training and development function; and professional self-development (Pinto and Walker, 1978). There should also be an understanding that there are a variety of people (internally and externally) who may be selected to develop, facilitate, and evaluate a training program.

One of several people may be selected to facilitate a training program, including the following:

—immediate supervisors

—coworkers, as in buddy systems

—members of the human resources or personnel staff

—specialists in other parts of the company

—outside consultants

Which of these people is selected to teach depends on where the training program is held, the KSAs that are to be taught, and the training necessary for the training personnel. Wehrenberg (1989) has recommended that those responsible for selecting and evaluating trainers decide to what extent the trainer will be involved in the training process. This problem-solving process can be broken down into five broad areas (roles) the trainer will perform: analysis, design, development, delivery, and evaluation. With this information in mind, Wehrenberg suggests the following be taken into consideration when selecting a trainer.

When selecting trainers for the analyzer role, look for evidence of

—experience in: observing work, occupational analysis, interviewing, negotiating with supervisors and line managers, discovery of performance discrepancies, and presenting information (written and oral)

—knowledge of: principles and current theories in the behaviorial sciences, motivation theories, learning theories, and job design

When selecting for the designer role, look for evidence of

—experience in: designing training programs, selecting alternatives to expensive classroom training when appropriate, and developing clear performance (training) objectives

—knowledge of: a wide range of performance-enhancing methods, classroom training, and the elements of a clear performance (training) objective

When selecting for the developer role, look for evidence of

—experience in: developing lesson plans, training schedules, training aids, and other instructional materials; writing such training materials as instructions, workbooks, and job aids; planning training events; and using a wide range of training media

—knowledge of: media selection, principles involved in developing written instructional materials, and adult-learning theories

When selecting trainers for the delivery role, look for evidence of

—experience in: speaking before groups, managing classroom process, dealing with conflict, giving performance feedback, and using various training media

—knowledge of: training objectives, individual and group behavior, specific techniques of public speaking (such as getting and keeping participants' attention), and the use of humor

When selecting trainers for the evaluator role, look for evidence of

—experience in: observing and measuring performance, presenting (in writing, visually, and orally) results of evaluation, applying statistical techniques to data, and comparing performance to standards

—knowledge of: work measurement techniques, statistical measurements analysis, and data collection

All the selection criteria (competencies) described above can be used to select trainers. These core competencies can also become categories on which to base evaluation of trainers once they are in the job. Looking for evidence of all the previously described competencies can enhance the selection of a trainer.

The next section will provide some insights into some common trainer pitfalls that may lead to program failure in spite of who is selected to do the training (Mealiea and Duffy, 1980; Spitzer, 1986; Leap and Crino, 1989), can aid in the selection of trainers, and should be provided during any training of trainers.

Common Trainer Pitfalls

Awareness of some common trainer pitfalls should increase the effectiveness of those responsible for selecting trainers. They include the following:

1. *Training and development are regarded as a cure-all for all organizational ills.* The belief that any problem can be solved through some type of training is unrealistic. For example, to believe that all communication problems can be solved through communications training, that all production problems can be solved through production training, and that inferior recruitment and selection processes can always be offset by some form of employee training is not reasonable. It must be appreciated that although training can prove a useful solution to many organizational problems, it cannot be applied to all of them with equal effectiveness.

2. *Trainees are not adequately motivated to capture their attention and commitment.* As was discussed earlier in this book, failure to motivate trainees is one of the best ways to ensure that a training program will fail. People cannot learn when they are inattentive, and they will not change their on-the-job behavior without reason to do so.

3. *One training technique is assumed to be applicable to all groups, in all situations, with equal success.* A single training technique simply cannot be equally effective in all situations, for all trainees. The technique selected must be suitable to the ability of the trainees, the content of the program, and the evaluation criteria selected.

4. *Trainee performance is not evaluated once the employee has returned to the job.* A training program based on needed performance improvement must ulti-

mately be evaluated with reference to the degree of positive transfer that takes place. Under these conditions, accomplishing training program goals can never take the place of improved employee job performance as the evaluation criteria.

5. *Cost-benefit information, in order to evaluate the training program, is not gathered.* The use of organizational resources brings with it certain responsibilities, especially the justification that the expense was merited.

6. *Management support is lacking.* Trainers must get the commitment of management to the training program. Without such commitment trainees and others may not take the program seriously.

7. *The central role of the supervisor is not recognized.* It is the supervisor who will manage the actual work environment. The success or failure of the training program depends on whether the work environment supports the results of the program (e.g., changes in work methods, employee behavior, attitudes, and so forth).

8. *Training alone is never powerful enough to lead to long-term, verifiable performance improvements.* Although the supervisor manages the work environment, considerable resistance to change may remain. Training transfer may not be possible if resistance to change cannot be overcome. The trainer must prepare the workplace to accommodate the newly trained personnel by anticipating the forces resisting change.

9. *There is little or no preparation or follow-up.* If you "drop an employee into a training program and plop him back on the job; little will change" (Spitzer, 1986).

Those responsible for selecting trainers should be aware of potential trainers' understanding and previous experience in addressing these common trainer pitfalls. In addition, trainer candidates should have an awareness of what constitutes unacceptable trainer behavior. A survey of members of the American Society for Training and Development provides insight into those behaviors considered unethical by professional trainers (Clement, Pinto, and Walker, 1978). These behaviors and some of the typical responses from those who participated in the study are as follows:

1. Lack of professional development–"Not 'keeping up' . . . expanding their own knowledge";
2. Violation of confidences—"Relating information gathered in the classroom back to the organization" or "Reporting information given in confidence";
3. Use of "cure-all" programs—"Consultants selling programs without any effort to even estimate the needs of the clients";
4. Dishonesty regarding program outcomes—"Concealing truth on program results" or "Falsifying training records to make results look better than they are";
5. Failure to give credit—"Failure to give credit for work done by others (includes materials, instruments, and even whole courses)" or "Copyright violations";
6. Abuse of trainees—"Racist and sexist remarks" or "Treating training participants as 'lesser' individuals of little importance";

7. Other improper behaviors—"Consultants designing programs that give people
   what they want rather than what they need" or "Lack of follow-up in order to
   see that programs are properly implemented after classroom training" (p. 11).

The selection of trainers can lead to more positive results when those
responsible for selecting trainers keep in mind common trainer pitfalls and
behavior considered improper or unethical for training professionals.
Where possible, reference checks on trainers should be conducted, which
partially focus on gathering information not only on the trainers' experience
and competencies, but their performance in avoiding common trainer pitfalls and unethical behavior. This same information should be discussed
by the training program designers with the potential trainer candidates.

Regardless of the organizations' training needs, many training programs
rely on both internal and external trainers. The remainder of this chapter
will discuss the internal/external team approach to training.

INTERNAL AND EXTERNAL TEAM APPROACH TO TRAINING

An organization's HRM department usually has responsibility for training the organization's employees. Developing and implementing a training
program that successfully meets the organization's training needs is a complex task, demanding attention to factors such as assessing participants'
needs, setting training needs, selecting training strategies, assessing training
staff resources, and selecting trainers to facilitate the program. As mentioned earlier in this chapter, a key to the success of a training program is
often the trainers themselves, especially when those responsible for training
decide to use an external-internal team approach to training (hereafter
referred to as the team approach). This section will examine some concerns
that may result from using such a team approach in training programs.

Why the Team Approach to Training?

In meeting their increased training needs, many organizations have created internal training departments composed of individuals responsible for
training organization members. Some organizations have used a combination training team to develop and implement training programs. This approach uses the resources and knowledge bases of both internal and external
trainers. Often, the approach designates an individual or small group within
the organization (often coming from the HRM unit) to work with the external
trainer to spearhead the training effort. In the team training approach both
the external and internal trainers share in planning, actual work with trainees, and subsequent reflection and replanning. Thus, the goal of utilizing an
external trainer is to improve the potential success of the training program.

Training magazine's 1989 Industry Report (*Training*, 1989) on the use of in-house and outside resources for training efforts provides some insight into the extent of the use of the team approach to training in organizations. The report showed that a combination of in-house and outside resources was the most popular option for delivering training to employees. Fifty-eight percent of organizations in the study provide production workers with training that is delivered solely by in-house trainers. At the opposite end of the spectrum, just 7.1 percent of organizations allowed in-house trainers to deliver all training to executives. Historically, the use of joint in-house and outside resource (trainer) has been the most popular option, and this was reconfirmed in the 1989 Industry Report.

An issue that contributes significantly to the success of a team training approach is the relationship built between the internal and external trainers. However unique the actual training experiences of both the internal and external trainers involved, a poor working relationship can severely impair a training program. It is the process of "joining up" between two different complex systems (trainers) with the expressed purpose of producing a common product (a successful training program) that often confronts the internal and external trainers. The issue of a team approach to training is an important and lively one wherever it occurs. As remarked by Tannenbaum, Weschler, and Massarik (1961).

Seeing different trainers at work can be most revealing. Each has his own personality, his theories of training and different skills in varying degrees of competence. Some act as catalysts; others as sources of wisdom; others as counselors; still others as teachers. Some respond to the overt, conscious needs of their trainees; others to what appear to them as more significant unconscious wants and drives. Some actually do what they think they do; others give lip service to one mode of operation while actually performing another. Some are blocked by their own personality difficulties from helping their trainees face up to similar problems within themselves; others appear reasonably well adjusted in the interpersonal area and are not bothered by undue tensions in the efficient execution of their jobs (p. 91).

This excerpt should give insight into what may happen if two or more trainers are at work and behave in the style or combination of styles portrayed above. Yet, this situation is not far-fetched because team training is usually a useful and practical occurrence in organizations.

Advantages of Team Approach. When an internal and external trainer work together on a training program, each trainer may bring complementary resources—that is, the advantages and strengths of one trainer may offset the disadvantages and weaknesses of the other. The external trainer brings expertise, objectivity, and new insights to organization training problems. The internal trainer, on the other hand, brings detailed knowledge of organization issues and norms, a long-time acquaintance with members, and an awareness of organization and training department strengths and weaknesses.

The collaborative relationship between the internal and external trainers integrates knowledge, skills, abilities, and resources. The relationship should embody such qualities as trust, respect, honesty, confrontation, and collaboration. The team approach to training allows for a division of training program work load and a sharing of the training needs diagnosis, objectives, plans, and strategies. The team approach is also less likely to accept watered-down or compromised training programs because each team member tends to support the other.

Another reason for using an internal-external training approach is to achieve greater continuity in the overall training department's programs. Because external trainers are involved in other outside training activities, they are generally available to the organization only a few days a month, with two- or three-week intervals between visits. The internal trainer, on the other hand, provides a continuing point or training contact for organization members if and when problems or questions arise.

The team approach also provides continuing support for maintaining the momentum of the organization's training programs. Most training programs will hit low spots or stumbling blocks, but team training has the potential to stimulate and motivate the organization's training program during periods of resistance and budget cuts. Finally, the team training approach combines the advantages of both the external and internal trainers while minimizing the disadvantages.

Anderson and Snyder (1989) have recently emphasized the importance of what they refer to as "team" training by pointing out that "two heads are better than one" and providing the following advantages to team training:

1. Colleagues can often supplement, emphasize, redirect, clarify, or enrich the contributions being made by the "up-front" team member, either during a pause or in the form of a graceful interruption.

2. Two people can deal with problems with clock, environment, materials, or substance more surely and easily than a "lone-wolf" trainer or consultant who is trying to mastermind and control the entire situation.

3. The initial stimulation that accompanies sharing with and playing off each other. Synergistic learning is at work: two can learn more together than the sum of what each can learn separately. And, the involvement of a talented colleague often causes each team member to perform at a high level. High-performance trainers lead to high-quality learning.

4. Team training keeps the pace and overall flavor of the experience at a stimulating level.

Just as there are advantages with the team approach to training, difficulties that the trainers must address also may arise; these are highlighted in the next section.

Disadvantages of Team Training—Carving Out a Piece of Turf. Both internal and external trainers must understand that they have a variety of ways of expressing their territorial feelings concerning an organization. In addition, they must also have the guts to confront one another directly with these feelings early in the game. Such feelings should become a part of the problem analysis, rather than being left unuttered to produce a normal collection of "territorial games." Openness makes it possible for the trainers to express their feelings and, thereby, better assess the specific interest areas in which both conflicting and complementary approaches are found.

It is quite easy to get a false view that the relationship-building process between the internal and external trainers will be a smooth one, requiring little effort. On the contrary, it may be as difficult as most joining-up processes, demanding many hours of conversation, feedback, observation, confronting, checking, etc. Experience shows that both the internal and the external trainer come to the organization with a unique set of skills, experiences, and preferences; both bring a sense of their "proper" roles in the organization.

The worlds of the two training professionals are distinctly different, not only in terms of experiences, but also in terms of focus and the way others respond to them. As external trainers respond to a pressing need to become part of the system by carving a niche for themselves, they run the risk of "stepping on the toes" of the internal trainer. For example, a trainer who prefers a particular training style may make general statements concerning training competence. This may lead to negative comparisons with the internal counterpart, regardless of the particular competencies of the internal trainer.

Nevertheless, the greatest problem presented by team training is the attempt to blend the members' training styles. As Lakin (1972) asserts,

By far the most difficult problem in co-training is the resolution of markedly differing conceptions of training procedures, goals and purposes. If they are sufficiently different, then the co-trainers will be uncoordinated much of the time, one calling to one kind of interaction, the other to another unrelated one. Such a signal crossing can become so confusing that the learnings are at cross-purposes and the process is essentially paralyzed (p. 125).

Depending on the particular positions these individuals hold in the organization, their verbal and nonverbal opinions can have serious effects on the relationship between the trainers and the training program in question. This makes the communication that develops between the internal and external trainers very important. The ability of the internal and external trainers to communicate and develop a positive rapport can reduce resistance to any forthcoming training efforts. Relationships of this nature will almost certainly be easier if not complicated by the comparative assessment of others. Such comparisons are inevitable, but members of training teams must work to blunt their impact.

Trainees' Responses to the Team Approach. Trainees have both positive and negative feelings about certain aspects of the team approach to training. Some of the positive aspects are: (1) stimulus provided by two or more training styles; (2) stimulus provided by two or more personalities; (3) good model of carrying appropriate workloads; (4) good model of cooperative behavior; (5) multiple points of view, which can enrich learning, and (6) permitting the trainers to be on top of situations—for example, when one is actively engaged, the other can observe and process, and vice versa.

On the other side of the coin, some problems trainees may have are: (1) difficulty adjusting to two or more different training styles; (2) difficulty adjusting to two or more different personalities; (3) one trainer not carrying his or her full share of the workload or responsibility; (4) confusing or contradictory messages or beliefs from training-team members; (5) apparent "power struggle," rivalry, or competitive behavior between or among team members; (6) interruptions, disagreements, and conflicts not gracefully handled; and (7) difficulty developing the kind of closeness and identification between a group of trainees and its trainer that a solo trainer generates.

For the trainees who make up the internal-external team's audience, problems may arise when the training team fails either to do its job well or to exhibit behaviors ascribed to successful training teams. The problems enumerated above can cripple the working relationship between internal training professionals and external trainers. Organizations that adopt the team approach must develop formal strategies for coping with these problems.

Obstacles to Team Thinking

There are some real obstacles to a team-based training approach. Some trainers find it hard to ask for advice, and even harder to take it. In some situations internal trainers have acknowledged fear of being perceived as failures if they participate in joint training efforts. Similarly, some trainers who are accustomed to working alone may find it difficult to share the limelight with colleagues, and to make suggestions to other HRM specialists and trainers. A training program should encourage both trainers to stick together. In order to work together successfully, the level of trust between the trainers must be raised, and participation must be voluntary. The desire to learn new skills of listening, problem-solving, and conducting joint training programs is an important one for most trainers.

Both trainers must want to develop a philosophy of mutual participation and ownership to help them distinguish the false training trails from the right ones. The distinction between decision making and cooperative problem solving should be at the heart of the trainers' working philosophy. Any HRM specialist can make decisions, but not everyone can solve today's training problems. Thus, participation works well between the external and internal trainers when training decisions are made that utilize the strengths of both trainers.

Characteristics of Successful Team Training

In a recent article, Anderson and Snyder (1989) provided the following tentative list of characteristics that may be related to successful team training. Successful team trainers:

1. Possess compatible but somewhat different personalities
2. Are obviously knowledgeable about the program material
3. Possess different skills, knowledge, and viewpoints that complement each other and add breadth or depth to the training
4. Function together efficiently and effectively
5. Capture and maintain the attention of the audience
6. Show mutual respect, courtesy toward each other, and acceptance of each other's contributions
7. Avoid "ego trips" at the expense of partners
8. Show strong evidence of advance planning (for example, content of presentation, charts, transparencies, and other resources is valid, up to date, relevant, and well organized; materials, equipment and other reference resources are sufficient, readily available, and efficiently distributed; logistical arrangements dealing with such subjects as time, space, and furniture reflect good anticipation and adaptation)
9. Relate well to trainees
10. Appear to be comfortable in their team planning roles
11. Cause trainees to "stretch" intellectually and professionally
12. Equip trainees with useful, practical skills
13. Appear to find professional pleasure in training-team membership
14. Provide for a good flow of activity (time is effectively used; events follow each other in a smooth manner; energy level of trainees is well maintained; group needs, such as breaks, are recognized and respected; and progress toward goals is made in an orderly manner
15. Show strong management skills while directing the program (provide good instruction and task clarification, handle training activities efficiently, encourage and enable active participation, reinforce desired behaviors, handle neg-

ative responses effectively, provider feedback and correctives, and keep the group on task)

16. Model behavior related to the aims of the training program

The following factors are important in creating a positive environment for training programs and the working relationship between external and internal trainers:

1. *Trainer initiative and skill.* Are there persons who are actively pursuing the external-internal team approach to training, and are they skillful in raising top administrators' interest, commitment, and resources for training innovations and program success?

2. *Linkage.* Are trainers well connected to the information, materials, and training skills they need to carry out the training program?

3. *Openness and tolerance.* Do the trainers actively seek to understand and appreciate new ideas, practices, or training products? Are training innovators and innovations respected and encouraged?

4. *Collaborative ownership.* Do the trainers responsible for the training programs feel that they value the need to collaborate and share ownership in pursuit of training goals they hold?

5. *Rewards.* Is the cooperative problem-solving process of identifying training needs, developing solutions, and carrying them out rewarding for those involved, both intrinsically and extrinsically?

6. *Administrative support.* Do training managers in the organization support the team approach to training?

In team training situations, trainers and trainees have experiences that differ from those of traditional, "solo" training presentations (Anderson and Snyder, 1989). As we learn more about those experiences and the perceived differences, we will be better able to test the hypothesis that the team approach is better, at least in many situations. Those responsible for the success of training programs must understand that internal and external trainers should each have the vision to identify critical training problems for the future of their working relationship, and the humility to be one voice among equals in resolving them. Possessing these values allows them to look beyond individual interests and specializations and toward a job well done together.

SUMMARY

The selection of those who will facilitate the training program is a key component in the overall design, implementation, and evaluation of a training program. Trainers differ in knowledge of the material, communication skills, ability to respond to questions and challenges, and ability to motivate trainees. Therefore, some trainers are more effective than others with specific training methods. These issues, among others, must be taken into consideration in the selection of trainers. In addition, prerequisites should be established and adhered to in determining who will be given final responsibility for the training program. The selection of trainers should also be based on an understanding of some common trainer pitfalls that may lead to program failure. Also, those responsible for the selection of trainers should be aware of what constitutes unacceptable trainer behavior.

Designers of training programs must understand that simply working together in a spirit of cooperation will not guarantee the success of training programs designed and executed by internal and external trainers. It is imperative that HRM specialists working in internal-external teams address differences when they arise. Avoiding conflicting objectives, training-style preferences, and strategies serves to limit trainers' abilities to construct the best program for a particular agency. It is only by dealing with these problems that both trainers grow to see that they share objectives that often transcend the conflict.

The selection of training teams should include time for the individuals to get acquainted with each other, socially and professionally, so that concerns about compatibility are minimal. Compatibility with respect to basic values, beliefs, and competencies is important in a team-training context. The internal and external trainer should possess talents and skills that complement and supplement other's. That mix of talents and skills can benefit not only the trainees, but the training-team members as well.

Enhancing the Effectiveness
of Training Programs

INTRODUCTION

Conducting training programs in organizations in a manner that fosters
employee development requires identification and management of those
aspects of the training program that influence the learning process. Learning is an interactive process that involves both trainers and employees.
Enhancing this interactive process can be accomplished by improving the
"fit" between training styles of trainers (Wheeler and Marshall, 1986) and
the cognitive or learning styles of employees (Kolb, 1985a, 1985b; Goldstein and Blackmon, 1978). A greater understanding of "successful" training may also emerge from answers to the following questions:

Are there certain trainer style profiles that work "best" with specific learning styles?
If so, what are they?

Do "effective" trainers adapt their training style to match the learning style of
specific employees and training programs?

Can trainers learn to "adapt" training styles to employees' learning styles?

Can training environment profiles be identified? If so, can the learning process be
managed in organizations?

Answering these questions can provide a basis for training strategies that
can help HRM specialists improve their training performance and the effectiveness of the training program in general. The goal of this chapter is
not to answer these questions in detail, but to present the importance of

adapting training methods to particular employee learning styles, and to discuss the importance of managing the learning process in training in organizations by adapting training methods to an employee's learning style. Such an approach creates training activities and training environments that should enhance and improve the effectiveness of training programs in organizations.

Most HRM specialists in organizations are aware of the ongoing changes in their organizations (mergers, acquisitions, down-scaling, and responding to foreign competition), themselves, and employees. As they facilitate growth and development in employees through training, HRM specialists struggle to improve themselves, to become more effective training leaders, planners, presenters, and facilitators. In addition, those responsible for training often are motivated to become more skillful in training employees in a variety of ways in order to be effective with as many employees as possible. Rather than using only the training style(s) with which they may be most comfortable, HRM specialists must learn to use new techniques and behaviors to suit different trainees' learning styles.

Learning, change, and growth become more meaningful, more useful, and more exciting for everyone involved when HRM specialists identify the areas in which they have the greatest expertise and attempt to increase their skills, thereby increasing their ability to address all aspects of the adult learning cycle (Kolb and Fry, 1979). The extent to which HRM specialists take time to manage the learning process determines the degree to which trainees' learning will be enhanced.

TRAINING PROGRAMS AND LEARNING STYLES

In the planning and development of too many training programs, very little attention is given to the interaction of trainer styles and the learning styles of HRM specialists and trainees. This results in several limitations. The first is the failure to take into account different learning styles. (As discussed in Chapter 5, learning style relates to how the employee prefers to learn—for example, through lecture, group discussion, or independent projects.) For instance: if, in a traditional training program taught by the lecture method, the HRM specialist decided to experiment with the case-study approach, the results, as measured by employee achievement and attitude scores, may be inconclusive. If trainees' preferences are randomly distributed with regard to learning styles, the gains to some trainees from a change in method may be offset by the losses to other trainees, unless one can control for the differences in employee learning styles.

A second limitation is the failure to control for differences in the HRM specialists' preferred training styles—highly structured lectures, group discussion, experiential learning, case studies, and so forth. Training styles are personal, develop over time, and are not usually subject to short-term change. For many HRM specialists, their training style reflects their learning style because they feel most comfortable presenting material in the way they best understand it. In many respects, the association is similar to many other relationships in life—likes attract, opposites repel. It is assumed that the preferred training style generally determines the training method and the learning or training environment of the training program that a HRM specialist uses and develops in an organization. For instance, a HRM specialist who believes that trainees learn best when the training program content is highly structured would probably use the lecture method.

A third limitation may occur if an organization's training programs fail to realize that simple achievement may not be the only goal of a training program from the employee's, the HRM specialist's, or the organization's viewpoint. Trainees may want to enjoy the training program, engage in dialogue with other trainees, understand their jobs better, or have other goals in mind as they attempt to maximize their job-related functions. HRM specialists may also be interested in diverse goals, such as obtaining good trainee evaluations and getting trainees to enroll in more advanced training programs.

An important step in developing and maintaining an effective training program is to determine the needs of the trainees and identify training opportunities or environments for satisfying these needs. Broadening trainee skills can be enhanced by (1) assessing the trainee's individual orientation toward learning or problem solving, (2) identifying the trainee's particular style, and then (3) adapting the training method(s) most likely to suit the trainee's learning style.

It is the premise of this book that people have learned something when either or both the following descriptions apply: they know something they did not know earlier, and can show it; and/or they are able to do something they were not able to do before. The descriptions require combining the characteristics of learning and problem solving. Thus we can come closer to understanding how it is that people generate from their experiences the concepts, rules, and principles that guide their behavior in new situations— and how they modify these concepts, rules, and principles to improve their effectiveness.

Like trainees, different HRM specialists have different training styles, related, for example, to how explicitly they give instructions, how much they expect trainees to learn on their own, and how actively they encourage group work. The Grasha-Reichmann Learning Style Questionnaire (GRLSQ) can be used to divide HRM specialists' training styles into three broad classifications (Dependent, Independent, and Collaborative), or Kolb's Learning Style Inventory (LSI) can be used to make similar classifications (Converger, Implementator, Diverger, Assimilator).

The LSI and Preference for Teachers/HRM Specialists and Learning Situations

Kolb (1984a, 1984b) performed several associations between the LSI and students' ratings of sixteen different situations that facilitate their learning. The learning situations included lectures, seminars, readings on theory, individual projects, examinations, talks by experts, and homework, among others. Significant results were found between these ratings and the students' learning styles. For example, students who were Concrete Experiencers tended to find theoretical readings of little aid to their learning. Reflective Observers tended to prefer lectures as the greatest aid to their learning. Abstract Conceptualizers preferred case studies and readings on theory. Finally, Active Experimenters disliked lectures and preferred small group discussions, projects, and student feedback.

The fact that an asssociation does exist between individuals' preferences for learning situations and their learning styles means that a HRM specialist may have to provide a variety of learning situations in a training program in order to facilitate the learning process of that training program. It also means that no one method satisfies all trainees in the training program. If a training program has a mixture of trainees from each of the four learning styles, the HRM specialist must present a diversity of learning situations.

A study by Sadler, Plovnick, and Snope (1978) indicates some of the difficulties of teaching in an environment in which the learning styles of the faculty and students differ. Their study noted that an incongruity in learning styles may result in a situation in which a faculty member may be required to use teaching methods which, although valuable to the students, are not appealing or intellectually rewarding to the teacher.

Correlations were also found between a student's learning style and his or her rating of the teacher who had influenced the student the most. Students oriented to concrete experience preferred teachers who had that same learning style, but these students reported a significantly negative preference for teachers with an abstract learning style. Reflective students preferred reflective teachers and did not prefer teachers with abstract learning styles. Students who learned best through abstract conceptualization significantly preferred teachers with abstract learning styles, and a significantly negative correlation was found between these students and teachers with either a concrete or reflective learning style. Finally, students with an active-experimentation learning style strongly preferred teachers with an active-experimentation learning style and did not prefer teachers with a reflective learning style. In summary, according to student ratings, teachers tended to have influenced students who shared their learning-style preference and to have had little influence on students who had other learning-style preferences.

The findings presented above may be generalizable to training efforts. As mentioned earlier, because HRM specialists' training styles are reflective of their learning style, each may feel more comfortable presenting material in the way he or she best understands it. If this is the case, then HRM specialists must pay particular attention to this tendency and spend time managing the training process.

The knowledge of a trainee's learning style, or of the styles of others, can help ensure more effective design of training methods and training environments aimed at broadening a trainee's skills. Once the predominant learning style of a trainee and HRM specialist are identified, then learning opportunities can be designed that match the trainee's learning strengths and weaknesses.

MANAGING THE TRAINING PROCESS IN ORGANIZATIONS

To conduct the training process in organizations in a manner that attends to the individual learning styles of trainees and fosters trainee development requires management of those aspects of the training system that influence the learning process. Such a training system must be soundly built on a valid model of the learning process. There has been a great burgeoning of training techniques designed to assist the learning process in recent years: computer-aided instruction, experience-based learning materials, programmed instruction, simulations and games, and so on. Although these techniques tend to be highly sophisticated and creative applications of their own particular fields of expertise, be it computer science or accounting, they are much less sophisticated in how they enhance trainee learning. The weakness of nearly all these techniques is the failure to recognize and explicitly provide for the differences in learning styles that are characteristic of both trainees and the training material covered in a training program.

Even though many of these training innovations have been developed in the name of individualized training and self-directed learning, there has been little attempt to specify along which dimensions individualization is to take place. For example, although computer-aided instruction and programmed learning provide alternative routes or branches for the individual trainee, these branches tend to be based primarily on various elaborations of the subject matter being covered in the training program. Little has been done to provide the individual employee with branches that provide alternative learning methods (such as those that differ from the HRM specialists' preferred style or method) based on the trainee's learning style. In addition, there has been little research to assess how the effectiveness of various training methods is contingent on either individual trainees' learning styles or the type of subject matter being taught.

Training Environments

Kolb's ELT provides one such system for managing the learning process in Fry's concept of the learning environment (Fry, 1978). The author has effectively used Fry's concept of the learning environment in the development of training programs in a variety of organizations. Any training program, training course, or training session can be viewed as having degrees of orientation toward each of the four learning modes in Kolb's ELT—labeled by Fry as Affective, Perceptual, Symbolic, and Behavioral, to connote the overall climate they create and the particular learning skill or mode they require (Kolb and Fry, 1975). Thus an affective training environment emphasizes the experiencing of concrete events; a symbolic training environment emphasizes abstract conceptualization; a perceptual training environment stresses observation and appreciation; a behavioral training environment stresses action-taking in situations with real consequences. Any particular training experience can have some or all of these orientations, to differing degrees, at the same time.

A typical lecture during a training program obviously has perceptual and symbolic orientations, because it requires trainees to listen to and interpret the presentation (reflective observation skills) and to reason and induce conceptual relationships from what they hear (abstract conceptualization skills). But there may be an affective orientation as well. Some trainees may be experiencing the HRM specialist doing the lecturing as a role model. Or, if we direct questions or pose dilemmas to the training group, we increase the behavioral orientation by urging trainees to take action by speaking up and testing their ideas out in public.

Each type of environmental orientation can be measured by observing the following variables in the context of a training program: the purpose of the major training activities, the primary source or use of information, the rules guiding trainee behavior, the HRM specialist's role, and the provision for feedback. These are useful cues, because to a great extent they are controlled by the HRM specialist, independently of the trainee. Most decisions affecting these aspects of training environments are made before the trainee–training program interactions take place. Using these variables, the following pictures of different types of training environments and trainers' roles result.

Affectively Complex Environments. Affectively complex training environments are ones in which the emphasis is on experiencing what it is actually like to be in a particular job. Trainees are engaged in activities that simulate or mirror what they would do as employees, or they are encouraged to reflect upon an experience to generate these insights and feelings about themselves. The information discussed and generated is more often current/immediate. It often comes from expressions of feelings, values, and opinions by the trainee in discussions with peers or the trainer.

Such expressions of feelings are encouraged and seen as productive inputs to the learning process.

In this training environment the training activities would often vary from any prior schedule as a result of the trainee's training needs. The HRM specialist serves as a role model for the trainees, relating to them on a personal basis and more often as a colleague than an authority. Feedback is personalized with regard to each trainee's needs and goals, as opposed to comparative. It can come from both peers and the HRM specialist. There is accepted discussion and critique of how the training program is proceeding, with the result that specific events within a single training session are often more emergent than prescribed.

Perceptually Complex Environments. Perceptually complex training environments are ones in which the primary goal is to understand something: to be able to identify relationships between the concepts, to be able to define problems for investigation, to be able to collect relevant information, to be able to research a question, and the like. To do this, trainees are encouraged to view the topic or subject matter from different perspectives (their own experience, expert opinion, literature) and in different ways (listen, observe, write, discuss, act out, think, smell). If a task is being done or a problem is being solved, the emphasis is more on how it gets done, the process, than on the solution.

In this training environment, the HRM specialist would not ask that success or performance be measured against rigid criteria. Trainees are instead left to conclude, answer, or define criteria or success for themselves. Individual trainee differences in this process are allowed—and used as a basis for further understanding. Trainees are thus free to explore others' ideas, opinions, and reactions in order to determine their own perspectives. In this process, the HRM specialist serves as a "mirror" or "process facilitator." He or she is nonevaluative, answers questions with questions, suggests instead of critiquing, and relates current issues to larger ones. The HRM specialist creates a reward system that emphasizes methodology of inquiry versus getting a particular answer. In training sessions, there is planned time spent on looking back at previous steps, events, or decisions in order to guide the trainee in future activities.

Symbolically Complex Environments. Symbolically complex training environments are ones in which the trainee is involved in trying to solve a problem for which there is usually a right answer or a best solution. The source of information, topic, or problem being dealt with is abstract, in that it is removed from the present and presented via reading, data, pictures, lecture inputs, and so on. In handling such information, the trainee is both guided and constrained by externally imposed rules of inference, such as symbols, computer technology, jargon, theorems, graphical keys, or protocols. There is often a demand on the trainee to recall these rules, concepts, or relationships via memory.

In this training environment, the HRM specialist is the accepted representative of the body of knowledge—judging and evaluating trainee output and interpreting information that cannot be dealt with by the rules of inference. The HRM specialist is also a timekeeper, a taskmaster, and an enforcer of schedules of events in order that the trainee can become immersed in the analytical exercise necessary to reach a solution without worrying about having to set goals and manage his or her own time. Trainee success is measured against the right or best solution, expert opinion, or otherwise rigid criteria imposed by the HRM specialist or accepted in the organization. Decisions concerning the flow and nature of activities in the training sessions are essentially made by the HRM specialist, mostly prior to the training program.

Behaviorally Complex Environments. Behaviorally complex training environments are those in which the emphasis is on actively applying knowledge or skills to a practical problem. The problem need not have a right or best answer, but it does have to be something the trainee can relate to, value, and feel some intrinsic satisfaction from having solved. This would normally be a "real-life" problem, case, or simulation that the trainee could expect to face on the job. In the attack on the problem, the focus is on doing. Completing the task is essential. Although there may be an externally imposed deadline or periodic checkpoints by which reports or other information are required, most of the trainee's time is his or hers to manage. The trainee's concern is on what effect present behavior will have vis-à-vis the overall task to be done. The next task the trainee engages in will not occur independent of the present one.

In this training environment, the HRM specialist ensures that the trainee is left to make decisions or choices about what to do next or how to proceed. The HRM specialist can be available as a coach or advisor, but primarily as a result of the trainee's request or initiative. A trainee's success is measured against criteria associated with the task: how well something worked, feasibility, salability, client acceptence, cost, testing results, aesthetic quality, and so on.

When HRM specialists view the trainee and training environment in terms of learning styles and learning environments, useful relationships can emerge concerning the design of training activities or situations in organizations. As a result, managing the learning process allows learning to become a skill that can be managed, improved, and coached. Managing the learning process by working with learning styles, training styles, and learning environments allows the HRM specialist to design training opportunities that match the trainee's learning strengths and weaknesses. Empathy and communication become central to the training process. The concern of the HRM specialist then becomes how trainees' learning styles can be addressed when trainees are in training programs that are foreign to their preferred learning styles.

Enhancing Training Program Effectiveness

To improve the potential success of a training program and to assist in the development (or broadening) of a particular skill or learning style, HRM specialists must remember that no single learning or training style has any overwhelming advantage over any other. Each style has its strengths and weaknesses (though it is important to be cautious about labeling strengths and weaknesses since, to some extent, which is which depends on the context in which they are viewed). Program effectiveness can be enhanced by being clear about the relative strengths and weaknesses of each style because selecting appropriate learning opportunities essentially involves finding activities where strengths will be utilized and where weaknesses will not prove too much of a handicap.

Trainees can also be screened before they attend a training program to provide advance warning about the predominant learning styles of the trainees in a given training program. This information is very useful for the HRM specialists. It helps them prepare for the training program and, possibly, slant parts of the training program to better accommodate the learning-style preferences of the group. If there are a number of interchangeable HRM specialists available to run a given training program, then the HRM specialists' styles can be taken into account to get the most compatible match between trainees and HRM specialist.

A rather more ambitious possibility is to use the learning-style information to allocate certain trainees to certain training programs. For example, if it was felt desirable to have together in one training program an equal number of Implementators, Divergers, Assimilators, and Convergers, this could be engineered by administering some sort of quota system. This ensures that the group, as a whole, is well balanced with all the different learning skills equally represented. If, on the other hand, it is considered more practical to have as homogeneous a group as possible, then it is possible to invite Implementators or Divergers or Assimilators or Convergers to attend separate training programs. The training programs, while attempting to achieve the same objectives, are easier to plan and run with the likes and dislikes or strengths and weaknesses of more homogeneous trainee populations clearly in mind. The training program therefore remains the same but the methods differ, catering to learning-style preferences. Thus, there could, for example, be many projects for Implementators, reading time built in for Divergers, question-and-answer sessions for Assimilators, and practical demonstrations for Convergers.

If it is considered impractical to offer different versions of the same training program, then it might be considered more feasible to design different options or branches within the same program. The training program would contain some core activities standard for all, irrespective of differences in learning-style preferences. At intervals, however, the program would split into branching activities tailor-made to meet the needs of trainees with specific learning styles.

Implications for Training. A greater understanding of HRM specialists' and trainees' learning styles and learning environments has several implications for training in organizations.

1. Matching of trainees and HRM specialists possessing similar learning styles and training styles should improve trainee achievement in training programs and employee attitudes toward training. If maximizing these outputs is the main goal of the training program, then such matching would increase training efficiency.

2. HRM specialists should take training and learning styles into consideration when reviewing trainees evaluations of training. These evaluations may be reflecting trainees' responses to differences in training styles rather than being evaluations of training or the HRM specialist.

3. Training researchers who evaluate different methods of training may need to control for training and learning styles.

4. HRM specialists who use only the dependent training style can improve trainees' understanding and attitudes toward training by utilizing a variety of training methods.

5. The inconclusive results reported in surveys of the literature on trainee evaluations of HRM specialists may occur not because a new training method is "bad," but because trainees with different learning styles will react variously to different methods. Thus, some trainees may gain, but others may lose, from using a new training method. Taking these different learning styles into account may provide more conclusive results of the evaluations of different training methods. Researchers may be able to discover which types of trainees gain (or lose) from different types of training methods.

6. Many training research designs are costly to implement and to replicate because the need for research data requires "artificial" changes in training methods. For example, switching to a case-study approach or a self-paced method requires that a number of HRM specialists deliberately and explicitly alter their method of training. Obtaining the necessary number of HRM specialists to do that (especially more than once) may be difficult. On the other hand, researchers in training could use existing training and learning styles as factors to help study differences in training outcomes, without imposing the above costs on the HRM specialists.

Management of the learning or training process also includes giving attention to the development of the learning climate in training. The remainder of the chapter provides a series of psychological-contracting activities intended to facilitate the start-up phase of a training program. Their objective is to assist HRM specialists and training programs participants in creating the kind of learning or training environment most responsive to the unique needs of trainees.

Developing the Learning Climate in Training

HRM specialists are responsible for managing the content, process, and learning environment of a training program. Content refers to the material to be covered and to the general sequence in which it will be presented. Process encompasses the approaches by which that content is delivered. Environment is the physical and psychological surroundings for the training session.

HRM specialists often spend the first hours or days of a training program developing a sense of community and deciding how to use experience and the interactions of participants for maximum learning. The training program becomes a learning community—a community in which participants support one another, are open with one another about their responses, and are willing to confront or compare different responses, insights, and experiences. Learning to learn is important enough (and difficult enough) for trainees to spend time building such a climate systematically. A key aspect of this sort of training environment is learning how to effectively utilize one's experiences and those of others.

Characteristics of a Training Environment. The training environment model presented earlier in this chapter differs in some key respects from the stereotype of traditional training programs. First, it is based on a psychological contract of reciprocity. Reciprocity is a basic building block of human interaction which emphasizes that relationships based on a mutual and equal balance of giving and getting thrive and grow, whereas those based on unequal exchange very quickly decay. This process of reciprocity is particularly important for creating an effective learning environment because many initial assumptions about learning run counter to it. Learning is most often considered a process of getting rather than giving.

The process of getting rather than giving is most evident in conceptions of trainees' and HRM specialists' roles—that is, that HRM specialists give and trainees get. Yet, for successful training, both giving and getting by HRM specialists and trainees are critical. In getting, there is the opportunity to incorporate new ideas and perspectives. In giving, there is the opportunity to integrate and apply these new perspectives and to practice their use.

A second characteristic of the training environment model suggested in this chapter is that it is experienced-based. The motivation for learning comes not from the HRM specialist's dispensation of rewards but from problems and opportunities arising from the trainee's own life experience. Third, this learning environment emphasizes personal application. Since the trainees' learning needs arise from their own experiences, the main goal of learning is to apply new KSAs to the solution of the trainees' practical problems.

Fourth, the training environment is individualized and self-directed.

Just as every trainee's experience is different, so are each trainee's learning goals and learning style. A major concern in the management of training environments is to organize program resources in such a way that they are maximally responsive to what each trainee wants to learn and how he or she learns it. Essential to achievement of this kind of training environment is the trainee's willingness to take responsibility for the achievement of those training objectives. Perhaps the most important of the trainees' responsibilities is that of evaluating how well they are getting the training resources they need to achieve their goals—and alerting the training community as problems arise—since they are in the best position to make this judgment.

A final characteristic important to enhancing a training environment is that it integrates learning and living. There are two goals in the learning process. One is to learn the specifics of a particular subject matter. The other is to learn one's own strengths and weaknesses as a learner (i.e., learning how to learn from experience). When the process works well, trainees finish their training experience not only with new intellectual insights, but also with an understanding of their own learning styles. This understanding of learning strengths and weaknesses helps in back-home work application of what has been learned and provides a framework for continuing learning on the job. In this instance, learning is no longer a special activity reserved for the training classroom; it becomes an integral and explicit part of work life itself.

The individual and group activities included in this section are designed to assist HRM specialists in contracting with members of their training program to build their own version of the training environment described above. In a sense they are intended as a catalyst for conversations among training program staff and participants directed toward building and maintaining a highly effective training community.

Psychological Contracts. In order to build an effective learning environment during training it is important to undestand the nature of the psychological contract and how it influences the functioning of trainees in training programs. A psychological contract is implicitly formed between the individual trainee and the training program of which he or she is a member. It deals with the training program's expectations of the trainee and the trainee's contributions to meet them. It also deals with the trainee's expectations of the training program and the program's contribution to meet these expectations. However, first it is important to more clearly define psychological contract in the context of training.

When an individual decides to participate in a training program, he or she enters into a psychological contract with the training program and staff. A psychological contract is a set of unwritten reciprocal expectations between the trainee and the training program. It is the bedrock of the trainee–training program link because training is based on an implicit exchange of beliefs and expectations about the actions of the trainee vis-à-vis the training program, and the training program vis-à-vis the trainee. As such, psychological contracts usually involve expectations about training conditions, requirements of the training program itself, and the level of effort (participation) to be expended by the trainee in the training program.

Unlike a legal contract, a psychological contract in a training program defines a dynamic relationship that may continually change and be renegotiated. Often both parties to the contract may have different levels of expectation clarity, since some of the items may have been explicitly discussed and others only inferred. Important aspects of the contract are not always formally agreed on.

Expectations are sometimes unstated, implicit premises about the relationship. Organizational contributions, such as a sense of challenge in the training program, and trainee contributions, such as active participation, are expected but not consciously weighed. Yet this contract is a reality that has many implications for the productivity of the training program and for trainee satisfaction. A training program that is filled with trainees who feel "cheated" and expect far more than they get is headed for trouble. The trainee who feels the training program does not meet his or her expectations becomes a stumbling block to a productive training program. On the other hand, a training program that demands total compliance to peripheral norms (such as manner of dress) will stifle trainee creativity and participation.

Expectations and contributions. The dynamic nature of the psychological contract developed in a training program program means that trainee and training program expectations and contributions usually influence one another. The trainees entering into the psychological contract contribute their productive and participative capacity directed toward achieving the training program's purpose. High expectations on the part of the training program can produce increased trainee contributions, and great contributions will likewise raise expectations. From the training program's point of view, the questions become: How can we train the trainees so that we can maximize their individual contributions? and How can we create a training environment that meets trainees' expectations and our norms? For the trainee the question is How can this training program improve my job performance, career, personal growth and development?

Entering a training environment the first time is very much like the first day on a new job. The typical orientation program in a training program is one-sided. Most communication flows from the training program to the individual: "These are our policies, procedures, and expectations."

One effect of this one-sided process is to cause the trainees to feel that the training program is much more powerful than they are as individuals. So instead of trying to formulate and articulate their own expectations, the trainees often say what they think the training staff wants to hear. Another effect is the training program's tendency to oversocialize trainees. The trainees' feelings of powerlessness often lead them to be more passive than they might ordinarily be in the situation.

The training staff often reads passivity as a sign that the trainees want and need more direction and control. This situation can create a feedback cycle that in the long run operates to the detriment of the trainee and training program relationship. Maintaining a balanced psychological contract is necessary for a harmonious relationship between the trainee and the training program. Since psychological contracts are entered into as the trainees enter the training program, whether or not the trainees' expectations about the contract are met is crucial to the tenor of their relationship with the training program. For example, if a trainee participates in a training program with the expectation that the psychological contract includes some input in evaluating the trainer's performance, only to find out that the trainer's views differ, then the trainee is likely to suffer considerable dissatisfaction with the training program, based primarily on the perception that the psychological contract has been violated.

The violation of the psychological contract can signal to the trainee that the parties no longer share (or never shared) a common set of values or goals. Once this happens, one can expect a breakdown of communications among the parties, a failure in mutual understanding, increasing levels of frustration (and subsequent emotional responses) on the part of both parties, and a training climate less conducive to learning.

In many situations trainees find a training environment dull, boring, and unexciting. They sit passively in training, uninvolved in their own learning, and work halfheartedly to meet the training program's expectations. Their own expectations for learning, involvement, and stimulation go unsatisfied, in large measure because they never get the opportunity to make such expectations explicit. This, of course, need not be the case. If trainees can initially share their expectations and goals and can establish a climate where a shared responsibility is maintained, then it becomes possible to better meet everyone's training needs.

A dynamic process. It is important, however, to recognize that the psychological contract is not set forever in the initial training meeting. As mentioned at the outset, the initial training meeting represents a starting point for a dynamic process that will necessitate continued discussion and updating of mutual expectations as old training needs are met and new needs emerge. The remainder of this section will introduce a model for thinking about the training process that should help create an "early warning system" for the identification of problems and reinforce a set of norms for the training community that will encourage trainees to evaluate their own training progress and to sound alarms when their training needs are not met.

The psychological contract may be the central determinant in whether a training program is working effectively, generating trainee commitment, loyalty, and enthusiasm for the training program and its goals. This may depend to a large measure on two conditions: (1) the degree to which the trainees' expectations of what the training program will provide them and what they must give to the training program match what the training program's expectations are of what it will give and get; (2) what is actually exchanged (assuming there is agreement on expectations). An example of such exchanges is the active participation and commitment by the trainees during the training program to enhance their personal and professional growth, on the one hand, and the development opportunities provided by the training program, on the other. Figure 10.1 illustrates the importance to a training program of the match between expectations and contributions. The more training-program participants establish psychological contracts that are made up of matches in expectations, the greater will be their satisfaction with the training program.

Often training-program participants are not clear on what they want or need, or what they are capable of contributing during a training effort. Unfortunately, training programs also are not always clear as to what their expectations of trainees are. As a result they don't talk about many areas or pay attention to them. Mismatches can occur by accident, out of neglect.

What is needed, then, is for training-program participants to carefully consider all areas of expectations in order to overcome the problem of clarity. Too often this step does not occur because training-program designers and participants do not regularly consider it important. Training-program effectiveness can be enhanced if those responsible for designing, implementing, and evaluating training programs attempt to increase the number of matches in the psychological contract depicted in Figure 10.1.

A model developed by Sherwood and Glidewell (1971), known as the "pinch model of contract negotiation," is cyclical and includes four phases that can be applied to the development of more matches in the psychological contract and the training community. The four phases adapted for the development of a training community are:

1. Sharing training information and negotiating expectations;
2. When properly conducted, the first phase leads to mutual commitment to defined roles by training staff and trainees;
3. With commitment and role definition come stability and productivity; but
4. The emergent and individualized nature of the training process will inevitably lead to a new state of disruption.

This disruption, depending on its seriousness, inevitably brings some degree of uncertainty, anxiety, and discomfort. The discomfort can in turn lead to a number of possible outcomes, depending on how it is handled.

Figure 10.1
The Importance of the Match between Training Contributions and Inducements in the Psychological Contract

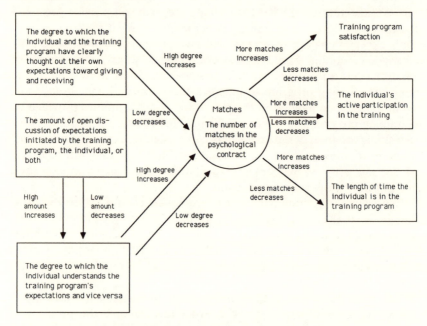

J. P. Kotter, The Psychological Contract: Managing the Joining-up Process, © [1973] by the Regents of the University of California. Adapted from the California Management Review, Vol. 15, No. 3. By permission of the Regents.

It can lead to termination or avoidance of the training environment altogether. It can lead to a kind of conservative return to the way things were, at the price of avoiding new training opportunities and resources, or it can lead to a renegotiation by a resharing of the new information and expectations that have been generated as a result of the disruption.

Sherwood and Glidewell (1971) suggest, however, that there is another approach to achieving stability in the psychological contract without all the unpleasant side effects of disruptions. This approach is called "planned renegotiation" and is based on the development of group norms that allow members to announce signs that they feel signal an imminent disruption. These signs are called "pinches." These signs, when noted in the stage of stability and productivity, can provide data for preventative renegotiation of expectations, which may avoid costly disruption of a productive training process. Examples of "pinches" that may signal the need for renegotiation in training environments are:

—a trainee feels bored or tuned out of a discussion

—a trainer senses that preparation assignments haven't been completed.

—training sessions don't start on time

—trainees are not actively participating or speaking up in discussions

If members of the training program let others know when they feel these subtle pinches, it becomes possible to make changes and minor adjustments without pressure, anxiety, and a crisis atmosphere.

In summary, there are a number of general points that result from developing the learning climate in a training program. First, the development of a psychological contract early in the training process is very important, and as such is worth carefully managing. Second, what you don't know *can* hurt you. A clear understanding of one's own expectations and the other party's will help form better contracts. Third, the key to contract formulation is achieving a match or a fit, not getting more, or the best, or whatever. Fourth, if a training program participant and a training program have one or more very central, basic mismatches, it may be counterproductive for all involved in the training program. Finally, with the development of matches in the psychological contracts, trainees can begin the process of self-directed learning and setting personal directions for learning throughout their training program experience.

Self-directed Learning in Training

Learning is a continuous process, with the question, "What do I want to learn from this training?" confronted after every training experience. In other words trainees choose training situations because they think they can answer questions and solve problems; at the same time, they expect the training experience to raise new questions and perhaps redefine old ones. From this perspective the criterion for a successful training experience is that it results in both conclusions and questions. While the conclusions represent an immediate practical outcome or problem solution, the questions provide guidelines for the choice of future training experiences. Questions are thus the basis for setting personal learning goals in training.

Setting Personal Learning Directions. An example may help describe how the questioning process can be used to set personal directions for learning in training. Let us say that various supervisors have begun to sense some questions about how to deal with the people factors in their work—how to motivate employees, improve quality and acceptance of their decisions, improve communication, and so on. One day they receive a brochure for a supervisory training program that proposes to deal with these topics and others. After some preliminary checking on such matters as the quality of the training staff, the feasibility of getting time off, and the desirability of the program location, they decide to attend. A month later they arrive at the conference center for the training program.

What we see in this example is a four-step problem-solving sequence: (1) a felt need or problem (to better deal with people factors), (2) data collection (the brochure, questions to other resources), (3) a goal or imagined solution to the problem (a plan to attend the program), and (4) action (arriving at the program). The supervisors' training goal has arisen from their attempts to solve a personally felt problem. How effectively that training goal will meet their needs is primarily a result of how well they have sensed and defined their problems, i.e., how well they have asked their training questions. The data they collect to analyze their situation, and their active attempts to use these data to generate and evaluate alternative solutions (goals), are two critical factors that will determine goal effectiveness.

Once the supervisors have arrived at the conference, what can they do to continue their control over their learning and problem solving? The answer lies in continuing to cycle through the problem-solving process that brought them to the program in the first place. While the four-stage problem-solving process has been defined in linear terms, it is really a continuing cycle leading to new experiences that cast old problems in a new light and offer new resources for re-solving the problems.

Thus, in the process of learning one moves in varying degrees from actor to observer, from specific involvement to general analytical detachment. The "Decision to Attend a Training Program" questionnaire presented below provides a mechanism for helping individuals to describe the problem-solving process they go through in deciding to attend a training program. The questionnaire allows the training program staff to share information about the objectives, content, and training techniques they have prepared for the training program.

The Decision to Attend a Training Program questionnaire is designed to help an individual describe the problem solving he or she went through in deciding to attend a training program. It is intended to increase trainees' awareness of the learning questions that influence their decisions to attend a training program as well as to provide a starting point for sharing with training staff and other trainees the kinds of training needs and concerns they bring to a training program. The design for sharing answers to the questionnaire during the first training session is such that individuals' responses can remain anonymous unless they choose to identify themselves in some way as they answer the questions. Information gathered from the Decision to Attend a Training Program questionnaire can also be used in enhancing the effectiveness of a training program as presented in the next section.

Exhibit 10.1
Decision to Attend a Training Program

1. Describe in a few sentences or phrases the problems or training needs that brought you to this training program.

    What questions are you seeking to answer?

    Check which of the following best characterizes how you feel about these training needs right now:

    _____ My needs are critical and specific. I need to come away from this program with specific action plans to satisfy them.

    _____ My needs are less pressing and more general. I am here to discover and explore.

    _____ Some of both of the above.

2. What made you decide to come to this specific training program? (What have you heard about it? What features of it most attracted you?) Again, answer briefly in a few sentences or phrases.

    Check which of the following best characterizes your decision to attend this program:

    _____ I freely chose to come myself, with no external pressure to attend.

    _____ I was basically sent here by forces or events beyond my control.

    _____ Some of both of the above.

3. Please indicate your expectations of this program by completing the following sentences:

    The best thing that could happen for me in the program is:

    The worst thing that could happen to me is:

    Thank you.

Building a Climate for Learning in Training

This section suggests a design for building a climate in a training program that will enhance the program's effectiveness. The purpose of the design is to provide the opportunity for training staff and trainees to share the information generated by trainees in the Decision to Attend a Training Program questionnaire, and information from the training staff about the objectives, content, and training techniques they have prepared for the training program. There are four specific objectives in this sharing process:

1. To inventory the learning needs of training program participants: both what they want to learn and how they tend to learn best
2. To have training staff present the overall design of the training program
3. To take whatever action steps are necessary to create a training environment that is maximally responsive to trainee needs
4. To have trainees and training staff become acquainted with one another

An overview of the design for this meeting is as follows:

Activity
1. Description of plans for the training program by the training staff
2. Anonymous sharing of data from the Decision to Attend the Training Program questionnaire
3. Sharing learning resources (discussion of Learning Style Inventory data)
4. Forming a reciprocal psychological contract (four homogeneous groups, by LSI type, list what they hope to give in the training program and what they hope to get from it)
5. Group reports
6. Identification of unmet training needs and untapped learning resources
7. Action planning to resolve problems
8. Discussion of "Learning Diaries"

A more detailed discussion of each of the above steps is presented below.
Description of Plans for the Training Program by the Staff. During this time the training staff presents its plans and preparations for the training program. The presentation includes the following:

—staff and trainees briefly introduce themselves

—a statement of program objectives/goals

—a description of the training modes and methods that will be used in the program

—a statement by the staff of its expectations of trainees

—an inventory of the major training resources that the program has to offer

Sharing by the Staff and Participants of Data from the Decision to Attend the Training Program Questionnaire. In order to limit the time for this portion of the meeting to approximately one hour, sharing questionnaires should be done in groups no larger than twelve. In a larger program, parallel groups can do this activity simultaneously. The suggested format for each group is as follows:

1. A staff member should collect the questionnaires within each group, shuffle them and then redistribute them randomly to the group members. (Occasionally a member may by chance get his or her own questionnaire back, but that is okay.)
2. The group task is the following. Each group member should read the question-naire responses aloud to the rest of the group. After each questionnaire is read, the rest of the group should try to empathize with the author of the question-naire—try to imagine how they would feel and act if they were in the author's position. From this position of empathy the group should try to answer the following questions: If I were this person,

    —How would I feel if I were faced with this problem or opportunity?

    —What alternatives would I consider to deal with it?

    —What would I do to benefit maximally from this program?

    —What aspects of the program as I have heard it described seem most critical?

The prime objective of this activity is to provide the author of each questionnaire with new perspectives and ways to deal with his or her training needs in this program. Trainees should keep this in mind as they make comments. The key to successful empathy is to capture how it would feel to be in the author's situation. Trainees should try to avoid judgmental statements ("That's a stupid problem") and know-it-all pre-scriptions. Also, the HRM specialists should try to budget their time so that everyone's questionnaire can be read. (If more than one group is in-volved it may be worthwhile at the conclusion of the group meetings to have the whole training group share some highlights of the group ses-sions.)

Sharing Learning Resources (Discussion of Learning Style Inventory Data). For this discussion training staff and trainees record their LSI scores and learning-style types on a blackboard or flipchart so that the group's scores are visible to everyone. Group members may then want to discuss answers to the questions following the LSI and examine the dis-tribution of learning styles that is represented in the training group.

Forming a Reciprocal Psychological Contract (Analysis of "Gives" and "Gets" by Learning-Style Types). Following the discussion in the preceding paragraph, the training group should divide into four groups representing the four learning-style types—Assimilator, Implementator, Converger, and Diverger. The training staff should join the groups that best fit their own learning styles. Any group too large for discussion should be divided into two separate sections.

The task for each of the groups is to prepare two lists—a give list and a get list. The give list should record what individuals and/or the group as a whole are prepared to contribute to meet the training needs of the program members. These can be arranged in two categories: (1) contributions to program content, such as specific areas of expertise, relevant work experience, books or other training materials, and (2) contributions to the program training process, such as willingness to help manage time constraints. The get list should record what individuals and/or the group as a whole want from the training experiences. This list can also be arranged in two categories: (1) content (specific knowledge, skills, or abilities needed) and (2) process (the kind of training-environment characteristics individuals feel they need to learn most effectively). The two lists should be prepared as large charts so that they can be viewed by the whole training group during the following group reports and discussion. The group should also choose a spokesperson to report the results of the group's work and answer questions about the charts.

Group Reports of Gives and Gets. The two lists should be posted for viewing by the whole training group. Trainees should be allowed about ten minutes to mill about and read the reports of other groups. Group spokespersons should briefly describe their groups' work and answer questions. If time permits, it is sometimes interesting to explore how the various learning-style groups went about their tasks and to examine whether the approaches the different groups used were consistent with Kolb's ELT predictions for the different learning-style types.

Identification of Unmet Needs and Untapped Resources. After the training group has had a chance to discuss and understand the subgroups' reports, the next task is to analyze these data to see if there are unmet training needs (i.e., people who want to get something without corresponding "gives" from others) or untapped resources (i.e., opportunities for training). This activity can take place in a large group discussion, although it is often easier to appoint a task force to complete this analysis after some preliminary discussion in the total training group. The task force can then report its findings at a later time.

Action Planning to Resolve Problems. Depending on how many unmet needs or untapped resources there are, this step may take only five minutes or may involve substantial time and energy to make some design changes in the training program and bring new resources to bear. As in the preceding step, in some cases a task force or temporary committee can serve as a useful vehicle for problem solving and the development of action recommendations.

Evaluating and Directing Learning Progress

The following section is concerned with trainees' responsibilities as learners. This section proposes a method for tracking trainees' training progress through the phases of the learning cycle by means of a training learning diary. The diary is intended as an aid to reflective observation, since the author's experience has suggested that adult learners, particularly in active, responsible positions, tend to be weakest on this particular learning skill.

The Training Learning Diary. At the close of each training day or whenever the trainees find it convenient, they can complete the training learning diary, which has proven to be an effective tool in getting trainees to look back on the activities of a particular training day or program. (You may want to provide several copies of the training learning diary for each trainee to complete at their convenience) What follows is a format for a "learning diary."

Each trainee should complete the following statements which ask the trainees to:

1. Think back briefly over your experiences during the day and describe briefly the most salient of these (Concrete Experience).

2. Articulate and record your most salient observations concerning the experience(s). What observations did you have about your own feelings/reactions to the experience? What observations/feedback did others share with you which seem important (Reflective Observation)?

3. Formulate some generalizations or concepts that seem to explain the above experience(s) and observations, and that can be used back on the job or elsewhere (Abstract Conceptualization).

4. Raise some questions or hypotheses that you feel will be important to test in future experiences. What new questions do the above raise for you? What new behaviors or approaches do you see a need to try in the future to be better able to answer these questions (Active Experimentation)?

The data gathered from the exercises and questionnaires presented in this chapter can be used in several ways by the trainees: (1) as each trainee's own private record, (2) as a starting point for discussion with others, (3) as a tool for forming questions that will help the HRM specialists and trainees decide on future training needs, or (4) as data for review and evaluation of the training program.

SUMMARY

Just as some trainees are heavily dominated by one learning style, or are particularly weak in one style, so some training activities are dominated by explicit or implicit assumptions about learning styles. An activity may be so geared to a particular style of learning as to cause a mismatch with any trainee whose major preferences are different. For example, participants in marketing training programs have generally been identified as having an Implementator learning style, learn primarily from "hands-on" experience, and have a tendency to act on "gut" feelings rather than on logical analysis. Many training programs tend to emphasize rationality, logic, and system-values—which are best suited to the Assimilator learning style—when training those interested in marketing. In addition, training programs most often reflect the training styles of HRM specialists, not the trainees.

Of course just as there are employees whose learning styles are widely varied, so there are training and training activities which contain opportunities to learn in different styles. An example of this would be an employee development training program that involves role plays. A trainee who has an Implementator learning style will enjoy actually playing roles if, as is likely, the person may feel uncomfortable and ineffective when asked to provide a logical analysis of the role play. The concern of the HRM specialist then becomes to establish how learners' styles can be addressed when they are designing training programs so as to develop aspects that are foreign to learners' preferred learning style.

Learning styles can be used to the advantage of all those involved during the development and implementation of a training program. First, learning styles can be used to predict learning difficulties, (for example, to anticipate who will talk most/least, find the program too fast/slow, be keen to observe or to take part). Predictions like these are useful because they open up the possibility of HRM specialists beiing able to handle more appropriately the design of a particular training environment from the start, rather than feeling their way for a period as trainees' behavioral tendencies gradually reveal themselves. Second, learning styles can help in discussing the learning process. Discussing the learning process helps trainees understand what is involved in the learning process, and can assist them in learning from the various opportunities built into the training program.

Third, the learning styles can help people plan and expand their learning. This suggestion is an extension of the last one, because it presupposes that trainees have completed an LSI or GRLSQ and scored and interpreted it. Instead of leaving it at that, however, the idea is now to invite trainees to analyze their responses to the questionnaire in more depth, with a view to producing some personal action plans. Fourth, the learning styles can be used to allocate roles in experiential exercises. Often, within the framework of an exercise in a training program, trainers are able to decide which roles to distribute to which trainees. Role-play exercises are an obvious opportunity to do this, but other exercises may also lend themselves.

Finally, using learning-style results can help in constituting groups or learning teams. Much has been written about methodologies for putting together individuals who can blend their different strengths to form a coherent team. The learning-style information offers another basis for mixing groups in a training situation. Perhaps the most obvious way to use learning styles is as a basis for putting groups or training programs together to ensure that all groups are matched and that the full range of learning styles is available to each group.

Early experiences in a training program can have a great effect on a trainee. Building a training climate that provides a series of psychological-contracting activities intended to facilitate the startup phase of a training program will create the kind of training environment most responsive to the needs of program participants. Such a training environment differs in some respect from the stereotype of traditional training programs. It is based on a psychological contract of reciprocity, is experience-based, emphasizes personal application, is individualized, and finally, integrates learning as an explicit part of the trainees' work life.

The individual and group activities discussed in this chapter are designed to assist the trainer in contracting with members of training programs to build their own version of a training (learning) environment. It is hoped that HRM specialists will see the value of using the approach presented in this chapter as a catalyst for conversations among training staff and participants directed toward building and maintaining a highly effective training environment.

Planning Evaluations of Training Programs: A Systems Analysis Approach

INTRODUCTION

Evaluation is the final formal phase of the training process (see Figure 1.3). As the preceding chapters suggest, evaluation results can be available to those responsible for developing and carrying out training program efforts in an attempt to facilitate improvement. When positive, they also can be used to justify the existence of the training activity to top-level HRM and line managers.

The previous chapters have focused on the design and development of a training system. The purpose of this chapter is limited to identifying precisely what is to be evaluated, who should do the evaluating, and when, why and how the evaluation is to be done. The purpose of evaluation in the training process is to determine whether trainees actually learned new KSAs and attitudes as a result of the training program. In the eyes of the trainee, training ends when trainer and trainee go their separate ways. Upon returning to the job duties, the employee hopes to perform more effectively or, perhaps, be better prepared for promotional opportunities. When direct involvement in the program has ended, as far as the employee is concerned, training is over. But though the instruction has ended, the training process has not yet run its full cycle.

One very important question remains: Was the training effective? This often overlooked question involves the third and final phase of training– evaluation. Over $200 billion a year is spent nationwide on training ac- tivities, and the cost of training to large organizations can run into the millions of dollars (*Training,* 1989). With training costs often consuming a sizable portion of the human resource management budget, any prudent manager should ask: Are we getting our money's worth?

In talking with anyone who is planning to implement a major training program, evaluation is likely to emerge as a major concern, if not a source of anxiety. Despite the hundreds of articles, books, and seminars devoted annually to the topic, evaluation remains largely misunderstood, neglected, or misused. More than one-third of the members of the American Society for Training and Development who responded to a survey reported that evaluation was the most difficult aspect of their jobs (Galagan, 1983).

In another study, Lusterman (1985) found that over two-fifths of the companies taking part reported significant change during the past five years in which they evaluated training effectiveness. Most appeared to be trying to measure behavioral change against predetermined performance goals, and in many companies it has become practice to specify expected results before training activities are undertaken. A tightening economy, increasing competition, and the need to boost productivity—among other factors—have renewed the importance, for HRM specialists, of determining the effectivenesss and value of training, and of demonstrating that training dollars are invested wisely. Evaluation has moved to the forefront as a significant and growing challenge of human resource development in addressing the above objectives.

HRM specialists are often sharply criticized for not doing better jobs of evaluating their programs. In point of fact, however, they probably are no worse than others in this respect, and most of them undoubtedly do about as much as can be expected given the pressures of their jobs and the resources at their disposal. Most seem to feel (apparently correctly) that management would rather see ten training programs that appear to be meeting employee training and development needs than six or eight that have been rigorously evaluated (some, perhaps, with negative results). Further, many know that negative results can be, and often are, used not in the "spirit of inquiry" but in the "spirit of retribution" (Heneman, Schwab, Fossum, and Dyer, 1989).

None of this condones present practices, but it does serve to direct whatever blame is in order to the right place—that is, to HRM specialists and line managers who are content to take training on faith rather than allocate a portion of available resources in a positive way toward eventual improvement. Regardless of the blame, as long as the objectives and benefits of evaluation of training programs are considered, HRM specialists must still attempt to facilitate improvement in training efforts.

THE OBJECTIVES AND BENEFITS OF TRAINING PROGRAM EVALUATION

The primary and overriding objective of training program evaluation is to collect data that will serve as a valid basis for improving the training system and maintaining quality control over its components. It must be emphasized that all components of the system and their interactions are the objects of scrutiny.

The potential benefits that evaluation offers include:

1. Development of training programs that produce the results for which they were intended
2. Greater visibility and influence for the program sponsor and potential sponsors of future programs and whether they should continue sponsoring similar programs
3. Greater credibility for the HRM specialist to include information on how to do a better job now or in their next training assignment or to redesign the program or future programs
4. Greater cost-effectiveness of training and a basis for deciding whether their resources are well spent
5. Stronger commitment to training by participants, so that they can understand the experience more fully, make up for deficiencies, and confirm or disconfirm subjective feelings about the value of the program
6. Better basis for managers to determine whether to send potential recruits to training in future programs
7. Quantifiable data enabling researchers and developers who are concerned with the training process to generalize the effects of a training effort

Planning, Designing, and Conducting an Evaluation

Because of the diversity of training programs and the techniques and methods used in training programs, the wide range of circumstances under which they are used, and the different purposes that evaluations serve, there can be no one best way of evaluating training programs. It is suggested in this chapter, however, that better evaluations can be performed through a systematic identification and organization of important factors that impact the planning and execution of training program evaluation efforts.

An assumption of this approach is that the training program should be designed with thought as to how it will be evaluated. This means that the evaluation should be planned at the same time the training program is being designed, and certainly before the training program is implemented. The advantages of this approach include:

1. Relevant audiences are defined early, so the evaluation can be designed to meet their interests and information needs. This refers to the "who," or audience for the evaluation. (Who will or might be interested in the evaluation? Who will receive a report?) It is important to specify the key players of an evaluation, because their needs may differ.
2. The evaluation complements the training program. Evaluative methods can be incorporated to minimize any disruptive effects on the training program.

3. The evaluation activities can be initiated before the training program begins, enabling more valid premeasures.

4. The material, data, and human resource requirements for the evaluation are delineated and included as part of the resources needed for the overall training program, not simply as an appendix to the training program.

5. The evaluation can be planned around key training program activities to provide timely information. This is crucial when results are used to modify or upgrade subsequent stages in ongoing training programs. This refers to the "what" or the information the audience wants to receive from the evaluation study. The answer will be a main determinant of when and how the evaluation study is conducted.

Designing the Training Evaluation. Two of the major components in a training system should be a plan of training activities and a plan of evaluation activities. Simply put, the training program plan is created by (1) defining the training needs, (2) deciding what has to be evaluated, (3) developing the training program with objectives and criteria clearly laid out to enable evaluation, and (4) developing an evaluation plan based on the training objectives, criteria, and activities of the training program. Figure 11.1 illustrates the process of developing a training program that includes evaluation. The process on the right is the development of the evaluation part of the plan. As in the design of the action plan, the design of the evaluation is a systems analysis approach with antecedents of training objectives, criteria, resources and constraints, and a repertoire of training methods.

The first and most important step in planning an evaluation is to decide on its purpose: what kinds of questions are being asked about the training program, and what is it that we want to know: Each kind of question necessitates consideration of how the evaluation should be designed to provide answers. Three kinds of evaluative purposes, described by Stufflebeam, Foley, Gephart, Guba, Hammond, Merrimam, and Provus (1971), are relevant to training program evaluation: First, evaluation can be used to identify differences in behavior—a group or individual may be compared to other individuals or groups, to an ideal or standard (as in performance appraisal), or with itself at different moments in time (a time-series study). This is *comparative* evaluation. Evaluation can also be used to investigate causes of behavior, to relate programs to outcomes by controlling for changes in other variables. This is *explanatory* evaluation. Finally, in *predictive* analysis, evaluation information from training programs is used to predict other, later outcomes (e.g., changes in on-the-job behavior or system performance).

The objectives and criteria used in a training evaluation will depend on its purposes. Whatever the purposes of the evaluation, five general categories may be used:

Figure 11.1
Designing a Training Program Evaluation

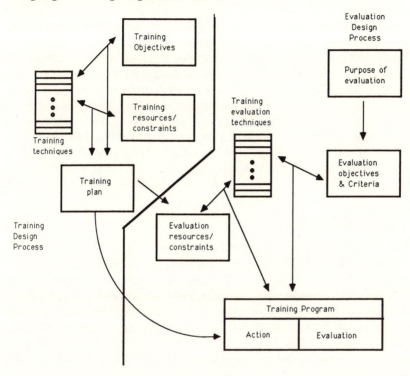

Adapted from "A Systems Analysis Approach for Planning Evaluation
of OD Interventions" by John M. Nicholas © 1977, pp. 358-362
Academy of Management Proceedings.: With permission of the
Academy of Management.

1. Evaluation of training *effort* assesses input, regardless of output. The questions "What did you do?" and "How well did you do it?" are addressed.

2. Evaluation of *performance* focuses on the results of the program. This requires clear statements of objectives; it asks "Did any change occur?" and "Were objectives achieved?"

3. Evaluation of *adequacy* determines how effective the program was. For example, participants in a training program may exhibit considerable back-on-the-job behavioral change, but the number of participants may be inadequate to alter conditions in the organization.

4. Evaluation of *efficiency* is concerned with alternate ways of achieving the same ends that are more efficient in terms of time, money, human resources, materials, and convenience.

5. Evaluation of *process* focuses on the operation of a training program, with emphasis on how and why it works or does not work.

A single evaluation may have several purposes and employ several kinds of evaluative criteria. As mentioned earlier, purposes and criteria depend on whom the evaluation results are intended to serve. Thus, an additional early step in evaluation planning is determining who the audiences of the evaluation are. Most often the source of evaluation will be a source of information for a variety of organizational members (supervisors, managers, CEOs, HRM specialists, trainees, and trainers). Determination of the audiences of the evaluation can improve the likelihood of not falling into one of the many pitfalls that can affect the potential success of a program evaluation. The next section presents some other potential evaluation pitfalls.

Pitfalls in Training Evaluation

Too often, training program evaluations have failed. Mainly these failures can be attributed to inadequate planning or designing, lack of objectivity, evaluation errors of one sort or another, improper interpretation of results, and inappropriate use of results. Poor systems of training program evaluation produce anxiety, resentment, budget reductions, and efforts to sabotage the program. But what is of even greater importance, poor training evaluation programs do not provide firm data for improving and controlling the quality of the training system. What follows are some of the most common pitfalls in training program evaluation.

Poor Planning. To be effective, a training program evaluation must be carefully planned. Some of the common deficiencies in planning are these:

1. Failure to work out the details of the program, failure to include data-collection instruments, specific procedures to be followed, and the scheduling of surveys, interviews and observations
2. Failure to train evaluators in the principles and techniques of evaluation, which includes the use of data-gathering instruments
3. Failure to make clear to all concerned the purposes of the evaluation program and the uses to be made of evaluations and recommendations

Lack of Objectivity. Although it is impossible to guarantee that training program evaluations will be completely objective, there are some steps that can be taken to make certain they will be more objective.

1. Select evaluators who are capable of making objective judgments
2. Train evaluators
3. Design appropriate data-gathering instruments

4. Look at all the components of the training situation as an integrated system

5. Focus on important details—avoid nitpicking

Rater Errors. When scales are used to evaluate quality of performance or materials, observers often differ in their ratings. These differences are rater errors, although this may not be the most accurate term to use for all these disparities. Some errors are caused by faults in the design of rating instruments; others, by the raters. Some errors occur only with certain groups of observers, and some occur only with individual observers. Other errors occur only when certain behaviors of individuals are rated. Some observers make errors when rating all persons, some when rating certain groups, and others when rating certain individuals. Some of the more typical rating-error categories are: central tendency, halo effect, and recency.

Improper Interpretation of Data. The collection of data on the training program is one thing; interpreting that data is quite another. Here, the meaning and impact of the data are judged. If this step is not handled properly, the value of the information collected will be completely lost. Here are some of the main pitfalls in interpretation of data from training programs:

1. Assuming that consensus among one category of data on a single training system element guarantees a valid and accurate judgment

2. Concluding that an observation or judgment made by only one observer or group of trainees for example, is inaccurate or invalid

3. Taking comments or responses to open-ended questions at face value, and not considering the nuances of language and the problems of semantics

4. Failing to take into consideration the perspective of the individuals providing the data

Inappropriate Use of Evaluation Results. When tabulated, data collected during the training program evaluation have the aura of complete objectivity and truth. Sometimes the results of evaluation are used for purposes other than that originally intended. This is a major error. Some of the inappropriate uses to which evaluative data have been put are:

1. Using data and reports on a single part of a training program to make decisions on the whole program

2. Using data and reports designed for evaluating the whole training program as a basis for denying or granting funding for future training programs

3. Using otherwise unsupported and unvalidated data as a basis for causing significant changes to a training program or system to be made

HRM specialists should be aware of the pitfalls that may befall the evaluation of a training program and the ability to measure the training's effectiveness as presented in the next section.

Four Levels to Measure Training Effectiveness

The way in which training is to be evaluated is best considered before the training begins in order to allow design flexibility in evaluating a training program's success. This is a point that cannot be overemphasized. One popular evaluation strategy includes four different levels of evaluation. In fact, it comprises four separate evaluation strategies. The matrix presented in Figure 11.2 illustrates the four bases for evaluating training. The designers of this system advocate applying each level of evaluation to a program (Kilpatrick, 1983; Newstrom, 1978). The system suggests measuring the participants' reaction, participants' learning, change in participants' behavior, and impact of the program on organizational effectiveness. Newstrom (1978) has demonstrated that different conclusions would be reached evaluating the same programs using only one of the four evaluation techniques: therefore a complete evaluation must use multiple criteria. Responses to the following questions for each level should be answered in developing an evaluation:

1. *Reaction*. How well did the trainees like the training? Are the trainees happy? Did the trainees respond favorably to the program?
2. *Learning*. To what extent did the trainees learn the facts, principles, and approaches that were included in the training? Do the materials used in the training session teach the concepts or skills specified?
3. *Behavior*. Are the concepts applied on the job? To what extent did trainees' on-the-job behavior change because of the program?
4. *Results*. Does the application of the concepts positively affect the organization? What final results (personal or organizational) were achieved (reduction in cost, reduction in turnover, improvement in production, etc.)?

Reaction. Reaction-level evaluation can be measured by conducting interviews or by administering questionnaires to trainees. However, the immediate reaction may measure how the people like the training, rather than how it benefited them.

Learning. Learning-level evaluation measures how well trainees have learned facts, ideas, concepts, theories, attitudes, and ability to use skills. Tests on the training material are commonly used for evaluating learning and can be given both before and after training to compare scores.

Figure 11.2
Evaluation Matrix

What We What to Know	What Might Be Measured	Measurement Dimensions	What to Look At (sources of data)	Alternative Data Gathering Method

1. Are the trainees
happy? If not, why?
 	
a. Concepts not
   relevant
b. Workshop design
c. Trainees not prop-
   erly positioned
	Trainee reaction
	during workshop
		Relevance
		Threat
		Ease of Learning
			Comments between trainees
			Comments to instructor
			Questions about exercises
			"Approach behavior" to
			   exercises
				Observation
				Interview
				Questionnaire

	Trainee reaction
	after workshop
		Perceived "worth"
		V-Relevance; or
		C-Learning energy
			"Approach behavior" to
			   project
			Questions about project
			   concepts
				Observation
				Interview
				Questionnaire

2. Do the materials teach the concepts? If not, why not?	Trainee performance during workshop	Understanding Application	Learning time Performance on exercises Presentations	Observation Document review

a. Workshop structure
b. Lessons
   -Presentation
   -Examples
   -Exercises
	Trainee performance
	at end of workshop
		Understanding
		Application
		Facility
		Articulation
			Action plan for project
			Use of tools on exercises
			Presentations
				Observation
				Document review
				Interview
				Questionnaire

3. Are the concepts used?
If not, why not
 	
a. Concepts
   -Not relevant
   -Too complex
   -Too sophisticated
b. Inadequate tools
c. Environment not
   supportive
	Performance improve-
	ment projects
		Analysis
		Action plan
		Results
			Discussions
			Documentation
			Results
				Observation
				Interview
				Document review
				Questionnaire
				(critical incident)

	Problem solving technique	Questions asked Action proposed Action taken	Discussions Documentation Results	Observation Interview Document review Questionnaire (critical incident)
	Ongoing management approach	Dissemination effort Language People management process	Discussions Meetings Documentation	Observation Interview Document review Questionnaire (critical incident)
4. Does application of concepts positively affect the organi- zation? If not, why not?	Problem solving	Problem identi- fication Analysis Action Results	Discussions Documentation Results	Interview Document review Questionnaire (critical incident)
	Problem prediction and prevention	Potential problem identification Analysis Action	Discussions Documentation Results	Interview Document review Questionnaire (critical incident)
	Performance measures Specific to a parti- cular workshop	Output measures Interim or diagnostic measures	Performance data	Document review

Behavior. Evaluating training at the behavior level attempts to measure the effect of training on job performance. This level is more difficult to measure than the previous ones. Interviews of trainees and their coworkers, observation of before-and-after job performance, and time-series analysis are ways of evaluating training at the behavior level.

Results. The results-level evaluation of training measures the effect of training on the achievement of organizational objectives. Because results such as productivity, turnover, quality, time, sales, and costs are more concrete, this type of cost-benefit evaluation can be done by comparing records before and after training (Kilpatrick, 1983). These evaluations typically involve determining the financial return, or cost effectiveness, of the training program.

From a managerial perspective, an important component of results-level evaluation involves whether the costs of training are offset by the training benefits. The difficulty with this measurement is pinpointing whether it was the training that caused any change outcomes. Other factors may have had a major impact as well. Correlation does not confirm causation. For example, Nandi Cele, a supervisor for an automobile manufacturer, has completed a supervisory training program. By comparing turnover in Nandi's department before and after training, some measure of results can be obtained. However, turnover is also dependent on the current economic situation, the demand for automobiles, and the quality of employees being hired. Therefore, when using results evaluation, Nandi's manager should be aware of all the issues involved in determining the exact effect of her training. Although cost-benefit information is unquestionably valuable to any organization sponsoring training, it is important to note that both cost and benefit sides of the ratio often are very difficult to compute with accuracy and, if not done carefully, may yield misleading results. Cost-benefit evaluation will be discussed in more detail later in this chapter.

Resources and Constraints

Resources are those items available to the HRM specialists for the development of a training evaluation plan and for subsequent implementation. Constraints are limitations on what can be included in the evaluation plan or implementation. Both are considerations in selecting among various methodologies and procedures to make up the evaluation plan. For example, a constraint existing for most evaluations is the amount of time available to collect and analyze data, and to report results. This influences not only procedures of data collection and analysis, but also the kind of data collected. Standardized questionnaires may be used if there is insufficient time to develop and test tailored ones. This further constrains the trainer to measuring what the instrument purports to measure. Some of the resources/constraints to training program evaluation that must be considered include:

1. *Funds*—dollars allowed to cover training evaluation planning and implementation
2. *Time*—limits imposed in developing and executing the evaluation; these may be thought of as a sequence of "milestones," such as completion of pretest and posttest data collection (for example, testing knowledge or skill, usually by paper-and-pencil), completion of data analysis, dissemination of results to appropriate audiences, etc.

3. *Human resources*—trained personnel (may include statisticians, computer specialists, research methodologists, other HRM specialists and trainers)

4. *Organizational climate*—the trust and openness of managers, employees, or trainees in general in providing and receiving evaluative feedback information

5. *Availability of data*—availability and quality of organizational information such as records of individual, group, department and organization performance, reports, personnel records; availability of employees for providing new data through surveys, interviews and observation

6. *Details of the training evaluation action plan*—objectives, timetable, procedures, participants, location; possible use of strategies that overlap evaluation strategies, such as survey feedback

7. *Audiences*—kind and number of key players of the evaluation, and their information needs and interests

8. *Technical ability and feasibility*—availability and feasibility of using standardized instruments, computerized analysis and storage of data; logistics in collecting and disseminating results; competencies and abilities of persons involved

9. *Ethical concerns*—privacy considerations, employee and organizational confidentiality, obtrusiveness, or harmful aspects of data collection and reporting

To a large extent, these factors are interdependent, and the training program planning analysis requires careful consideration of each and all of them.

Training Evaluation Technique Options

There are many ways to evaluate what the effect of training has been. The optional training evaluation techniques include all possible methods available to the HRM specialist for conducting training program evaluations. Some of these techniques include:

1. Experimental and quasi-experimental designs
2. Methods of data collection, including observation, questionnaires, interviews, organizational records
3. Criteria for evaluating training programs
4. Instrumentation
5. Methods of data aggregation, storage, and quality control
6. Methods of executing and maintaining the integrity of the training program evaluation design
7. Methods of analyzing and interpreting data
8. Methods of preparing and reporting results

Each of the elements of the options contains several alternatives from which particular ones are selected. For example, among the alternative

kinds of experimental and quasi-experimental designs there are considerations of randomization of subjects, comparison of groups, timing of observations, and experimental validity. Although the evaluation of a training
program takes place after the training has been completed (posttest), it is
essential that some measure of the KSAs and attitudes of the trainees be
determined prior to the program (pretest). Evaluation designs that do not
allow for pre- and posttraining comparisons of the appropriate attributes
do not provide sufficient information to evaluate trainees' progress in the
program. Even when a determination of trainee progress can be made, it
remains to determine whether the training, or some other events that took
place at the same time as the training, caused the measured progress. These
two issues (amount of change and source of change) require that an organization consider the evaluation process and options in depth, at a point
prior to the actual training programs. Figure 11.3 provides some examples
of training evaluation designs. The Xs represent the training program, the
Os represent the observations of some trainee reactions (knowledge acquisition or retention), and the subscripts represent sequential time periods.

The first design (Design One) represents a training program in which
no observations are taken prior to the training program. Although the
relevant trainee attributes (KSAs) are measured after the training program,
it is impossible to determine whether any improvement has been made.
No comparison of the level of trainee attributes before training (pretraining) is known. The only situation in which this type of design may provide
useful information on the changes that took place during the training program is when the trainees had no relevant knowledge or skill at the start
of the training. (Pretraining level of the attribute is zero). This is a very
weak design and, unfortunately, one that is used often—as a result of
convenience, ignorance, a deliberate attempt to hide the ineffectiveness
of a training program, or some combination of the three.

The second design (Design Two) allows for the critical pre- and posttraining comparison. This design can provide information on the degree
of improvement (or change) but not the source of that improvement. Thus,
the training program may receive credit for causing changes that are due
to other events. Nevertheless, this design represents an improvement over
Design One, and can be used with slightly more confidence. It is especially
effective when the organization can logically eliminate any alternative
sources for the changes that took place during training. To the extent that
such alternative sources cannot be eliminated, and there is reason to believe
that they may have influenced the changes seen, this design is inadequate.

The third design (Design Three) attempts to deal directly with both of
the evaluation issues of concern to an organization. In this design the
organization divides the trainees into two groups, with one group receiving
the pretest, the training, and the posttest, and the other group receiving

Figure 11.3
Research Designs

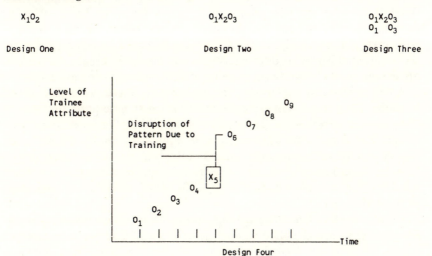

X_1O_2 $O_1X_2O_3$ $O_1X_2O_3$
                                                                                      $O_1 \quad O_3$

Design One   Design Two   Design Three

Design Four

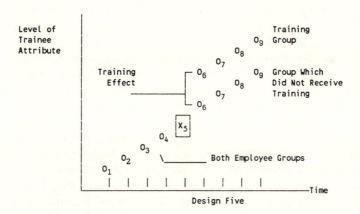

Design Five

the pretest and the posttest only. The logic is that the changes in the group receiving the training should be significantly greater than the changes in the group that received no training. Assuming that the two groups are equivalent and that the administration of the pre- and posttests, when coupled with the training, does not somehow create an impact separate from the training itself, this design will meet the needs of most organizations. Sometimes there are problems generating two equivalent groups of employees. For example, an organization may compose the two groups from different shifts, or physical locations. This will minimize the contact between the employees who receive the training and those who do not (contact between the two groups might allow for an exchange of information regarding the training and compromise the effectiveness of comparisons). Unfortunately, many differences can exist between employees on different shifts or in different locations. Those differences may show up as measured change when training effectiveness is being evaluated.

A design that can effectively cope with most of these problems, as well as additional problems not presented in this discussion, requires four groups of equivalent employees. The design is called the Solomon four-group design. Because it requires four groups of equivalent employees, it is often impractical for an organization to use. For this reason, the two-group design (Design Three) may be the most practical design (see Campbell and Stanley, 1963, for a complete discussion of issues surrounding the use and misuse of these designs).

There is another type of design that may be useful for evaluating training. These designs are classified as *time-series* designs. They require multiple observations of the status of trainee attributes over time. Many of these observations are taken prior to training (baseline data), with the remaining observations taken after the training has taken place.

The first of these to be discussed (Design Four) uses only one group of employees. This design is referred to as an *interrupted time-series design*. The pretraining observations establish a pattern or baseline for these attributes. The posttraining observations can provide information on whether a pattern has been disrupted by the training. A disruption of this pattern may be considered evidence of a training-program effect. Note this design is similar to Design Two, in that observations are made immediately before training (O^4), and immediately after training (O^6). The difference is that with the baseline data to refer to, it is less likely that an observed upward or downward trend in the data would be interpreted as a significant training effect. Design Four can be expanded to include two groups of employees, thereby significantly increasing the power of the design (Design Five). This type of design is referred to as a *multiple time-series design*.

A final note on statistical analysis should be added. Simple differences in observed employee attribute levels should not be interpreted as meaningful differences. Statistical analyses should be performed on the data. Analyses for Designs Two and Three (Design One cannot be analyzed) are rather straightforward, and guidance may be found in many elementary statistics textbooks. However, statistical analyses for time-series designs can become very complex and are best left to professional statisticians and others trained in data analysis. Further, statistical significance does not necessarily mean that the differences found are sufficiently large to justify continued existence of the training program.

The final success of the training program evaluation, in terms of how well it meets an intended purpose, depends on how well the HRM specialists can overcome problems through a well-thought-out design and implementation scheme. The training program evaluation plan should be developed through selection of alternatives by assessing each against the objectives of the evaluation and within the constraints and existing resources. A familiarity with available resources, imposed constraints, and methodological alternatives is thus a requirement for developing accurate, useful, and practical training program evaluations.

The Training Program Plan: Action and Evaluation

Evaluation can take place at any of the four levels (reaction, learning, behavior, and results) suggested by Kilpatrick (1983) or at any of the levels of training program planning, designing, and implementation: micro training design (MTD), training session (TS), and training program (TP). At the MTD level, training evaluation focuses on the process and products of the exercises, activities, and training methods. For most training programs, not every MTD (perhaps none) will be rigorously evaluated. Simple observation may be all that is needed to indicate achievement of objectives at this level or a need to modify MTD procedures.

At the training session (TS) level, evaluation focuses on the process and outcomes of individual training components. This can be achieved through aggregation of evaluative data from the MTD level, or separately at the TS level, such as taking measures before and after a TS to analyze individual effects.

And at the training program (TP) level, evaluation focuses on the process and outcomes of the total training program. Evaluation can be performed by aggregating data from evaluations performed at lower levels, or, for example, by taking observations prior to and following the program. Typically, evaluation at the TP level has a purpose of measuring program effects on the total organization or system, and evaluative measurement continues for months or years after the program has ended, to determine these effects. At this level, where evidence of outcomes or results is more mediated and distal than at lower levels, the training evaluation is more difficult to carry out and is usually more complex in design.

The major components of the final training program plan are schematically represented in Figure 11.4, which is intended as a guide to be kept in mind—a mental checklist of the various components of the plan and how they relate to one another. The training program objectives, criteria, procedures, and activities (methods) are represented by columns 1 and 2. When evaluation is desired, the objectives and criteria must be specified as represented by column 3. Corresponding to these objectives are the evaluation techniques and procedures as indicated by column 4. This includes the methodology and scheduling for collection of data, analysis,

Figure 11.4
Training Plan and Evaluation

Level	Training Plan		Training Evaluation Plan	
	1 Objectives	2 Procedures	3a Objectives	4b Procedures
Program		c		
1		d		
2		d		
Training Session :		:		
M		d		
1.1		e		
:		:		
1.		e		
Micro-Training : design		:		
M.1		e		
:		:		
M.Q		e		

a.   Evaluation objectives and criteria are specified only for those levels, sessions, and micro-designs where evaluation is to be done.
b.   Evaluation procedures are specified only for those levels, training sessions, and micro-training designs where evaluation is to be done.
c.   At the training program level, procedures roughly outline what is to take place at the session level: number of sessions, timetable, etc.
d.   At the training session level, procedures roughly outline what is to take place during each session: kinds of micro-training designs, participants, etc.
e.   At the micro-training design level, procedures define in detail step-by-step procedures, activities and timing for each.

Adapted from "A systems analysis approach for planning evaluations of OD Informations" by John M. Nicholas, 1977, pg. 358-362, Academy of Management Proceedings, 1977: With permission from Academy of Management.

and reporting. Also included should be the expected outcomes in terms of the objectives and criteria in columns 1 and 3. Specifying what is expected to occur is useful and important for two reasons.

First, it forces the HRM specialists to reconsider if the intended outcomes can reasonably be expected from what they plan to do, or if perhaps some aspects of the training program should be redesigned; second, it forces them to reconsider if the evaluation as planned will tell them whether these results have been achieved, and then whether they will be able to believe the results.

The final training program evaluation plan should enable the HRM specialist to visualize the total training program process and to anticipate further problems or design considerations. Thinking about expected outcomes forces the HRM specialist to check all previous steps and to determine if desired results can reasonably be expected and measured.

Guidelines for Planning, Designing, and Conducting a Training Program Evaluation

HRM specialists can enhance the potential success of their training program evaluations by using a systems analysis approach to planning the evaluations. In addition, taking into consideration other helpful guidelines will prove very beneficial in planning, designing, and conducting evaluations. First, the training program evaluation plan should be kept as simple as possible while still meeting the specified objectives. Often there is a tendency to overevaluate—to address too many questions in one study. If the goals of the evaluation prove too ambitious, conducting the study may overburden available resources and become counterproductive. Alternatively, the evaluation may promise its audience too much, leaving them disappointed with the value of results.

Although the training evaluation plan should be simple, it also should maintain a broad focus. These two principles appear incompatible, but really are not. By keeping a broad focus, the evaluator should not limit himself or herself to considering only one source of evidence of a program's effectiveness, such as end-of-program evaluation sheets, supervisor ratings, anecdotes, or cost-benefit estimates. Not only do programs produce a variety of effects, changed attitudes, improved skills, new ideas, better productivity, and so on, but their effects can be measured in a variety of ways. By keeping an open mind toward collecting data, being creative, and "triangulating" with several sources of information where possible, the evaluator can gain a better understanding of what effects the program has produced (Brinkerhoff, 1981).

Finally, the training evaluation plan should be tested with the audience before the evaluation is conducted. In this way, the evaluator can determine in advance if the evaluation matches and responds to the audience's needs, and then begin to build value for the results. In particular, the credibility—and thus the usefulness—of the potential results should be determined. That is, will the audience believe the findings? Will they find them useful in making decisions? Even a training program evaluation study that is conducted rigorously and yields scientifically valid results is unlikely to prove useful if it is not understood, considered believable, and responsive to the needs of its audience (Foulkes, 1989).

Guidelines for Training Program Evaluation Implementation. HRM specialists should also pay particular attention to the methods used to collect, analyze, and use the training program evaluation data. Guides to collecting, analyzing, and using training program evaluation data can be of immense help to HRM specialists.

Data collection involves gathering information on specific training program features. Careful attention to collecting data helps to promote the three goals of data collection. The first and most immediate objective is to obtain valid information about the training program. Data collection can also rally energy for constructive training program change. Finally, data collection helps develop the collaborative relationship necessary between HRM specialists and trainees for effecting training program improvements and changes. The following procedures developed by Tracey* should serve as guides in collecting data:

1. The most effective technique should be selected to collect required information. Great skill is necessary if the data collected are to be pertinent, objective, and error-free

2. Develop a plan for collecting data; this plan should indicate the technique(s) to be used

3. Determine the type of data to be collected: nonquantitative or quantitative

4. Identify the aspects of the training system where data will be collected

5. Establish a schedule for collecting data with dates, times, and individuals affected

6. Make certain that the rationale for collecting data is made clear to all participants

7. Edit the completed data collection forms and scales

8. Establish summarizing categories for both closed and open-ended responses

9. Determine the mathematical treatment to be applied to each summarizing category; for example, mean, median, mode, percentage, range, rank order, percentile, or standard deviation

10. Make a preliminary list of responses under each summarizing category for the open-response type of item to determine the nature and range of responses

11. Establish a final list of responses for each summarizing category (1971, 1984)

After collecting data on the training program, it is necessary to analyze the information and put it into a form from which HRM specialists can draw conclusions and devise appropriate responses. Specific analytical tools help organize the data so that observed patterns in the data are lawful and not simply caused by chance. The techniques for analyzing data vary from relatively simple methods for assessing qualitative information to highly sophisticated tools for statistically analyzing quantitative data. The following procedures should serve as guides to analyzing data:

1. Study each response on all returns (item 1 on all forms, then item 2, item 3, and so forth), and tabulate them in the proper category by placing a tally beside them

2. Sum the tally marks in each category for each item and/or apply the mathematical function required

3. Prepare a summary report of significant items

4. Analyze the summaries for each item in turn, and write a brief statement of their meaning and possible significance

5. Compare the statements derived from the previous step with the findings of other evaluative instruments dealing with the same category to determine areas of agreement and disagreement; consider the nuances of language, the problem of semantics, and the perspectives of the respondents

6. Draw your conclusions, and state them in simple and concise language

7. Draft your recommendations (Tracey, 1971, 1984)

The most critical step in gathering evaluation data on a training program is using the data. Properly analyzed and meaningful data can have an impact on the training effort if relevant HRM specialists and managers use the information to devise appropriate action plans. The success of using the data depends largely on its ability to arouse action and to direct energy toward issues, concerns, and problems with a training program. The following procedures should serve as guides to using information results gathered from training program evaluations:

1. Submit recommendations to key training program players, HRM specialists, trainees, managers

2. Meet with key players to discuss the findings and recommendations

3. Establish a priority listing of recommendations or changes

4. Determine the resources required to improve the training effort and potential constraints

5. Establish who will take responsibility for incorporating knowledge gained from the training program evaluation to current or future training programs

6. Establish a procedure for follow-up and re-evaluation of the training system (Tracey, 1971, 1984)

An important use of evaluation results is to reinforce the effects of training. As Humphrey stated: "The issue is not evaluation—Did the training work?—but reinforcement—Make it work! (Humphrey, 1985, p. 5). The results of evaluation should be used to not only report the data, but should educate the audience on how and why the study was conducted, what valid conclusions can be drawn from the results, and how the results can be used. In addition to these guidelines, training program evaluators will do well to make use of Hawthorne's (1987a) "decision points" in planning an evaluation:

1a. Should the evaluation be prospective or retrospective?

b. What time period should be included in the assessment of the program?

2. Should the evaluation be a formative or a summative evaluation?

3. Would single or multiple evaluation criteria be preferred?

4. Should resource costs be included?

5a. If this is a multiple-criteria evaluation, is it better to aggregate the criteria or to present the findings criterion by criterion?

b. If data will be aggregated, which common scale should be used?

c. Should weighting be included in the evaluation?

6a. Should attention be paid to the concerns of different groups with an interest/ investment in the program?

b. Is it desirable to factor into the evaluation the impact of the program on different groups of affected individuals?

7a. What sources should be used to find evaluation criteria?

b. What selection process should be used to determine which evaluation criteria will be included in the study?

8. How will the evaluator demonstrate causality?

9. Will the evaluation findings be applied to future versions of the program?

Once all of the above guidelines have been addressed and the questions answered, the training program evaluator(s) will have clear parameters within which to plan, design, and conduct a training program evaluation. While these guidelines and questions are helpful in the training evaluation process, the HRM specialist or trainer must still determine which one or more of the many evaluation techniques they will ultimately use. The next section discusses two of the many techniques available to evaluate training programs: training audit and cost-benefit analysis.

Selected Training Program Evaluation Techniques

Training Audit (TA). The concept of the TA as a vehicle for evaluating training programs has recently been introduced by several authors (Buckley and Caple, 1984; Bramley and Hullah, 1987). A TA is usually for senior management when they are seeking to review the activities (training program) of the training and development department. There are two major aspects to auditing training: (1) auditing the training system in order to discover how professional it is and to what extent it contributes to the well-being of the organization, and (2) auditing a specific training event to discover how well run it is and also how well it fits into the organizational context.

Auditing a training activity has four stages: familiarization, examining the pre-activity preparation, auditing the training program itself, and examining the postprogram learner support.

Stage One: Familiarization

The intent in the familiarization stage is to take a thorough look at what the training program is supposed to be doing, where it has come from, and why it is there. It is also necessary to discover if there is any evidence that the training program is actually of value to the organization. Some of the key questions that need to be asked are listed below.

Aims, intentions and objectives:

1. What changes are expected to result from this program in terms of individual performance levels? Organizational effectiveness?

2. How do these changes relate to overall corporate objectives?

3. Whose objectives are controlling the program? The organization (i.e., training committee/department, human resource manager, etc.)? The trainees (i.e., for fine tuning of course objectives)? HRM specialists?

Needs analysis

1. How was the needs analysis done? When? By whom? By what methods?

2. How wide was the consultation on needs?

3. Where is the emphasis on needs? Individual? Organizational? Remedial/Developmental?

Target population/Demand

1. How are people selected for this training? Line manager/appraisal system? Self-nomination? Human resource management department?

2. On which basis is the selection made?

3. To what extent are trainees ready for the program and the standards implicit in the training objectives?

4. What, if any, procedures are used to integrate nominations with the overall human resource planning system?

Evaluation

1. Is a report on the training program available?

2. Has a previous audit been undertaken? What were the recommendations?

3. What evaluative and implementation feedback data about this program does the training department have?

4. What is the cost of the program?

5. What evidence is there of benefits?

According to Bramley and Hullah (1987) this stage could sometimes be the complete audit. If the activity is not linked to organizational requirements and does not appear to be meeting a need, the audit could be stopped at the end of this stage.

An important aspect of the familiarization stage is that it ought to be possible to find some links between the training program or activity and the organization's objectives. To take a simple case:

—sales trainers will have objectives of trying to impart new product knowledge and the techniques for using it in selling

—sales personnel attending the training will have objectives of learning something that will help them to get orders for the new products

—sales managers will have objectives of reaching targets and obtaining new sales; and

—the organization will have the intention of obtaining sales volume that matches the potential product volume and that will maintain or increase their share of the market

Collecting information about this chain of intentions can only be done by visiting and listening to supervisors and managers along the chain, in the areas where they work. This is standard procedure for external trainer consultants, but it is often neglected by internal HRM specialists.

Stage Two: Preprogram Preparation

It is important to determine the extent to which individuals attending a training program know why they are attending. If they are not aware of their reasons for attending, then the first part of the training program is an uphill battle to establish objectives for these individuals that will commit them to learning something and thus underpin motivation.

The training policy document should lay down the clear responsibilities and roles for supervisors and managers as well as HRM specialists. If the "right" people are not being selected, and if the purpose of their attending training is not clarified, there is little likelihood of the training resulting in improved performance. The questions that might be asked in this part of the training program audit are:

1. What form does the preprogram briefing take? Who does the briefing? Are learning objectives clarified and agreed on? What is the extent of trainer involvement?

2. How are the training objectives communicated? Do the supervisors and line managers understand them?

3. What is the individual expected to do differently at the end of the program?

4. How long before the program did the briefing take place?

5. Was any preprogram preparation necessary? Activity? Reading? Other?

6. Was it carried out?

Stage Three: Auditing the Training Program

A good place to start the examination of the training program in a training audit is by looking at which objectives are actually controlling the learning. During the familiarization phase of the training audit, the auditor will have discovered what the objectives are; the emphasis now changes to the way in which they are being used.

The questions that might be asked at this point in the training audit are:

Training program objectives

1. *Have the training staff openly discussed and agreed on the objectives?*

2. *Are the objectives clear and unambiguous?*

3. *Does the achievement of the objectives mean complete achievement of the training need, or is some on-the-job training required?*

4. *To what extent are HRM specialists familiar with the trainees' own learning objectives? When did they find these out?*

Training program structure

1. On what principles is the training program structured?

2. Is there a satisfactory balance between practice reflection and theory input?

3. How satisfactory are the duration of the training program and the length of the working day?

4. Does the balance of the training program reflect the different degrees of importance attached to the objectives?

Training methods and media

1. On what basis have the training methods been chosen?

2. Are optimal training methods being used, given the characteristics of the learners?

3. Do training methods and media provide variety and encourage learning?

4. What is the quality and readability of handouts and other training aids?

Evaluation/Feedback

1. What form of assessment of progress is being used during the training program?

2. Is each assessment method reliable and timely?

3. Where practical or written tests are being used: Are the test items appropriate? Are there sufficient test items? Have the tests been piloted? How reliable is the marking guide?

4. How is feedback given to the trainees?

5. How is feedback used by the trainers? Is there sufficient flexibility to allow remedial work, etc.?

6. Are summarizing and consolidating sessions built into the training program?

7. Are training program evaluation reports written? To whom are they sent? Is any action taken as a result of these reports?

Stage Four: Posttraining Program Learner Support

The learning model that underlies most training is:

1. Individual wants to improve
2. Learning through training
3. Changes in individuals' KSAs, and attitudes
4. Changes in individuals' work performance
5. Changes in organizational effectiveness

The focus is on the individual and the process is one of encouraging him or her to learn something said to be useful and then expecting the trainee to find uses for the learning. The transfer of learning needs to be supported by an action plan, a suitable organizational climate, and usually a sympathetic line manager. The training auditor should investigate the extent to which posttraining program learner support is given. The kinds of questions that should be asked during the investigation of the posttraining program learner support are:

Posttraining program debriefing

1. What form does the posttraining program briefing take?
2. Who does it?
3. Are action plans reviewed, priorities set?

Constraints

1. What constraints, if any, have been placed on the employees' ability to put into effect what they have learned?
2. What level of support is being given to the achievement of action plans?

Performance levels

1. Is there a gap between the levels achieved on the training program and competent job performance?
2. Is support available to close this gap?

Evaluation

1. What changes have been achieved in terms of different individual performance levels? Increased levels of organizational effectiveness?
2. What criteria of effectiveness are being used?
3. Who is responsible for assessing changes?

4. How do the changes achieved relate to those planned (and discovered by the auditor during the familiarization stage)?
5. What objectives have been achieved in terms of: Organizational objectives? Individual learning objectives? Additional HRM specialists' objectives?

In conclusion, the TA must concern itself, first, with the fit between training program activities being offered and aspects of organizational effectiveness. This can only be done in discussions with line managers and supervisors. Similarly, when examining a particular component of the training program, the first focus is the link with organizational needs. If this cannot be established, then examining the quality of the process itself seems not to be indicated (Bramley and Hullah, 1987). The TA should not be seen as merely an assessment, but rather as an opportunity to improve the effectiveness of the training function. It is recommended that the training audit should pay particular attention to the examination of these three aspects:

1. The pretraining program preparation must be carried out in order to produce participants who are attending the right program for the right reasons.
2. The training program must be designed as a continuous set of activities structured to complement each other in facilitating learning.
3. Posttraining program learning support for the learners is necessary to extend the training period and allow time for new methods of working to become established.

A cost-benefit analysis approach can also be employed in evaluating a training program. The next section will highlight the use of cost-benefit analysis in the evaluation of training programs.

Cost-Benefit Analysis. The ultimate evaluation questions on training programs evolve around utility. More specifically: is the gain to the organization in increased performance greater than the cost of the training to justify the investment? Answering this question requires that dollar values be placed on various levels of performance and that various training costs be computed. Because of its focus on utility, cost-benefit analysis (CBA) is a natural choice of evaluation methodology for HRM specialists who are consistently confronted with a "bottom-line" approach to making decisions about training programs. CBA presents information on economic efficiency.

The most common application of CBA is to decide which of a set of alternative projects is economically feasible and which of those is most satisfactory should only one be affordable (Mishan, 1976; Hawthorne, 1987a). Thus a preview of a project or training program can be afforded by CBA. In addition, one can employ CBA methodology in retrospective analyses that examine which completed project or training program was most successful in terms of cost-benefit criteria. Retrospective cost-benefit analysis is more straightforward to accomplish than prospective analysis because it depends on data generated in the training program in places where prospective analysis relies on economic theory, projections, and assumptions. Retrospective CBA, however, may also use economic theory and similar assumptions (see Hawthorne, 1987a, for an excellent discussion of retrospective and prospective cost-benefit analysis).

Costs. Chapter 1 suggested that training has become big business. For individual human resource managers, even more compelling evidence of training costs comes from the budget allocated to training programs. Training costs are fairly easy to compute. They consist of nonrecurring and recurring expenses. Nonrecurring costs are those associated with the development of training programs (such as materials used by the developer, and his or her salary), while recurring costs are those associated with conducting such programs. Recurring costs can be further broken down into those that are fixed (such as facilities) and those that are variable (such as handouts provided to trainees, and trainees' salaries while they are off the job).

One case cited by McKeon (1981) calculated costs of $134,000 to develop an off-site program (including training department overhead, staff salaries, consultants, equipment, and materials), plus $16,500 to deliver one two-day meeting for twenty people (including lost work time of participants, facility costs, and transportation). A more recent study calculated the costs of a supervisory skills training program applied to sixty-two bank employees in five sessions. One-time costs involved developing materials and video-tapes ($10,000) plus salaries, benefits, and travel for trainers for five days ($2,800). Total costs over the five sessions included trainers' salary ($3,350), equipment and materials ($755), facilities ($580), and trainees' salary costs of $17,791. Thus, the total cost to train sixty-two bank employees was $35,276—that is, $569 per trainee (Mathieu and Leonard, 1987). Of course, the particular training costs differ with each training program.

Some of the more typical training cost categories and examples are: (1) equipment—training devices (computers, videos, trainers), telecommunications, and laboratory equipment; (2) personnel—instructors, managers/administrators, clerks, programmers, analysts/designers, consultants, and artists; (3) facilities—classrooms, laboratories, offices, libraries/learning centers, and carrells; (4) materials—workbooks, texts, slides and tapes, programs, tests, paper and film (Kearsley, 1982, p. 24). Generally, training costs should include all resources that must be required or shifted from other uses to develop and conduct the program.

The substantial budget costs of training often lead organizations to see only the cost per trainee and consider cutting training programs to save costs. Although it may often be appropriate to cut ineffective training programs, it is impossible to judge effectiveness by costs alone. Very often, such shortsighted decision making may cost more in lost productivity than it saves in program expenses. HRM specialists must also pay attention to the benefits of training.

BENEFITS. While training costs are fairly easy to conceptualize and compute, the same is not true of the gains or benefits from training. How much, for example, is the performance improvement noted below worth to the company involved? How would this be determined (Latham and Saari, 1979)?

In a large international company, a training program that consisted of two hours of training each week for nine weeks was undertaken to improve leadership skills among the first-level supervisors. Sessions focused on: (1) orienting new employees, (2) giving recognition, (3) motivating poor performers, (4) correcting poor work habits, (5) discussing potential disciplinary action, (6) reducing absenteeism, (7) handling a complaining employee, (8) reducing turnover, and (9) overcoming resistance to change (Latham and Saari, 1979).

Each session followed the same format: (1) introduction to the topic, (2) a film demonstrating effective behaviors, (3) group discussion of the film, and (4) role playing with class feedback. Trainees were encouraged to use the learned skills with one or more employees during the following week and to report the results during the next session. Problems were role-played and discussed. Superintendents of the trainees were given an accelerated training program and encouraged to reinforce desirable behaviors by their subordinates on the job.

The evaluation design was (mostly) to be done after training only, with control group and random assignments, involving the first twenty supervisors to be trained and a like number of controls. Evaluation criteria and reaction measured by questionnaire were: knowledge learning measured by a specially constructed paper-and-pencil test, skills learning measured by evaluations of role plays, and job behavior change measured by performance appraisals. Timing of the measures was as follows: reactions—immediately following and eight months after the training; knowledge learning—six months after training; skills learning—three months after training and job behaviors—one month before (an exception to the overall design) and one year after the training.

Trainees expressed high opinions of the program both immediately after training and eight months later and scored significantly better than the controls on both the knowledge and skills tests. While the two groups had been rated the same on performance before training, the trained group performed significantly better afterward. Further, when the control group was eventually trained, it caught up to the original group on all of the criteria.

Latham and Saari (1979, p. 245) concluded that "leadership skills could be taught in a relatively short time period (i.e., eighteen hours), providing that the trainees: (1) are given a model to follow, (2) are given a specific set of goals and guidelines, (3) are given an opportunity to perfect the skills, (4) are given feedback as to the effectiveness of their behavior, and (5) are reinforced with praise for applying the acquired skills on the job."[*]

The estimation of gains requires that evaluators not only place a dollar value on various levels of performance, but also take into account several factors that can affect these dollar values (e.g., the diminishing effect of training over time, and turnover rate among those who have been trained). Major conceptual and methodological advances in the measurement of training benefits have been made in recent years, but actual applications are few (Boudreau, 1988). In the Mathieu and Leonard (1987) application presented earlier in this chapter, it was shown that a training program to develop the managerial skills of sixty-five bank supervisors, which cost $50,000 to run, returned two to three times that much (depending on the assumptions made) in from three to five years.

Break-even Analysis for Training Programs. Clearly, precise estimates of training costs and benefits are seldom, if ever, available. However, one could say the same thing about any human resource management activity. In fact, the same thing could be said about management activities in general, including marketing, finance, and production. Figure 11.5 presents information on a training program's costs and benefits.

As shown in Figure 11.5, total costs of the program are $1 million including first-year start-up costs of $500,000. However, the leverage of the program (the number of person-years of productivity affected by it) is 1,200 as shown in the top of the figure.

Rather than dwell on the imperfections of the training effectiveness measures, one can compute the minimum level of training benefits necessary to cover the training costs. This minimum return equals $833 (that is, $1 million divided by 1,200). If the increase in work-force value created by the training program (per person, per year) is greater than $833, the investment pays off, and vice versa. Several studies have suggested that break-even analysis often produces break-even effect levels that are quite low (Boudreau, 1984, 1988; Florin-Thuma and Boudreau, 1987; Rich and Boudreau, 1987). When this is true, it may be possible that even imperfect training assessments based on only a portion of the possible training outcomes may be sufficient to justify the training investment. Such an approach is certainly superior to attempting to measure training program effects down to the last dollar (Boudreau, 1984; Milkovich and Boudreau, 1988).

---

*G. P. Latham and L. M. Saari, "Application of Social Learning Theory to Training Supervisors through Behavior Modeling," *Journal of Applied Psychology* 64 (1979), pp. 239–264. Copyright 1979 by the American Psychological Association. Reprinted/adapted by permission of the publisher.

Figure 11.5
Example Cost-Benefit Analysis for a Training Program

<u>Computing Quantity/Leverage</u>

Year	Trained Employees Added to the Work Force	Trained Employees Leaving the Work Force	Net Increase in Trained Employees in the Work Force	Total Trained in the Work Force
1	200	0	200	200
2	25	5	20	220
3	25	5	20	240
4	25	5	20	260
5	25	5	20	280

Total person-years of productivity affected = 1,200

<u>Estimating Program Quality</u>

Supervisors were asked to estimate the dollar value of the expected increase in employee service value from the training program, on a per-person, per-year basis, less the increased service costs that would have to be incurred to maintain that increased service value. The estimates of net value ranged from a low of $1,000 to a high of $10,000 per person-year.

<u>Computing Program Costs</u>

Year	Start-Up Costs	Ongoing Program Costs	Total Costs
1	$500,000	$100,000	$600,000
2	0	100,000	100,000
3	0	100,000	100,000
4	0	100,000	100,000
5	0	100,000	100,000

Total program costs over five years = $1,000,000

<u>Computing Total Program Returns</u>

Total program returns = (Program quality x leverage) - Program costs

Program Quality	Leverage	Program Costs	Total Program Returns
$ 833/person-year	1,200	$1,000,000	$ 0
1,000/person-year	1,200	1,000,000	200,000
10,000/person-year	1,200	1,000,000	11,000,000

Adapted from: John W. Boudreau, "Utility Analysis: A New View of Strategic Human Resource Management," in ASPA/BNA Handbook of Human Resources Management, vol. 1, ed. Lee D. Dyer (Washington, D.C.: Bureau of National Affairs, 1988).

In conclusion, HRM specialists should take into consideration the following criteria for evaluating a training design (Tracey, 1971):

1. *Objectives*: Does the design fit the objectives?
2. *Targeting*: Does the design hit the right level in terms of: (a) trainee needs and expectations? (b) trainee learning style? (c) trainee culture (expectations about authority, how hard to work, etc.)?
3. *Congruence*: Is the design method congruent with what the HRM specialists are teaching?

4. *Structure*: Does the structure provide a framework within which emergent issues can be productively utilized? Can the design be modified to keep in touch with the trainees felt needs without sacrificing objectives?

5. *Scheduling*: Can the design be carried out in the time allotted? (a) appropriate amount of work? (b) suitable pacing?

6. *Variety*: Does the design provide a mix of activities along the dimensions of: (a) appealing to different learning styles? (b) activity (listening, discussing, behaving)? (c) perspectives or viewpoints on the material to be learned?

7. *Sequencing*: Is the material in proper sequence: (a) logically? (b) psychologically?

8. *Communication of Important Points*: Is there redundancy (a) at different levels (e.g., written, spoken, acted)? (b) over time (introductions and summaries)?

9. *Learning Climate*: Does the design allow for ongoing development of learning climate (a) implicit through training activities? (b) explicit through process analysis exercises?

10. *Evaluation*: Does the design include evaluation? (a) interim? (b) terminal?

The above criteria should assist the HRM specialist in more effectively evaluating training programs during each phase. In addition, early on in the training development process, the HRM expert will have to focus on very key parts of the training design.

SUMMARY

The need for evaluation of training programs is currently at the forefront in many organizations. There have been some estimates that U.S. organizations spend at least $200 billion each year on training (*Training*, 1989). While that figure is astonishing, even more astonishing is that we know so little about how to effectively manage this investment. Historically, evaluation has been touted as the measurement of "learning" from a training experience. In today's organizations, this expectation is refined through a focus on enhanced individual and organizational performance. Evaluations of training programs have traditionally asked four increasingly complex questions:

1. Did you enjoy the training experience?
2. Did you learn/retain the information presented?
3. Has your performance improved as a result of the training experience?
4. What return on this training investment will the organization realize?

The last question acknowledges that decisions on organizational training investments are made in the wider context of other investment opportunities: to improve performance. But the lack of quantitative return on investment (ROI) information about training places these investments at a disadvantage. The HRM specialist must frequently cite hollow reassurances about the value of training to employees and the organization. As a consequence, training programs are frequently vulnerable when resource allocations are made throughout the company. This scenario forces HRM specialists to be more ROI-oriented.

The four levels of evaluation cause the trainee to revisit the training experience. This intervention reinforces learning and increases the positive transfer between the training experience and the work environment. As this occurs, the measurement process exerts a positive influence, such that the act of measuring training effectiveness increases training effectiveness. A cycle of positive training outcomes is thus set in motion. HRM specialists can do well for themselves and the training program by understanding the importance of training program evaluation and problems typically associated with it. A problem with many training programs is that they are not designed with consideration as to how they will be evaluated. Evaluation should be planned at the same time the training program is designed. In this way the training program objectives and procedures can be integrated with evaluation purposes and procedures. Additionally, the information needs and interests of key organizational members and other audiences are determined early; training program evaluation results are likely to be more credible, and be perceived as such, especially when audiences are included in initial development and are informed of procedures and expected outcomes prior to evaluation. Suggested in this chapter is a "systems" approach to planning, designing, and conducting, that is, an orderly, systematic approach, goal-oriented, that considers the range of options available to utilize existing resources and cope with constraints.

While there are no facile solutions to the problems facing HRM specialists in the evaluation of training programs, evaluations can nonetheless be rewarding and "if proper care is given to the manner in which findings are obtained and interpreted, the positive contributions [of the evaluator] will far outweigh the negative implications deriving from the imperfection of his tools" (Brooks, 1971, p. 62). By continually measuring the effects of training, improving programs based on evaluation data, and keeping decision makers informed of and involved in the evaluation process, the full value of evaluation as a powerful organizational tool can be realized.

A Selected Recapitulation

INTRODUCTION

Training, in one form or another, has become part of most corporate and organizational cultures (Dodge, 1989). Most organizations have accepted training as a critical component in maintaining an effective organization. Staff training undertaken by industry, the service sector, and the public sector represents a large volume of adult education and a significant amount of money. For example, as noted earlier in this book, $44.4 billion was budgeted for training by American organizations in 1989, up from $32 billion in 1987 (*Training*, 1989; Lee, 1987).

The training challenge that faces the HRM specialist during these times of rapid change is ensuring that employees are prepared to keep in step with helping the organization meet its needs and goals. This requires that the HRM specialist have a clear understanding of the organization's future direction and objectives, combined with a framework for focusing on both organizational and individual development.

It has been the contention throughout this book that one way an organization can meet this challenge is by using a systematic approach to training. The training model presented in this book (see Table 2.4) suggests that the success of training programs is dependent on a systems approach that considers a number of interacting components. It is necessary not only to attend to careful needs assessment and evaluation but also to understand that training programs are one element in a complex organizational system. This chapter will briefly revisit some of the key components of the systems model discussed in this book and highlight some current and future training concerns that will merit special attention.

KEY COMPONENTS IN SYSTEMATIC TRAINING

Unlike too many training programs that focus on the trainee's needs, the systems training approach merges key components of training that are driven by the organization's needs. The result is a relevant, cost-effective method of supporting employee and organization development that ensures competent employees will be available to meet the organization's long-term needs.

In the public sector, organizational and employee development programs strive to enhance service. In the private sector, however, the aim is to realize greater profit (Darkenwald and Merrian, 1986). Because a systems approach to training is evaluated on its relevance to organizational objectives, the question is what contribution training made to the desired result (e.g., employee skills in problem solving).

Typical training programs focus on giving employees additional knowledge, skills, and abilities relating to their current jobs. Some organizations, such as Westinghouse, Beatrice Foods, and Holiday Inns, use these programs to reduce real or anticipated deficiencies in performance resulting from past behaviors. Another purpose of training is to make managers more aware of new manufacturing techniques for the firm's goods and services. In 1987, IBM estimated that it spent more than $100 million in that one year alone training managers how to introduce new products to customers and how to maintain effective interpersonal relationships with clients (Hellreigel and Slocum, 1989).

Important Steps in the Training Process

Regardless of the purpose of training or how much money is being spent on it, the literature on training suggests that organizations frequently omit important steps that would increase its effectiveness (Lien, 1979; Donnelly, 1987). First, an HRM specialist must not go straight into the organization-wide assessment of training without going through a preassessment phase. Factors that make up the preassessment phase (availability of training resources, management and other key stakeholders' attitudes toward training, professionalism of HRM specialists, and the potential capacity of the organization to undertake change within the cultural constraints of the organization's current value system) will largely determine the extent, content, and viability of subsequent assessments and the acceptability and potential for success of a training activity. When HRM specialists take the time to complete the preassessment phase they are in a better position to move into the needs-assessment phase of a training activity.

Second, a needs assessment should precede the planning and execution of a training program. In a needs assessment, the HRM specialist determines exactly what the training needs are before designing a program to meet them. While this seems an obvious step, many training programs are initiated simply because "Marie over in Production Materials heard a good speaker last week; she thought we should bring the guy in to talk to Marketing." Such programs may be entertaining for employees, but they do not address the real needs of the organization or department. Further, they may be a wasteful use of the training budget.

A third step in the effective management of training that is frequently omitted is training program evaluation, in which the HRM specialist determines the program's effectiveness in terms of the costs and benefits of the organization. In many instances training is given to some groups but not others. Tests are then given to all groups to measure whether those who received training score higher on test performance. If not, the training program is redesigned or replaced. Training program evaluation at its simplest must project the potential benefits at the outset of any training effort.

Needs assessment—analyzing an organization's internal and external environment to find out how much, if any, new training—has almost become a buzz word (Gent and Dell'Omo, 1989). The management literature in the past few years has covered the topic thoroughly. Unfortunately, it has tended to recommend specific tools without giving an overall plan to follow (Gent and Dell'Omo, 1989).

For instance, a recent article by Cureton, Newton, and Teslowski (1986) lists various information-gathering approaches to needs assessment; another focuses on methods of job analysts training evaluation; and a third refers to needs assessment as a particular approach to job analysis, planning for training, and performance evaluation. Needs assessment is more than just a set of job-related information-gathering and planning techniques. In reality, it brings training into the heart of organizational performance and growth by focusing on the major employee factor in productivity: employee job performance.

The HRM specialist must perceive needs assessment as a proactive process that attacks training problems as problems of employee job performance. In conjunction with conducting the organization-wide assessment, the HRM specialist has to determine whether there is a perceived discrepancy between desired and actual levels of organizational and employee performance. The desired level is not only what the organization needs now, but also what it will need in the future to accomplish its objectives. If there is no discrepancy between the two levels, there is no need to train. If a discrepancy is found to exist, the HRM specialist must resist the temptation to jump blindly into a training solution.

The next step in the process is to determine exactly what is causing the problem. If the discrepancy is due to a skill or knowledge deficit, then training is a relevant solution. If not, then the problem is due to other factors in the organizational environment and requires different solutions, perhaps changing something in the environment to make it more attractive to the employee. Such changes may include modifying organizational structure, supervisory practices, performance appraisal and feedback systems, resources, organization climate, job duties, and so on.

In most situations, the discrepancy is due to both KSA, deficits and environmental causes. Most likely, when the HRM specialist performs needs assessment correctly, he/she will uncover more than purely training needs. The HRM specialist can carry out a needs assessment by using the well-known three-part model of McGehee and Thayer (1961) as a guide. This traditional framework includes task (job) analysis, organizational analysis, and person (employee) analysis.

Job analysis requires the HRM specialist to determine and understand the nature of an employee's job. The HRM specialist could obtain preliminary information about the position from job postings, a recent job description, and a discussion with a supervisor/employee about "visions and perceptions" of the job in the future. In addition, the HRM specialist could use responses to a set of detailed questions about the position, asked in interviews with employees and their supervisors.

From this background information, the HRM specialist would be in a position to develop a series of statements reflecting the responsibilities and duties mentioned as being important elements of the job (these statements would constitute a "worker-oriented" job analysis for the position). The statements could then be included in a questionnaire that would be administered to all employees holding the particular job in question, asking them to evaluate the frequency and importance of each element.

The job analysis will provide key information in terms of duties and requirements, both now and in the future. In addition, the job analysis often highlights what may appear to be obvious: that many human resource concerns outside the training arena are affected by how jobs are formally designed—including selection, performance appraisal, compensation, and career management.

As previously mentioned, an organization usually turns to training as a response to some felt discrepancy in employee performance. This discrepancy, however, may be due in part to organizational environment factors not amenable to training, such as deficits in supervision or in resources for doing the job, poor employee interaction, or ineffective communication processes.

Even where training is called for, its success in improving performance (by upgrading employee knowledge, skill, and ability) is partially dependent on these very same organizational environment factors. Success may depend on management's support for training in the form of resources allocated, on employee interaction to reinforce training, and on effective communication of the training issues.

Organizations may not always be eager to have this information as part of a needs assessment. They may argue, for instance, that they do not want to open a "Pandora's box" for fear that unwanted employee expectations beyond training may be raised. Such arguments may be a sign that management is burying its head in the sand. Information from the organizational analysis provides important insights into possible environmental and motivational reasons for performance problems. It also gauges the potential for training success. Therefore, if the organization is truly serious about gaining maximum value for its expenditures, it cannot ignore the fact that organizational changes may be needed.

In essence, the organizational analysis should add to the findings in the job analysis—for example, showing that more thought may need to be given to the context for training, including more visible top management support for training efforts and increased attention to the other issues unrelated to training.

The employee analysis should gather information on how employees perceive their abilities to perform their job duties—for instance, by having employees rate themselves on the degree of difficulty they have in performing a particular aspect of their job or in operating some specialized equipment. This information should help to produce a more accurate diagnosis of a performance problem and to provide targeted solutions, including specific recommendations for training.

Employees could also be given tests covering many different knowledge, skill, and ability areas required for the job. This aspect of needs assessment can identify specific knowledge, skill, and ability deficiencies—actual training needs—of the individual employees. The HRM specialist should remember that the development of these types of tests requires in-depth research into the actual knowledge, skills, and abilities needed to perform a job. This is one of the areas in which the employees themselves should be actively involved. This will help the employees take ownership of the process and, more importantly, become motivated to participate in the training that may result.

The HRM specialist must involve the employee in the training process beyond identifying required knowledge, skill, and ability levels. Employees should be included, where possible, in planning what topics will be covered and in what order; in choosing, evaluating, and upgrading the specific training courses or programs; and in some instances, in presenting the training themselves.

Needs assessment should focus on performance problems seen as organizational systems problems, and requiring organizational solutions to rectify. Needs assessment, when conducted appropriately, will lead to a prescription for some training. If the training is to have long-lasting effects on performance, however, it needs to be supported by management efforts to upgrade the work environment and to improve employee motivation to apply training outcomes in productive ways. If the HRM specialist does not see that these concerns are dealt with in the needs assessment, any training that follows may turn out to be little more than an expensive waste of financial and human resources.

Enhancing Training Effectiveness

As mentioned throughout this book, all organizations engage in employee development through training. Available evidence suggests that this activity has become increasingly important in the face of ever more intensive international competition, deregulation, accelerated technological change, and the inexorable march toward the postindustrial society (Choate and Linger, 1986). Training is one way to develop a more flexible work force. According to a recent study (Stephan, Mills, Pace, and Ralphs, 1988), technological change is the driving force behind much of today's training, especially in technical areas. In a period of rapid change, training is a must for such companies as IBM and Hewlett-Packard, which are committed to full employment. Without continuous learning and investment in training, these companies could not make the constant internal adjustments needed to avoid layoffs (Work in America Institute, 1987).

Most training is carried out on the job, and most of this is done informally (Carnevale and Goldstein, 1983). Still, a study of 1,006 employers in seven different industries found that more than two-thirds engaged in some type of formal training. The median expenditure was between $75 and $100 per employee (Prentice-Hall Editorial Staff, 1979). IBM and other companies—Xerox, AT&T, GE, GM, Wang, and Motorola—operate their own "universities," in which a wide variety of technical and managerial subjects are taught (Bowen, 1985; Noble, 1985). Again, collectively, U.S. organizations with one hundred or more employees were estimated to have budgeted $44.4 billion to formally train employees—and close to $200 billion to cover all training programs in 1989.

Is this money well spent? Although the organizations involved apparently think so, the fact is that the benefits of employee training are largely taken on faith. Evaluation efforts have lagged. Yet we know that it is extremely difficult to design training experiences that will result in desired learning, let alone change behavior leading to better organizational results. Adequate theory and research to guide the process are emerging only slowly, and organizations have been somewhat slow to capitalize on that which has become available (Latham, 1988). In fact, of all the Personnel/Human Resource activities, training has been the one to be most consistently seduced by the alluring array of fads and folderol offered by consultants and "educators."

The costs of this promiscuous behavior are becoming ever more apparent, however, forcing HRM specialists to ensure that their training efforts are (1) directed toward organizational objectives, (2) undertaken only when

they are the most effective way to attain these objectives, (3) solidly designed, using the latest proven methods, and (4) carefully implemented
and thoroughly evaluated.

Understanding Trainees and Trainers. "The wise man shows his wisdom
in separation, in gradation and in his scale of creatures and of merits is as
wide as nature . . . The foolish have no range in their scale, but suppose
that every man is as every other man" (Krauthammer, 1983, p. 30). This
quote from Emerson gets to the very heart of the content of a major premise
of this book: understanding individual differences in training. Whereas the
truth in Emerson's statement may seem self-evident, the fact of the matter
is that there is a persistent tendency in people to overgeneralize about the
similarity existing among others. Even more troublesome is the tenacious
habit that some HRM specialists have of assuming that everyone else is
just like them. This belief that the whole world "is just like me" is called
"the mirror image fallacy." It is a particularly attractive belief because it
makes the world seem much easier to manage (as well as making the world
seem a lot less lonely). That is, an HRM specialist responsible for a training
activity believes that everyone in the training program shares the HRM
specialist's interests, values, beliefs, abilities and learning styles, wherefore
organizing these people in order to harmoniously pursue a common goal
should be an easy matter.

Unfortunately the mirror image fallacy is just that—a fallacy. Moreover,
when the philosophy behind this belief is put into practice in the real world
of training it becomes a very dangerous one at that. Especially for the
HRM specialist, given the need to tailor training to individual differences,
it often leads to incorrect diagnosis and implementation of training programs. In particular, the belief that "deep down we're all alike" causes
people to attribute to assorted factors many training problems that are
actually due to individual differences. For example, if two trainees do not
seem to be learning the material in a training program, the HRM specialist
holding on to the mirror image fallacy immediately assumes that there is
some misperception or some miscommunication. The problem would go
away if only the trainees had the right "attitude" about the training program. It is often the case, however, that both individuals have different
styles of learning.

The HRM specialist in the above situation has probably not taken into
consideration that individual differences in learning styles and motivation
to learn will impact the amount of learning that each trainee absorbs. Thus,
the HRM specialist must understand that there is a wide variety of ways
that individuals learn and that individual differences affect a training program. HRM specialists who ignore these differences or assume that everyone else is just like them, are making a very large mistake that could be
costly to them, the organization, and the trainees. The HRM specialists
must also take into consideration that individual differences exist among

those responsible for a training program and make use of this information in the selection of trainers for specific training programs.

When considering a given training program, HRM managers must determine whether to use internal HRM specialists, external trainers, or the team approach. The choice should depend on the nature of the skills to be taught, the underlying assumptions about how people learn, and the anticipated role of the trainer. Wehrenberg (1989) recommends that training managers match trainers to the task. That is, if a task is complicated and requires years of on-the-job experience for an employee to become proficient, it makes good economic sense to turn a craftsman into a trainer. For example, welders learn their trade from years of experience, not from a book.

The HRM manager must remember that just because a worker can perform a task, and may be an expert, it does not follow that he or she can be a good trainer—or even an adequate one. If the task is more knowledge-based, such as a mathematical or computer procedure, experience may not be required to have a working knowledge of the subject. For softer skills, such as giving positive feedback for a job well done, performance appraisal interviewing, or disciplining a problem employee, there may be no precise answers or processes. Therefore, there may not be any real experts.

Those responsible for selecting and evaluating trainers must decide to what extent the trainer will be involved in the total training process—information gathering (needs analysis), implementation, and evaluation. That is, what role the trainer is expected to fill. Many times, the HRM specialist's role ends with presentation (delivery), and prospective trainers should be assessed accordingly. In other cases, the trainer is expected to be an active participant in resolving performance problems and can be assessed on the additional competencies implied in the following paragraphs.

If the trainer's role is to step into a classroom and present a prepared lecture or demonstration, presentation skills predominate. When combined with subject-matter expertise, presentation skills may be sufficient. If the trainer is expected to be involved in a broader scope, from identifying performance problems to implementing and evaluating training solutions, additional skills are required.

Trainer selection can be enhanced by evaluating prospective trainers on:

1. Specific knowledge of the most recent theories of work motivation, job design, and enough knowledge of the behavioral sciences to understand why people do what they do (both of which are necessary if the trainer is to be effective);

2. Familiarity with a broad range of teaching methods, from simple instructions to formal classroom and on-the-job training, plus the ability to select the appropriate mix for the problem to be solved.

3. Ability to develop clear and accurate training objectives that are observable, attainable, measurable, results-oriented, contain the critical elements of the job to be performed, and communicate expectations;

4. Skills in planning and writing, knowledge of training media, timing, presentation methods, sequencing of training materials, and the capabilities and limitations of the trainers and the trainees;

5. Skill in actually implementing the training solution (instructing in a classroom or seminar environment, introduction of job aids, explanation of new operating instructions, delivery of workbooks or whatever) or getting the message across to trainees (ability to speak comfortably and with authority, to think quickly so as to capitalize on classroom events, responding to trainees in a non-threatening manner, skill in giving feedback, and a willingness to hold trainees accountable for learning);

6. Skills in comparing measurement, statistics, and presentation of findings.

The situation surrounding selection plays a large role in a systems approach to training. Selection of trainers requires that the HRM manager look for evidence of all the previously mentioned competencies, regardless of whether an internal, external, or team approach to training will be used in the training program. Of course, expertise in the areas listed above represents only part of what impacts trainer selection. How a trainer's activities contribute to the health and well-being of the organization is as much a part of the evaluation as is the trainer's experience and competence.

Current and Future Training Concerns

As introduced earlier in this book, economic and technological trends provide clear signals that training is a growth industry. The pace of innovation, change, and development is faster, faster, year by year. Obsolescence bedevils all of us. Perhaps the Paul Principle expresses this phenomenon most aptly: *Over time, people become uneducated, and therefore incompetent, to perform at a level they once performed at adequately* (Armer, 1970). Training is an important antidote to obsolescence. In addition to the many productivity-enhancing programs provided in Table 2.1, many firms are also offering the kinds of training that will enhance the quality of work life as well (e.g., personal growth, career planning, and safety). This trend is likely to continue.

What is also likely, however, is continued research that will provide stable and accurate estimates of the percentage improvements in job performance and productivity expected from various kinds of training interventions (Guzzo, Jette, and Katzell, 1985). Such estimates are crucial to the widespread application of utility analysis in training evaluation. This type of research will enable us someday to provide managers with accurate dollar gains in productivity of alternative training strategies, and it can also guide HRM specialists in adjusting their programs so as to make them more attractive from a cost-benefit viewpoint. As a conclusion to this book, the remaining pages will discuss four areas (retraining, career planning, management development, and cross-cultural training) in which HRM specialists have started to more regularly adjust their training programs.

Retraining. Many organizations and HRM specialists have become increasingly involved in retraining employees whose skills have become obsolete with the continuing introduction of rapidly changing technologies. Retraining employees requires the HRM specialist to develop training programs that continually expose trainees to new learning challenges— with the result that they are continually being brought up to date. To accomplish this task the HRM specialist must use current and future needs-assessment methods to determine what KSAs are necessary for employees to remain technically competent in their jobs. Concerns about needs-assessment methods that can determine KSAs for jobs that do not exist but are on the planning board are also important to the massive retraining efforts that will continue to confront the HRM specialist in training—as evidenced in the following examples.

To help dislocated workers in Des Moines, two transition centers were set up to retrain people for banking and insurance careers—the two main professional service industries in the area. The two centers recruit participants and place them in programs offered by local educational institutions. Area employers have provided funding to these programs and hire many of the displaced workers once their retraining is completed. The efforts of this task force have been successful: 80 percent of the retrained workers find new jobs within a year of termination from the factories.

Dislocated workers are not all unskilled or semiskilled. Even highly skilled (professional) workers are feeling the effects of a changing labor market. Labor Department grants have been used to teach new skills and to relocate geologists, petroleum engineers, and other professionals in Oklahoma and Texas. Officials have said that oil and gas geologists who wish to change careers can be retrained in two months to fill a need for hydrologists; engineers are becoming science teachers. Other workers in Texas and Oklahoma are being given the opportunity to learn new computer skills, and then, if they wish, they are sent to cities with high-tech jobs (*Wall Street Journal*, April 28, 1987, p. 1).

An innovative California program funded by the state has encouraged such experiments as the $1.4–million mobile classroom operated by the Los Angeles City College system. The trailer, filled with computer-controlled lathes and other modern equipment, is trucked out to aerospace plants to retrain assembly workers as skilled machinists. The costs: $2,600 per worker for 410 hours of training; the benefits: shorter periods of unemployment for trainees, and a 55 percent average increase in their wages. What is the bottom line on all of this? Even executives who have trouble believing that any government program could turn a profit are finding in their own plants and offices that investments in human capital have a high payback (Brody, 1987).

Other examples are not hard to find. General Electric, as in the case of the company's mid-1980s layoffs in Schenectady, New York, makes a point of either retraining workers within G.E. or helping them find work locally. Retraining has also become more prevalent in the case of older workers. Control Data Corporation, AT&T, Kelly Services, Inc., and others run programs to keep their older workers employed. Nevertheless, there must be more effort put into retraining the older worker if organizations are to come to terms with a work force that is aging too quickly and with other demographic changes.

HRM specialists can help in the coordination of retraining efforts in several ways: (1) providing feedback on proposed and existing retraining and training programs, (2) developing needs-assessment methods that determine KSAs required for persons to remain technically competent in their jobs, (3) determining through needs-assessment methods KSAs for jobs that are on the planning board, (4) identifying occupations for the development of retraining programs, and (5) serving on review boards that assess the effectiveness of retraining efforts.

Career Planning and Management Development. Organizations are providing more and more opportunities for their employees to advance through positions of increasing responsibility, and the HRM specialist and employees often share the responsibility for both the planning and preparation of employees for those moves. This planning and preparation include career-planning training and management development programs. Career-planning training helps employees define and establish their own roles in the planning of their careers. Employees may meet formally or informally with HRM specialists to discuss their personal goals, the KSAs necessary to accomplish these goals, a realistic timetable against which to evaluate goal accomplishment, and how the organization can help them achieve their goals (very often through some kind of organization-sponsored training).

The HRM specialist may also distribute useful career-planning materials, or assist the employee in locating them. This career counseling provides benefits to both the organization and the individual employee. It provides employees with a long-term perspective on their employment with the organization, creates a motivation for them to seek out and participate in training programs, and demonstrates the organization's interest in employees' well-being. From the organization's perspective, employees are willing to identify closely with the organization, more likely to perceive it to be in their own self-interest to earn high performance evaluations, and are more likely to establish realistic personal goals.

The HRM specialist has realized that prior to instituting a career-planning program for employees, an organization must address concerns regarding the components of the program, the desirability of employee involvement, and the level of resources to be invested. All of these concerns have been recognized by those responsible for organizational training as deserving serious consideration before the HRM specialist has the organization commit its resources to a career-planning program.

Although career-planning training is useful for employees at all levels of the organization, management development (training reserved for those who currently are, or are about to become, managers) continues to require new innovations and attention by the HRM specialist responsible for an organization's training. A variety of training falls under the management development umbrella. Management development is characterized not so much by training content as by the overall objective—to develop managers (Newburg, 1980; Eastburn, 1986). One management researcher has provided an illustrative and useful definition of management development training: "The goals of management development are to support the strategic objectives of the corporation; provide for interdivisional consistency in management philosophy; support the integration of human resource functions, such as career development, appraisals; and encourage an open, flexible, participatory management style" (Galosky, 1983).

Consistent with the goals presented above, the HRM specialist realizes that development training may take many forms, including university courses and degrees, job rotation (transfers) within the lower managerial ranks (Moore, 1982), and seminars on sexual harassment, motivation, discipline, corporate finance, time management, stress reduction strategies, problem solving, management theories, leadership, strategic planning, and human relations, among other topics. The HRM specialist has also realized that typically it is very difficult to evaluate the tangible benefits of a management development program. In most situations it may take many years before the KSAs developed in those programs are necessary to the job. The ongoing and future orientation of management development will continue to make it difficult for the HRM specialist to determine when such benefits should be evaluated. However, the HRM specialist must continue to adjust training programs to increase their potential benefit to the organization.

Cross-Cultural Training. The increased emphasis on a global economy has found many organizations and HRM specialists recognizing the need for training programs that successfully respond to cross-cultural training. The HRM specialist with responsibility for training employees and managers who will be working in other cultures has started to recognize that such training can be fraught with difficulties, because management is culture-specific. This view holds true for organizations, nations, and internationally defined cultures. Different perspectives on life may not be translated easily from one culture to another. Indeed, conscious or unconscious ethnocentrism, the belief that one's native life-style is the "best" or the most appropriate for everyone, can result in value judgments that cause misperceptions about other cultures. With proper preparation, however, today's HRM specialist must get the organization's employee ready for the shock that invariably comes when he or she is thrust into a cross-cultural encounter.

Cross-cultural training for employees has presented and will continue to present new challenges for the HRM specialist. The challenges have resulted in the HRM specialist's designing training programs that help orient employees to new cultures by teaching them some of the target culture's specific characteristics, to include (1) the range of acceptable and unacceptable behaviors or norms for different social situations, (2) role structures, including role perceptions, which can differ among cultures, (3) subtle behaviors that can express general intentions and attitudes, (4) difference in self-concepts that may be quite different from the employees' country's norms, and (5) certain kinds of behavior that will be acceptable or rejected in the host culture.

Training employees for cross-cultural assignments can be somewhat like walking on eggs. The HRM specialist must continue to develop methodologies that help employees develop important KSAs and a life-style that fit the norms and the traditions of the host culture.

CONCLUSION

Before completing this book, it should be noted that the success of training programs is dependent on the active participation of the HRM specialist. HRM specialists are playing an increasingly important role in organizations; they affect not only the welfare of the organization but the attitudes and behavior of employees in the organization. Because of this, they are a force to be reckoned with whenever organizations go through periods of decline or growth.

In the future there will be little significant change in organizations without the collaboration or at least the acquiescence of HRM specialists and their training contributions. Any HRM specialist who is working in the field of training should therefore know the importance of viewing training as but one element of interacting components within a broader organizational system—a system that includes many components that can affect the proposed training system.

The HRM specialist must also understand that the various interacting components that exist—from preassessment, through needs assessment, into training program development and design, and the program evaluation phase—must be congruent with the organization's overall goals. In spite of sizable budgets, good intentions, and real needs, training programs will not succeed or achieve lasting results if the purported goals of the training are vague and unresponsive to practical training needs. If HRM specialists don't know where they're going, they can't tell if they got there. Nor can they tell if it's where they wanted to be! The systems orientation toward training can do nothing but increase the effectiveness of the HRM specialist and training in general within the organization and in HRM specialists' eyes.

Bibliography

American Society for Training and Development. (1986). *Servicing the new corporation*. Alexandria, VA: American Society for Training and Development.

American Society for Training and Development. (1986, July). Employee training in America. *Training and Development Journal, 37.*

Anderson, R.H., & Snyder, K.J. (1989, February). Team training. *Training and Development Journal, 43* (2), 59–61.

Argyris, C. (1982). *Reasoning, learning and action*. San Francisco: Jossey-Bass.

Armer, P. (1970). The individual: His privacy, self-image, and obsolescence. *Proceedings of the Meeting of the Panel on Science and Technology*, 11th Science and Aeronautics. Washington, DC: U.S. Government Printing Office.

Ash, R.A. (1988). Job analysis in the world of work. In S. Gael (Ed.), *The job analysis handbook for business, industry, and government* (Vol. 1, pp. 3–13). New York: John Wiley.

Ash, R.A., & Levine, E.L. (1980, November-December). A framework for evaluating job analysis methods. *Personnel, 57*(6), 53–59.

Baker, R.E., Simon, J.R., & Bazeli, F.P. (1986, Spring). An assessment of the learning style preferences of accounting majors. *Issues in Accounting Education, 1*(1), 1–12.

Bandura, A. (1986). *Social foundations of thought and action: A social cognitive theory*. Englewood Cliffs, NJ: Prentice-Hall.

Bartlett, C.J. (1978, July). Equal employment opportunities in training. *Human Factors, 20*(2), 179–188.

Bass, B.M., & Vaughn, J.A (1966). *Training in industry: The management of learning*. Pacific Grove, CA: Wadsworth.

Baumgartel, H., & Jeanpierre, F. (1972, November-December). Applying new knowledge in the back-home setting: A study of Indian managers' adoptive efforts. *Journal of Applied Behavioral Science, 8*(6), 674–694.

Beckhard, R. (1982). The changing shape of management development. *Journal of Management Development, 1*(1), 51–62.

Bemis, B.E., Belenky, A.H., & Soder, D.A. (1983). *Job analysis: An effective management tool.* Washington, DC: Bureau of National Affairs.

Berke, E.I. (1984, February). Keeping newly trained supervisors from going back to old ways. *Management Review, 73*(2), 14–16.

Bernardin, H.J., & Beatty, R.W. (1984). *Performance appraisal: Assessing human performance at work.* Boston: Kent.

Bernstein, A., Ticer, S., & Levine, J.B. (1986, July 7). IBM's fancy footwork to sidestep layoffs. *Business Week*, pp. 54–55.

Biddle, R.E. (1976). *Guidelines oriented job analysis manual.* Sacramento, CA: Biddle & Associates.

Bloom, B.S. (1956). *Taxonomy and educational objectives.* New York: McKay.

Boudreau, J.W. (1984, Spring). Decisions-theory contribution to HRM research and practice. *Industrial Relations, 23*(2), 198–217.

Boudreau, J.W. (1988). Utility analysis: A new view of strategic human resource management. In *ASPA/BNA handbook of human resource management.* Vol. 1., ed. L. Dyer. Washington, DC: Bureau of National Affairs.

Bowen, E. (1985, February 11). Schooling for survival. *Time*, pp. 74–75.

Bownas, D.A., & Bernardin, H.J. (1988). Critical incident technique. In S. Gael (Ed.), *The job analysis handbook for business, industry, and government* (Vol. 2, pp. 1120–1137). New York: John Wiley.

Bownas, D.A., Bosshardt, M.J., & Donnelly, L.R. (1985, Spring). A quantitative approach to evaluating training curriculum content sampling adequacy. *Personnel Psychology, 38*(1), 117–31.

Bramley, P., & Hullah, H. (1987). Auditing training. *Journal of European Industrial Training, 11*(6), 5–10.

Brinkerhoff, R.O. (1981, December). Making evaluations more useful. *Training and Development Journal, 35*(12), 66–70.

Broadwell, M.M. (1975). *The supervisor and on-the-job training.* Reading, MA: Addison-Wesley.

Brody, M. (1987, June 8). Helping workers to work smarter. *Fortune*, pp. 86–88.

Brooks, M. (1971). The community action program as a setting for applied research. In F. Caro (Ed.), *Readings in evaluation research* (pp. 53–62). New York: Russell Sage Foundation.

Buckley, R., & Caple, J. (1984). The training audit. *Journal of European Industrial Training, 8*(7), 3–8.

Buckly, R. (1980). *Integrated job analysis* (2nd ed.). Los Angeles: Psychological Services.

Buckly, R. (1986). *Integrated job analysis and selection.* Glendale, CA: Psychological Services.

Buckner, K.E. (1989). *A review and empirical analysis of court standards for employee selection.* Unpublished doctoral dissertation, Auburn University, Auburn, AL.

Bureau of National Affairs. (1975). *On-the-job training: Personnel Management*. Washington, DC: Author.

Butler, F.C. (1978, January). The concept of competence: An operational definition. *Educational Technology, 18*(1), 7–18.

Campbell, D.T., & Stanley, J.C. (1963). *Experimental and quasi-experimental designs for research*. Chicago: Rand McNally.

Campbell, J.P. (1980, August). What we are about: An inquiry into the self-concept of industrial and organizational psychology. Presidential address to Division of Industrial and Organizational Psychologists, 86th annual meeting of American Psychological Association, Toronto.

Campbell, J.P., Dunnette, M.D., Lawler, E.E., & Weick, K.E. (1970). *Managerial behavior, performance, and effectiveness*. New York: McGraw-Hill.

Canfield, A.A., & Lafferty, J.C. (1970). *Learning styles inventory*. Detroit: Humanics Media (Liberty Drawer).

Carnevale, A.P., & Goldstein, H. (1983). *Employee training: Its changing role and an analysis of new data*. Washington, DC: American Society for Training and Development.

Carrell, M.R., Kuzmits, F.E., & Elbert, N.F. (1989). *Personnel: Human resource management*. Columbus, OH: Merrill.

Carroll, S.J., Paine, F.T., & Ivancevich, J.M. (1972, Autumn). The relative effectiveness of training methods—Expert opinion and research. *Personnel Psychology, 25*(3), 495–509.

Cascio, W.F. (1987). *Applied psychology in personnel management* (3d ed.). Englewood Cliffs, NJ: Prentice-Hall.

Cascio, W.F. (1989). *Managing human resources: Productivity, quality of work life, profits*. New York: McGraw-Hill.

Center for the Study of Teaching and Learning Styles. (1983). *Learning styles network instrument assessment analysis*. Jamaica, NY: St. John's University.

Choate, P., & Linger, K. (1986). *The high-flex society*. New York: Alfred A. Knopf.

Christal, R.E. (1974). *The United States Air Force occupational research project*. Lackland Air Force Base, TX: Air Human Resources Laboratory.

Christal, R.E., & Weissmuller, J.J. (1988). Job-task inventory analysis. In S. Gael (Ed.), *The job analysis handbook for business, industry, and government* (Vol. 2, pp. 1036–1050). New York: John Wiley.

Clark, H.F., & Sloan, H.S. (1958). *Classroom in the factories: An account of educational activities conducted by American industry*. Rutherford, NJ: Fairleigh Dickinson University, Institute of Research.

Clement, R.W., Pinto, P.R., & Walker, J.W. (1978, December). Unethical behavior by training and development professionals. *Training and Development Journal, 32*(12), 10–12.

Clement, R.W., Walker, J.W., & Pinto, P.R. (1979, March). Changing demands on the training professionals? *Training and Development Journal, 33*(3), 3–7.

Cohen, A.R., Fink, S.L., Gadon, H., & Willits, R.D. (1988). *Effective behavior in organizations*. Homewood, IL: Irwin.

Cole, G.A. (1986). *Personnel management: Theory and practice*. Maidenhead, Berkshire: D.P. Publications.

The Conference Board. (1985). *Trends in corporate education*. New York: Author.

Coop, R.H., & Brown, L.D. (1970, October). Effects of cognitive style and teaching method on categories of achievement. *Journal of Educational Psychology, 61*(5), 404–405.

Corbett, S.S., & Smith, W.H. (1984, Autumn). Identifying student learning styles: Proceed with caution! *The Modern Language Journal, 68*(3), 212–221.

Cornelius, E.T. (1988). Practical findings from job analysis research. In S. Gael (Ed.), *The job analysis handbook for business, industry, and government* (Vol. 1, pp. 48–68). New York: John Wiley.

Cureton, J.H., Newton, A.F., & Teslowski, D.G. (1986, May). Finding out what managers need. *Training and Development Journal, 40*(5), 106–107.

Darkenwald, G.G., & Merrian, D.B. (1986). *Adult education: Foundation of practice* (p. 64). New York: Harper & Row.

Davis, L.E., & Wacker, G.J. (1988). Job design. In S. Gael (Ed.), *The job analysis handbook for business, industry, and government* (Vol. 1, pp. 157–172). New York: John Wiley.

Digman, L.A. (1980, Winter). Determining management development needs. *Human Resource Management, 19*(4), 12–17.

Dilauro, T.J. (1979, November-December). Training needs assessment: Current practices and new directions. *Public Personnel Management, 8*(6), 350–359.

Dodge, R.B. (1989, September). Learner-centered development. *Personnel Journal, 68*(9), 100–105.

Donnelly, E. (1987). The training model: Time for a change? *Industrial and Commercial Training, 19*(3), 3–6.

Dunn, R., & Dunn, K. (1978). *Teaching students through their individual learning styles: A practical approach.* Reston, VA: Reston Publishing Division, Prentice-Hall.

Dunn, R., & Dunn, K. (1972). *Practical approaches to individualizing instruction.* Englewood Cliffs, NJ: Parker Division of Prentice-Hall.

Dunn, R., De Bello, T., Brennan, P., Murrain, P. , & Krimsky, J. (1981). Learning style researchers define differences differently. *Educational Leadership, 38*(5), 372–75.

Dunnette, M.D., & Borman, W.C. (1979). Personnel selection and classification systems. *Annual Review of Psychology, 30*, 477–525.

Eastburn, R.A. (1986, March). Developing tomorrow's managers. *Personnel Administrator, 31*(3), 71–76.

Elliot, R.H., Boyles, W.R., Hill, J.B., Palmer, C., Thomas, P., & Veres, J.G. (1980). *Content-oriented personnel selection procedures: A training manual.* Montgomery, AL: Center for Government and Public Affairs, Auburn University at Montgomery.

Equal Employment Opportunity Commission, Civil Service Commission, Department of Labor, & Department of Justice. (1978). Adoption by four agencies of uniform guidelines on employee selection procedures. *Federal Register, 43*, 38290–38315.

Erez, M. (1977, October). Feedback: A necessary action for the goal-setting performance relationship. *Journal of Applied Psychology, 62*(5), 624–627.

Feild, H.S., & Gatewood, R.D. (in press). Development of a selection interview: A job content strategy. In G.R. Ferris & R.W. Eder (Eds.), *The employment interview: Theory, research, and practice.* Beverly Hills, CA: Sage.

Ferrell, B.G. (1983, February). A factor analytic comparison of four learning styles instruments. *Journal of Educational Psychology, 75*(1), 33–39.

Fine, S.A. (1988). Functional job analysis. In S. Gael (Ed.), *The job analysis handbook for business, industry, and government* (Vol. 2, pp. 1019–1035). New York: John Wiley.

Fine, S.A., & Wiley, W.W. (1971). *An introduction to functional job analysis: A scaling of selected tasks from the social welfare field.* Kalamazoo, MI: W.E. Upjohn Institute for Employment Research.

Fine, S.A., Holt, A.M., & Hutchinson, M.F. (1974). *Functional job analysis: How to standardize task statements.* Kalamazoo, MI: W.E. Upjohn Institute for Employment Research.

Flanagan, J.C. (1954, July). The critical incident technique. *Psychological Bulletin, 51*(4), 327–358.

Florin-Thuma, B.C., & Boudreau, J.W. (1987, Winter). Effects of performance feedback utility analysis on managerial decision processes. *Personnel Psychology, 40*(4), 693–713.

Ford, J.K., & Wroten, S.P. (1984, Winter). Introducing new methods for conducting training evaluation and for linking training evaluation to program redesign. *Personnel Psychology, 37*(4), 651–665.

Foulkes, F.K. (1989). *Human resources management.* Englewood Cliffs, NJ: Prentice-Hall.

French, W.L. (1982). *The personnel management process: Human resources administration and development.* Boston: Houghton Mifflin.

Fry, R.E. (1978). *Diagnosing professional learning environments: An observational framework for assessing situational complexity.* Unpublished doctoral dissertation, Massachusetts Institute of Technology, Cambridge.

Gael, S. (1988). Job descriptions. In S. Gael (Ed.), *The job analysis handbook for business, industry, and government* (Vol. 1, pp. 71–89). New York: John Wiley.

Gael, S. (Ed.). (1988). *The job analysis handbook for business, industry, and government* (Vols. 1–2). New York: John Wiley.

Gagne, R.M. (1962, February). Military training and the principles of learning. *American Psychologist, 17*(2), 83–91.

Gagne, R.M. (1977). *The conditions of learning.* New York: Holt, Rinehart & Winston.

Galagan, P. (1983, August). The numbers game: Putting value on HRD. *Training and Development Journal, 37*(8), 48–51.

Galosky, J.R. (1983, January). Curriculum design for management training. *Training and Development Journal, 37*(1), 48–51.

Gane, C. (1972). *Managing the training function.* London: George Allen & Unwin.

Gardner, R.W., Holzman, P.A., Klein, G.S., Linton, H.B., & Spence, D.P. (1959). Cognitive control: A study of individual consistencies in cognitive behavior. *Psychological Issues, 1*(4).

Gatewood, R. D., & Feild, H.S. (1987). *Human resource selection.* Hinsdale, IL: Dryden.

Gent, M.J., & Dell'Omo, G.G. (1989, July). The needs assessment solution. *Personnel Administrator, 34*(7), 82–84.

Ghorpade, J., & Atchison, T.J. (1980). The concept of job analysis: A review and some suggestions. *Public Personnel Management, 9*(3), 134–144.

Gilpatrick, E. (1977). *The health services mobility study method of task analysis and curriculum design basic tools: Concepts, task identification, skill scales and knowledge system.* Springfield, VA: National Technical Information Service.

Goldstein, A.P. (1974). *Changing supervisor behavior.* New York: Pergamon.

Goldstein, G.P. and Sorcher, M. (1974). *Changing supervisory behavior.* New York: Pergamon.

Goldstein, I.L. (1974). *Training: Program development and evaluation.* Belmont, CA: Wadsworth.

Goldstein, I.L. (1986). *Training in organizations: Needs assessment, development and evaluation.* Monterey, CA: Brooks/Cole.

Goldstein, K., & Blackmon, S. (1978). *Cognitive style: Five approaches and relevant research.* New York: John Wiley.

Gordon, J. (1986, October). Where the training goes. *Training, 23*(10), 49–63.

Gray, I., & Borecki, T.B. (1970, March-April). Training programs for the hard-core: What the trainer has to learn. *Personnel, 47*(2), 23–29.

Gregorc, A.F. (1979). Learning/teaching styles: Their nature and effects. In *Student learning styles: Diagnosing and prescribing programs* (pp. 39–54). Reston, VA: National Association of Secondary School Principals.

Greiner, L.E. (1987, Winter). Confessions of an executive educator. *New Management*, pp. 35–38.

Guion, R.M. (1978, August). Scoring of content domain sample: The problem of fairness. *Journal of Applied Psychology, 63*(4), 499–506.

Guzzo, R.A., Jette, R.D., & Katzell, R.A. (1985, Summer). The effects of psychologically based intervention programs on worker productivity: A meta-analysis. *Personnel Psychology, 38*(2), 275–291.

Hagedorn, H.J. (1984, July). Training as a way of life for line managers. *Management Review, 73*(7), 8–13.

Haig, C. (1984, October). A line manager's guide to training. *Personnel Journal, 63*(10), 42–45.

Hamblin, A.C. (1974). *Evaluation and control of training.* London: McGraw-Hill.

Havelock, R.G., & Havelock, M.C. (1973). *Training for change agents.* Ann Arbor, MI: Institute for Social Research.

Hawthorne, E.M., Libby, P.A., & Nash, N.S. (1983). The emergence of corporate colleges. *The Journal of Continuing Higher Education, 31*(4), 2–9.

Hawthorne, E.M. (1987a). *Evaluating employee training programs.* Westport, CT: Greenwood.

Hawthorne, E.M. (1987b). *A research-based guide for human resources managers.* New York: Quorum Books.

Hay, E.N., & Purves, D. (1954, July). A new method of job evaluation: The guide chart-profile method. *Personnel, 31*(2), 72–80.

Hayenga, B.S., & Isaacsen, H.B. (1980). Competence-based education for adult learners. *New Directions for Community Colleges, 29*, 39–46.

Hellreigel, D., & Slocum, J.W., Jr. (1989). *Management* (5th ed.). Reading, MA: Addison-Wesley.

Heneman, H.G., Schwab, D.P., Fossum, J.A., & Dyer, L.D. (1989). *Personnel/ Human resource management*. Homewood, IL: Irwin.

Hess, L., & Sperry, L. (1973, September). The psychology of the trainee as learner. *Personnel Journal, 52*(9), 781.

Hicks, W.D. & Klimoski, R.T. (1987, September). Entry into training programs and its effects on training outcomes: A field experiment. *Academy of Management Journal, 30*(3), 542–552.

Hilgard, E.R., & Bower, G.H. (1966). *Theories of learning*. New York: Appleton-Century-Crofts.

Hill, J. (1971). *Personalized education programs utilizing cognitive style mapping*. Bloomfield Hills, MI: Oakland Community College.

Hogan, P.M., Hakel, M.D., & Decker, P.J. (1986, August). Effects of trainee-generated versus trainer-provided rule codes on generalization in behavior-modeling training. *Journal of Applied Psychology, 71*(3), 469–473.

Holley, W.M., & Jennings, K.M. (1983). *Personnel management: Functions and issues*. Chicago: Dryden.

Honey, P., & Mumford, A. (1982a). *The learning styles questionnaire*. Maidenhead, Berkshire: Peter Honey.

Honey, P., & Mumford, A. (1982b). *The manual of learning styles*. Maidenhead, Berkshire: Peter Honey.

Honey, P., & Mumford, A. (1986a). *The learning styles questionnaire*. Maidenhead, Berkshire: Peter Honey.

Honey, P., & Mumford, A. (1986b). *The manual of learning styles*. Maidenhead, Berkshire: Peter Honey.

Houle, C. (1961). *The inquiring mind*. Madison: University of Wisconsin Press.

Humphrey, J.W. (1985). The role of training in corporate repositioning. *Forum Issues, 4*, 4–6.

Hunt, D.E. (1979). Learning style and student needs: An introduction to conceptual level. In *Student learning styles: Diagnosing and prescribing programs* (pp. 23–28). Reston, VA: National Association of Secondary School Principals.

Ilgen, D.R., Fisher, C.O., & Taylor, M.S. (1982, May). Consequences of individual feedback on behavior in organizations. *Journal of Applied Psychology, 64*(4), 349–371.

Ivancevich, J.M., & Glueck, W.F. (1989). *Foundations of personnel: Human resource management*. Homewood, IL: BPI/Irwin.

Jung, C.J. (1970). *Generalizations about training*. Portland, OR: Northwest Regional Educational Laboratory.

Kagan, J., Moss, H., & Sigel, I. (1963). Psychological significance of styles of conceptualization. *Monographs of the society for research in child development, 28*, 73–112.

Kearsley, G. (1982). *Costs, benefits, and productivity in training systems*. Reading, MA: Addison-Wesley Publishing.

Keirsey, P., & Bates, M. (1984). *Please understand me: Characters and temperament types*. Del Mar, CA: Prometheus Memsis Book Company.

Kenney, J., & Reid, M. (1986). *Training interventions*. London: Institute of Personnel Management.

Kidd, J.R. (1973). *How adults learn*. New York: Cambridge.

Kilpatrick, D.L. (1983, November). Four steps to measuring training effectiveness. *Personnel Administrator, 28*(11), 19–25.

Kimble, G.A., & Garmezy, N. (1963). *Principles of general psychology*. New York: Ronald.

Kirby, P. (1979). *Cognitive style, learning style and transfer skill acquisition*. Columbus, OH: National Center for Vocational Education.

Kirkland v. New York Department of Corrections, 374 F. Supp. 1361 (S.D. NY 1974).

Knowles, M.S. (1980). *The modern practice of adult education: From pedagogy to andragogy* (rev. ed.). New York: Cambridge.

Knowles, M.S. (1984). *The adult learner: A neglected species* (3d ed.). Houston: Gulf.

Knowles, M.S., & Associates. (1984). *Andragogy in action: Applying modern principles of adult learning*. San Francisco: Jossey-Bass.

Kolb, D.A. (1971a). Individual learning styles and the learning process. Working paper, Alfred P. Sloan School of Management, Massachusetts Institute of Technology.

Kolb, D.A., (1971b). *Organizational psychology: An experiential approach*. Englewood Cliffs, NJ: Prentice-Hall.

Kolb, D.A. (1976). *Learning style inventory: Technical manual*. Boston: McBer & Company.

Kolb, D.A. (1984a). *Experiential learning: Experience as the source of learning and development*. Englewood Cliffs, NJ: Prentice-Hall.

Kolb, D.A. (1984b). *Organizational psychology: An experiential approach* (2nd ed.). Englewood Cliffs, NJ: Prentice-Hall.

Kolb, D.A. (1985a). *The learning style inventory*. Boston: McBer & Company.

Kolb, D.A. (1985b). *Learning style inventory: Technical manual*. Boston: McBer & Company.

Kolb, D.A., & Fry, R.E. (1975). Toward an applied theory of experiential learning. In C. Cooper (Ed.), *Theories of group processes*. London: John Wiley.

Kolb, D.A., & Fry, R.E. (1979). Experiential learning theory and learning experiences in liberal arts education. *New Directions for Experiential Learning, 6*, 79–92.

Krauthammer, C. (1983, August 15). Deep down, we're all alike, Right? Wrong. *Time*, pp. 30–31.

Labor Letter (1987, April 28). *Wall Street Journal*, p. 1.

Lakin, M. (1972). *Interpersonal encounter theory and practice in sensitivity training*. New York: McGraw-Hill.

Latham, G.P. (1988). Human resource training and development. *Annual review of psychology, 39*, 545–582.

Latham, G.P., & Locke, E.A. (1979, Autumn). Goal setting: A motivational technique that works. *Organizational Dynamics, 8*(2), 68–80.

Latham, G.P., & Saari, L.M. (1979, June). The application of social learning theory to training supervisors through behavior modeling. *Journal of Applied Psychology, 64*(3), 239–246.

Leap, T.L., & Crino, M.D. (1989). *Personnel/Human resource management*. New York: Macmillan.

Ledvinka, J. (1982). *Federal regulation of personnel and human resource manage-ment* (pp. 121–123). Belmont, CA: Wadsworth.

Lee, C. (1987, October). Where the training dollars go. *Training, 24*(10), 51–65.

Levine, E.L. (1983). *Everything you always wanted to know about job analysis and more: A job analysis primer*. Tampa: Mariner.

Levine, E.L., Ash, R.A., & Bennett, N. (1980, October). Exploratory comparative study of four job analysis methods. *Journal of Applied Psychology, 65*(5), 524–535.

Levine, E.L., Ash, R.A., Hall, H., & Sistrunk, F. (1983, June). Evaluation of job analysis methods by experienced job analysts. *Academy of Management Journal, 26*(2), 339–348.

Lien, L. (1979). Reviewing your training and development activities. *Personnel Journal, 58*, 791–807.

Lienert, P. (1983, October 19). Discrimination settlement will cost GM $42.5 million. *Denver Post*, p. 3A.

Likert, R. (1961). *New patterns of management*. New York: McGraw-Hill.

Locke, E.A. (1968, May). Toward a theory of task motivation and incentives. *Organizational Behavior and Human Performance, 3*(2), 157–189.

Lopez, F.M. (1986). *The threshold traits analysis technical manual*. Port Washington, NY: Lopez & Associates.

Lopez, F.M. (1988). Threshold traits analysis system. In S. Gael (Ed.), *The job analysis handbook for business, industry, and government* (Vol. 2, pp. 880–901). New York: John Wiley.

Lusterman, S. (1977). *Education in industry*. New York: The Conference Board.

Lusterman, S. (1985). *Trends in corporate education and training* (Report No. 870). New York: The Conference Board.

McAshton, H.H. (1979). *Competency based education*. Englewood Cliffs, NJ: Educational Technology.

McCormick, E.J. (1976). Job and task analysis. In M. Dunnette (Ed.), *Handbook of industrial and organizational psychology*. Chicago: Rand McNally.

McCormick, E.J. (1979). *Job analysis: Methods and applications*. New York: American Management Association.

McCormick, E.J., DeNisi, A.S., & Shaw, J.B. (1979, February). Use of the Position Analysis Questionnaire for establishing the job component validity of tests. *Journal of Applied Psychology, 64*(1), 51–56.

McCormick, E.J., Jeaneret, P.R., & Mecham, R.C. (1972, August). A study of job characteristics and job dimensions as based on the Position Analysis Questionnaire (PAQ). *Journal of Applied Psychology, 56*(4), 347–368.

McGehee, W. (1979). Training and development: Theory, policies, and practices. In D. Yoder and H. Heneman, Jr. (Eds.), *ASPA handbook of personnel and industrial relations*. Washington, DC: Bureau of National Affairs.

McGehee, W., & Thayer, P.W. (1961). *Training in business and industry*. New York: John Wiley.

McGregor, D. (1960). *The human side of enterprise*. New York: McGraw-Hill.

McKeon, W.J. (1981). How to determine off-site meeting costs. *Training and Development Journal*, p. 117. Adapted in Wayne F. Cascio, *Costing human resources* (2nd ed., pp. 224–225). Boston: Kent.

Macey, W.H. (1982). Linking training needs assessment to training program design.

Paper presented at the 90th annual meeting of the American Psychological Association, Washington, DC.

Mager, R.F. (1962). *Preparing objectives for programmed instruction.* San Francisco: Fearon.

Mager, R.F. (1984). *Preparing instructional objectives.* Belmont, CA: Pitman Learning.

Mahler, W.R. (1976). Executive development. In R.L. Craig (Ed.), *Training and Development Handbook* (2nd ed.) New York: McGraw-Hill.

Manis, M. (1966). *Cognitive Processes.* Monterey, CA: Brooks/Cole.

Margolis, F.H., & Bell, C.R. (1984). *Managing the learning process: Effective techniques for the adult classroom.* Minneapolis: Lakewood.

Mathieu, J.E., & Leonard, R.L. (1987, June). Applying utility concepts to a training program in supervisory skills: A time-based approach. *Academy of Management Journal, 30*(2), 316–335.

Mathis, R.L., & Jackson, J.H. (1985). *Personnel: Human resource management.* St. Paul: West.

Mathis, R.L., & Jackson, J.H. (1988). *Personnel: Human resource management* (5th ed.). St. Paul: West.

Matsui, T., Kakuyama, T., & Onglatco, M.L.U. (1987). Effects of goals and feedback on performance in groups. *Journal of Applied Psychology, 72*(3), 407–415.

Mealiea, L.W., & Duffy, J.F. (1980, November). Nine pitfalls for the training and development specialist. *Personnel Journal, 59*(11), 929–931.

Menne, J.W., McCarthy, W., & Menne, J. (1976, November-December). A systems approach to the content validation of employee selection procedures. *Public Personnel Management, 5*(6), 387–396.

Mento, A.J., Steele, R.P., & Karren, R.J. (1987, February). A meta-analytic study of the effects of goal setting on performance: 1961–1984. *Organizational Behavior and Human Decision Processes, 39*(1), 52–83.

Michalak, D., & Yager, E. (1979). *Making the training process work.* New York: Harper & Row.

Milkovich, G.T., & Boudreau, J.W. (1988). *Personnel: Human resource management.* Plano, TX: Business Publications.

Mishan, E.J. (1976). *Cost-benefit analysis.* New York: Praeger.

Moore, J.M. (1982, December). The role relocation plays in management development. *Personnel Administrator, 27*(12), 31–34.

Moore, M.L., & Dutton, P. (1978, July). Training needs analysis: Review and critique. *Academy of Management Review, 3*(3), 532–545.

Moses, J.L., & Byham, W.C. (Eds.). (1977). *Applying the assessment center method.* New York: Pergamon.

Mumford, A. (1984). Review of action learning in practice. *Industrial and Commercial Training, 16*(2), 11–16.

Munsterberg, H. (1913). *Psychology and industrial efficiency.* Boston: Houghton Mifflin.

Murrell, K.L. (1987). The learning-model instrument: An instrument based on the learning model for managers. *The 1987 annual: Developing human resources.* (pp. 109–119). San Diego, CA: University Associates.

Newburg, T.A. (1980, October). Exercises for better management development. *Personnel Management, 59*(10), 850–852.

Newstrom, J. (1978, November). Catch–22: The problems of incomplete evaluation of training. *Training and Development Journal, 32*(11), 22–24.

Newstrom, J., & Lilyquist, J. (1979, October). Selecting needs analysis methods. *Training and Development Journal, 33*(10), 52–56.

Noble, K.B. (1985, April 14). Where Xerox hones skills. Spring survey of education (Section 12). *New York Times*, p. 49.

Noe, R.A. (1986, October). Trainees' attributes and attitudes: Neglected influences on training effectiveness. *Academy of Management Review, 11*(4), 736–749.

Noe, R.A., & Schmitt, N. (1986, Autumn). The influence of trainee attitudes on training effectiveness: A test model. *Personnel Psychology, 39*(3), 497–523.

Norton, E.H. (1987, May 13). Step by step, the court helps affirmative action. *New York Times*, p. A27.

Olsen, L. (1986, September). Training trends: The corporate view. *Training and Development Journal, 40*(9), 32–35.

Osborn, A.F. (1963). *Applied imagination* (3d rev. ed.). New York: Charles Scribner's Sons.

Peterson, G.W., & Stakenas, R.G. (1981, July/August). Performance-based education: Method for preserving quality, equal opportunity, and economy in public higher education. *Journal of Higher Education, 52*(4), 352–368.

Pettigrew, A.M., Jones, G.R., & Reason, P.W. (1982). *Training and development roles in their organizational setting*. London: Manpower Services Commisson.

Pfeiffer, J.W., & Jones, J.E. (1980). Introduction to the structured experience section. In J.W. Pfeiffer & J.E. Jones (Eds.), *The 1980 annual handbook for group facilitators*. San Diego: University Associates.

Pierce, E.A., & Wentorf, D.A. (1970, March). Training objectives–philosophy or practice? *Personnel Journal, 49*(3), 235–240.

Pinto, P.R., & Walker, J.W. (1978, July). What do training and development professionals really do? *Training and Development Journal, 32*(7), 58–64.

Pitre, L.F. (1980). *Credit and noncredit education opportunities offered by large industrial corporations*. Unpublished doctoral dissertation, University of Texas, Austin.

Prentice-Hall Editorial Staff. (1979). *Employee training: Personnel management: Policies and practice series*. Englewood Cliffs, NJ: Author.

Price, G.E., Dunn, R., & Dunn, K. (1982). *PEPS (Productivity environmental preference survey manual* (rev. ed.). Lawrence, KS: Price Systems.

Prien, E.P. (1977, Summer). The function of job analysis in content validation. *Personnel Psychology, 30*(2), 167–174.

Primoff, E.S. (1975). *How to prepare and conduct job element examinations*. Washington, DC: Personnel Research and Development Center, U.S. Civil Service Commission.

Quackenboss, T.C. (1969). White collar training takes many forms. *Training and Development Journal, 23*(4), 16–26.

Rackham, N., & Morgan, T. (1977). *Behavioral analysis in training*. London: McGraw-Hill.

Ramirez, M., & Castaneda, A. (1974). *Cultural democracy, bicognitive development and education*. New York: Academic.

Reber, R.A., & Wallin, J.A. (1984, September). The effects of training, good setting, and knowledge of results of safe behavior: A component analysis. *Academy of Management Journal, 27*(3), 544–560.

Reichmann, S. (1974). *The refinement and construct validation of the Grasha-Reichmann student learning styles scales*. Master's thesis, University of Cincinnati.

Reinert, H. (1976, April). One picture is worth a thousand words? Not necessarily! *Modern Language Journal, 60*(4), 160–168.

Renzulli, J.S., & Smith, L.H. (1978). *The learning styles inventory: A measure of student preference for instructional techniques*. Mansfield Center, CT: Creative Learning.

Rich, J.R., & Boudreau, J.W. (1987, Spring). Effects of variability and risk on selection utility analysis: An empirical comparison. *Personnel Psychology, 40*(1), 55–84.

Robertson, I., & Downs, S. (1979, February). Learning and the prediction of performance: Development of trainability testing in the United Kingdom. *Journal of Applied Psychology, 64*(1) 42–50.

Rothwell, W.J. (1983, November). Curriculum design in training: An overview. *Personnel Administrator, 28*(11), 53–57.

Russell, J.S. (1984, Summer). A review of fair employment cases in the field of training. *Personnel Psychology, 37*(2), 261–276.

Sadler, G.R., Plovnick, M., & Snope, F. (1978). Learning styles and teaching implications. *Journal of Medical Education, 53*, 847–89.

Schmeck, R.R., Ribich, F., & Ramanaiah, H. (1977). Development of a self-report inventory assessing individual differences in learning processes. *Applied Psychological Measurement, 1*, 413–431.

Schmidt, F.L., Caplan, J.R., Bemis, S.E., Dewir, R., Dunn, L., & Antone, L. (1979). *The behavioral consistency method of unassembled examining*. Washington, DC: U.S. Office of Personnel Management.

Schneier, C.E. (1974, April). Training development programs: What learning theory and research have to offer. *Personnel Journal, 53*(4), 288–300.

Schuler, R.S., & Youngblood, S.A. (1986). *Effective personnel management*. St. Paul: West.

Shelton, H.R., & Craig, R.L. (1983). Continuing professional development: The employer's perspective. In M.B. Stern (Ed.), *Power and conflict in continuing professional education*. Belmont, CA: Wadsworth.

Sherwood, J., & Glidewell, J. (1971). Planned renegotiation: A norm OD intervention (Paper No. 338). Purdue University, Lafayette, IN: Herman C. Krannert Graduate School of Industrial Administration.

Siegel, A.I. (1983). The miniature job training and evaluation approach: Additional findings. *Personnel Psychology, 36*(1), 41–56.

Siegel, G.B. (1987). Education and training for the job analyst. *Personnel, 64*(7), 68–73.

Sims, R.R. (1981). *Assessing competencies in experiential learning theory: A person-job congruency model of effectiveness in professional careers*. Unpublished doctoral dissertation, Case Western Reserve University, Cleveland.

Sims, R.R. (1983, July). Kolb's experiential learning theory: A framework for assessing person-job interaction. *Academy of Management Review, 8*(3), 501–508.

Sims, R.R., & Noel, J. (1983). Management Development. *Business Education, 7,* 1.

Sims, R.R., & Veres, J.G. (1985, Summer). A practical program for training job analysts. *Public Personnel Management, 14*(2), 131–137.

Sims, R.R., Veres, J.G., Locklear, T.S. (in press). An investigation of a modified version of Kolb's Revised Learning Style Inventory. *Educational and Psychological Measurement.*

Sims, R.R., Veres, J.G., & Shake, L.G. (1989). An exploratory examination of the convergence between the learning styles questionnaire and the learning style inventory II. *Educational and Psychological Measurement, 49*(1), 227–233.

Skinner, B.F. (1969). *Contingencies of reinforcement: A theoretical analysis.* East Norwalk, CT: Appleton-Century-Crofts.

Smith, E.I. (1978). *Small climber development.* Basking Ridge, NJ: AT&T.

Smith, J.E., & Hakel, M.D. (1979, Winter). Convergence among data sources, response bias, and reliability and validity of a structured job analysis questionnaire. *Personnel Psychology, 32*(4), 677–692.

Sparks, P. (1979). *Job analysis under the new Uniform Guidelines.* Houston: Personnel Research, Exxon Corporation.

Sparks, P. (1981). Job analysis. In K. Rowland & G. Ferris (Eds.), *Personnel management.* Boston: Allyn & Bacon.

Spitzer, D. (1986, June). Five keys to successful training. *Training, 23*(6), 37–39.

Steadham, S.V. (1980, January). Learning to select a needs assessment strategy. *Training and Development Journal, 34*(1), 56–61.

Steinmetz, C.S. (1976). The history of training. In R.C. Craig (Ed.), *Training and development handbook* (2nd ed.). New York: McGraw-Hill.

Stephan, E., Mills, G.E., Pace, R.W., & Ralphs, L. (1988, January). HRD in the Fortune 500. *Training and Development Journal, 42,* 26–32.

Stufflebeam, D., Foley, W., Gephart, W., Guba, E., Hammond, R., Merriman, H., & Provus, M. (1971). *Educational evaluation and decision making.* Itasca, IL: Peacock.

Tannenbaum, R., Weschler, I.R., & Massarik, F. (1961). *Observations on the trainer role: A case study in leadership and organization.* New York: McGraw-Hill.

Taylor, J.W. (1974, May). Ten serious mistakes in management training and development. *Personnel Journal, 53*(5), 357–362.

Tessin, M.J. (1978, February). Once again, why training? *Training, 15*(2), p. 7.

Thompson, D.E., & Thompson, T.A. (1982, Winter). Court standards for job analysis in test validation. *Personnel Psychology, 35*(4), 865–874.

Tiffin, J., & McCormick, E.J. (1965). *Industrial psychology.* Englewood Cliffs, NJ: Prentice Hall.

Tough, A. (1979). *The adult's learning projects: A fresh approach to theory and practice in adult learning* (2nd ed.). Austin, TX: Learning Concepts.

Tough, A. (1982). *Intentional changes: A fresh approach to helping people change.* New York: Cambridge.

Tracey, W.R. (1971). *Designing training and development systems*. Washington, DC: American Management Association.

Tracey, W.R. (1984). *Designing training and development systems* (rev. ed.). Washington, DC: American Management Association.

Training. (1989, October). 1989 Industry Report. *Training, 35*(10), pp. 49–64.

Tyler, L. (1978). *Individuality: Human possibilities and personal choice in the psychological development of men and women*. San Francisco: Jossey-Bass.

U.S. Civil Service Commission. (1977). *Instructions for the factor evaluation system*. Washington, DC: Government Printing Office.

U.S. Department of Labor, Employment and Training Administration. (1977). *Dictionary of occupational titles* (4th ed.). Washington, DC: Government Printing Office.

United States v. State of New York, 82 FRD 2 (D.C. NY 1978) dec on *merits*, 475 F. Supp 1103 (D.C. NY 1979).

Van De Voort, D.M., & Stalder, B.K. (1988). Organizing for job analysis. In S. Gael (Ed.), *The job analysis handbook for business, industry, and government* (Vol. 1, pp. 315–328). New York: John Wiley.

Veres, J.G., Lahey, M.A., & Buckly, R. (1987). A practical rationale for using multi-method job analyses. *Public Personnel Management, 16*(2), 153–157.

Veres, J.G., Locklear, T.S., & Sims, R.R. (1990). Job analysis in practice: A brief review of the role of job analysis in human resource management. In G.R. Ferris, K.M. Roland, & M.R. Buckley (Eds.), *Human resource management: Perspectives and issues*. Boston: Allyn & Bacon.

Veres, J.G., Sims, R.R., & Shake, L.G. (1987). The reliability and classification stability of the learning styles inventory in corporate settings. *Educational and Psychological Measurement, 47*(4), 1127–1133.

Vroom, V.H. (1964). *Work and motivation*. New York: John Wiley.

Wehrenberg, S.B. (1989, August). Match trainers to the task. *Personnel Journal, 68*(5), 69–76.

Wernimont, P.F. (1988). Recruitment, selection, and placement. In S. Gael (Ed.), *The job analysis handbook for business, industry, and government* (Vol. 1, pp. 193–204). New York: John Wiley.

Werther, W.B., Jr., & Davis, K. (1989). *Human resources and personnel management*. New York: McGraw-Hill.

Wexley, K.N. (1984). Personnel training. *Annual Review of Psychology, 35*, 527.

Wexley, K.N., & Baldwin, T.T. (1986). Post-training strategies for facilitating positive transfer: An empirical exploration. *Academy of Management Journal, 29*(3), 503–520.

Wexley, K.N., & Latham, G.P. (1981). *Developing and training human resources in organizations*. Glenview, IL: Scott, Foresman.

Wheeler, M., & Marshall, J. (1986). The trainer type inventory (TTI): Identifying training style preferences. In J.W. Pfeiffer & L.D. Goodstein (Eds.), *The 1986 Annual: Developing human resources* (pp. 87–97). San Diego: University Associates.

Wircenski, J.L., Sullivan, R.L., & Moore, P. (1989, April). *Training and Development Journal, 43*(4), 61–64.

Witkin, H.A. (1975). Some implications of research on cognitive style for problems of education. In J.M. Whitehead (Ed.)., *Personality and learning*. London: Hodder & Stoughton.

Wolfe, D.M. (1980). Developing professional competence in the applied behavioral sciences. *New Directions for Experiential Learning, 8*, 1–16.

Wood, R.E., Mento, A.J., & Locke, E.A. (1987, August). Task complexity as a moderator of goal effects: A meta-analysis. *Journal of Applied Psychology, 72*(3), 416–425.

Work in America Institute. (1987). The continuous learning/employment security connection. *Report*. Scarsdale, NY: Work in America Institute.

Index

Adult learner, 125–128
Adult learning theory, 126–128
Alabama Merit System Method, 66.
    See also Job analysis methods
American Academy of Management,
    146
American Educational Research Asso-
    ciation, 146
American Management Association,
    146, 147
American Psychological Association,
    146
American Society for Training and
    Development (ASTD), 17, 120, 146,
    151, 188
Anderson, Robert, 154, 157–158
AT&T, 162, 224, 229

Baldwin Locomotive Works, 19
Beatrice Foods, 220
Behavioral Consistency Method, 64.
    See also Job analysis methods
Behavior modeling, 130–131
Bureau of National Affairs, 118

California, 228
Career planning, 229–230

Civil Rights Act, 37, 105, 112–113
CMDC Corporation, 53
College Board Study, 51
Competency development, 73
Competency levels, 12, 77–79
Control Data Corporation, 229
Criterion Scoring Guide, 100, 102–103.
    See also Tracey, William
Critical incident technique (CIT), 64.
    See also Job analysis methods

Dartmouth College, 19
Data collection technique, 61–63;
    sources, 59–61. See also Job analysis
Decision points, 206. See also Training
    team evaluation
Decision to Attend a Training Pro-
    gram Questionnaire, 178–181
Denver, Colorado, 53
Dictionary of Occupational Titles, 61,
    64, 107
Dunn, Kenneth, 138–139
Dunn, Rita, 138–139
Dunn and Dunn's Five Elements of
    Learning Style, 140. See also Learn-
    ing styles

Equal Employment Opportunity Act, 37
Equal Employment Opportunity Commission (EEOC), 61, 65, 111, 113
Evaluation phase, 6, 15–16, 187–217
Experiential Learning Model, 13, 14–15, 73, 79. *See also* Kolb, David
Experiential Learning Theory, 45–46. *See also* Kolb, David
External/internal team training, 152–158

Fry, Ron, 15, 46, 162, 166
Functional Job Analysis (FJA), 64, 66. *See also* Job analysis methods

General Electric (GE), 19, 24, 50, 224, 229
General Motors (GM), 113, 224
Goal setting, 129–130
Goldstein, Irwin, 6, 57, 116, 118, 120
Grasha-Reichmann Learning Styles Questionnaire (GRLSQ), 139–140, 163. *See also* Learning styles
Guidelines Oriented Job Analysis, 65. *See also* Job analysis methods

Harvard, 19
Havelock, Mary, 74
Havelock, Raymond, 74
Hawthorne, Elizabeth, 18, 19, 206, 211
Health Services Mobility Study Method, 65. *See also* Job analysis methods
Hewlett-Packard, 224
Hoe and Company, 18
Holiday Inns, 220
Honey and Mumford Learning Styles Questionnaire, 139. *See also* Learning styles
Human resource management specialists: 145–159; role of, 146–147; selection of, 14, 147–150; understanding of, 225–227. *See also* Trainers

IBM, 36, 50, 220, 224
Integrated job analysis, 65, 66. *See also* Job analysis methods
Internal/external team training, 152–158. *See also* Training; Training team evaluation
Iowa Merit Employment System (IMES), 64, 66. *See also* Job analysis methods

Job agent, 59
Job analysis, 11, 55–71, 221–223; defined, 56–57; importance of, 57; and training, 79
Job Analysis Handbook for Business, Industry and Government, 61
Job analysis methods, 63–71; Alabama Merit System Method, 66; Behavioral Consistency Method, 64; Critical incident technique (CIT), 64; evaluation of, 65–66; Functional Job Analysis (FJA), 64, 66; Guidelines Oriented Job Analysis, 65; Health Services Mobility Study Method, 65; Integrated Job Analysis, 65, 66; Iowa Merit Employment System (IMES), 64, 66; Job Element Method (JEM), 64; multimethod approach in action, 66–71; Task Inventory/Comprehensive Occupational Data Analysis Program (TI/CODAP), 64; Threshold Trait Analysis System (TTAS), 64; Versatile Job Analysis System (VERJAS), 65, 66; worker-oriented, 64; work-oriented, 64
Job analysts, 58–59
Job Element Method (JEM), 64. *See also* Job analysis methods
Job incumbents, 59
Job supervisors, 59–60
Journal of Applied Psychology, 61

Kelley Services, 229
Knowledge, skills and abilities (KSAs), 10, 15, 21, 38, 42, 53, 54, 55–71, 74, 76, 98, 99, 122, 154, 182, 198, 220, 222–224, 229–231

Knowles, Malcolm, 126, 127, 143
Kolb, David, 13, 15, 45–46, 127, 136, 138, 139, 143, 161, 162, 166; Experiential Learning Model, 13, 14–15, 73, 79, 89–91; Experiential Learning Theory, 45–46, 166; Learning Style Inventory, 163

Learning, 12–15; climate, 171–177; defined, 126; environments: affective, behavioral, perceptual, symbolic, 166–168; principles of, 128–135; self-directed, 177–179
Learning Style Inventory, 163, 181–182. *See also* Learning styles
Learning styles, 12, 79–83, 135–142; assessing, 138–141; defined, 81–83; Dunn and Dunn Model, 140; Grasha-Reichmann Model, 139–140; Honey and Mumford model, 139; implications for training, 171; Kolb's model, 143; Murrell model, 140–141; and training programs, 163–164; use of, 143
Los Angeles City College, 341
Louisville, Kentucky, 24

Management development, 229–230
Modeling. *See* Behavior modeling
Motorola, 17–18, 224

Needs assessment phase, 11–13, 220–223
New York Board of Regents, 20
New York City, 18

Objectives, 13; criteria for selecting, 99–100; procedures and selection criteria for, 99–103; uses of, 95–97; worksheet for, 100–101; writing of, 103–105. *See also* Training objectives
Organizational analysis, defined, 36

Peripheral skills, 77
Personnel Psychology, 61
Pivotal skills, 12, 76–79, 94; key principles, 83–89

Preassessment phase, 8–11, 220
Princeton University, 19
Psychological contracts, 172–178, 181–182; contributions, 173–177, 182; dynamic process, 174–175; expectations, 173–177, 182
Public Personnel Management, 61

Saari, Lise, 131, 213–214
Sharp and Oughton, Inc., 19
Sherwood, John, 175–177
St. John's Center for the Study of Learning and Teaching Styles, 141
Subject matter experts, 55–71
System, 1; defined, 2–4

Task Inventory/Comprehensive Occupational Data Analysis Program (TI/CODAP), 64. *See also* Job analysis methods
Texas Instruments, 51–52
Threshold Trait Analysis System (TTAS), 64. *See also* Job analysis methods
Title VII, 65, 105, 112
Tracey, William, 4; Criterion Scoring Guide, 100, 102–103, 104, 105, 204, 205, 215
Trainees, 125–143; identifying, 14; selection of, 112, 125–143; trainability of, 115–116; understanding, 225–227
Trainers, 145–159; pitfalls of, 150–152; role of, 146–147; selection of, 14, 147–150, 226–227; understanding, 225–227. *See also* Human resource management specialists
Training, 2; benefits of, 25–27; cross-cultural, 230–231; defined, 20–21; history of, 18–20; internal/external team training, 152–158; learning climate, 256; purposes of, 27–32; reasons for, 21–25; responsibility for, 109–111; transfer of, 116–117
Training and development phase, 5, 13–15
Training environments, 166–168; affectively complex, 166–167; behaviorally complex, 166, 168;

characteristics of, 171–172; perceptually complex, 166, 167; symbolically complex, 166, 167–168
Training learning diary, 183
Training magazine, 27, 28, 31
Training magazine's 1989 Industry Report, 17, 153
Training methods: kinds of, 117–120;
off-the-job, 119–120; on-the-job,
117–119; selection of, 13–14, 120–
122
Training needs: analysis of, 36–39;
prioritizing, 52–53
Training needs methods, 40–53; adaptive competency, 45–46; nominal
group technique, 46–48; performance discrepancy, 43–45; selection
of, 50–52
Training objectives, 13; principles of,
74–76; setting, 97–103; uses of, 95–
97; worksheets, 100–101; writing of,
103–105. *See also* Objectives
Training program, 109–124; content,
105–107; designs, 12–13, 73–91; effectiveness, 14–15, 161–185, 169,
170; managing, 165–183
Training program evaluation, 187–218;
benefits and objectives, 188–189;
break-even analysis, 214–215; cost-
benefit analysis (CBA), 195–196,
211–214; decision points, 206; designing, 190–192; guidelines for,
203–206; plan, 201–203; pitfalls in,
192–194; resources and constraints,
196–197; technique options, 197–
201; training audit (TA), 206–211
Training system, 1–17, 220–232; analysis of, 4–5; models, 5–8; phases of,
8–16
Training team approach, 152–158; advantages of, 153–154; characteristics
of successful, 157–158; disadvantages of, 155–156; internal/external
team training, 152–158; obstacles to,
156–157; trainees' responses to, 156

"Uniform Guidelines of Employee Se-
lection Procedures," 65, 105, 112,
122
United States v. State of New York, 65
United Steel Workers v. Weber, 113
U.S. Department of Labor, 61, 64

Versatile Job Analysis System (VER-
JAS), 65, 66. *See also* Job analysis
methods

Wang, 224
Westinghouse, 19, 220
Wexley, Kenneth, 105, 106, 112, 116,
117, 119, 120, 126, 132
Work in America Institute, 224

Xerox, 50, 224

About the Author

RONALD R. SIMS is Associate Professor of Business Administration at The College of William & Mary. His more than forty articles have appeared in journals such as *International Journal of Management, Public Personnel Management, Journal of Management Development,* and *Academy of Management Review.*

About the Author